THE LEADER IN THE GROUP

ALEXANDER WOLF, M.D.

The Leader in the Group

In Honor of Alexander Wolf, M.D., for His
35 Years of Outstanding Teaching, Supervision,
Writing, and Clinical Practice

Edited by

ZANVEL A. LIFF, PH.D.

*Director of Psychology and Senior Supervisor of
Group Psychotherapy,
Postgraduate Center for Mental Health
Visiting Professor of Psychology, Graduate Faculty,
New School for Social Research*

JASON ARONSON • NEW YORK

In Remembrance of

EMANUEL K. SCHWARTZ

*His serious contemplation of our
struggle, his generous concern for
our welfare, and his genuine
dedication to our mutual fulfillment;
these alone made Mannie great and
glorious, a towering leader in groups.*

ALEXANDER WOLF

Contributors

ARONSON, MARVIN L., Ph.D., Director, Group Therapy Department, Postgraduate Center for Mental Health

BATTEGAY, RAYMOND, M.D., Professor, University of Basel, Basel, Switzerland

CHRIST, JACOB, M.D., Clinical Director, Georgia Mental Health Institute, Atlanta, Georgia

COHN, RUTH C., M.A., Consultant Psychologist, Workshop Institute for Living-Learning, New York

FIDLER, JAY W., M.D., Medical Director, Union County Psychiatric Clinic, Plainfield, N. J.

FIELDING, BENJAMIN, Ed.D., Dean of Fellowship Training, Postgraduate Center for Mental Health

FOULKES, S. H., M.D., Member of the British Psychoanalytic Society; Honorary President and Founder, Group Analytic Society, London, England

GLATZER, HENRIETTE T., Ph.D., Training Analyst, Group Therapy Department, Postgraduate Center for Mental Health

GROTJAHN, MARTIN, M.D., Training Analyst, Los Angeles, California

KOSSEFF, JEROME W., Ph.D., Senior Supervisor, Group Therapy Department, Postgraduate Center for Mental Health

LEBOVICI, SERGE, M.D., Associate Professor of Child Psychiatry, University of Paris, Paris, France

LEOPOLD, HAROLD S., M.D., Associate Clinical Professor, Albert Einstein College of Medicine

LIFF, ZANVEL A., Ph.D., Director of Psychology, Postgraduate Center for Mental Health

McCARTY, GERALD J., Ph.D., Consulting Psychologist, Seattle, Washington

MENDELL, DAVID, M.D., Clinical Professor of Psychiatry, University of Texas School of Medicine, Houston, Texas

ROSENBAUM, MAX, Ph.D., Faculty, National Psychological Association for Psychoanalysis

STRACHSTEIN, HARRIET, Ph.D., Supervisor, Group Therapy Department, Postgraduate Center for Mental Health

WOLBERG, ARLENE R., M.S.S., Training Analyst, Postgraduate Center for Mental Health

Contents

PART II

THE GROUP LEADER: PSYCHOANALYTIC FUNCTIONS
AND OBJECTIVES 79

A MEMORIAL TO THE LEADERSHIP OF
EMANUEL K. SCHWARTZ

APPENDIX

Preface

Because of the current sociopolitical situation in the United States the larger theme reflected in this book, that of leadership, is in the foreground of public preoccupation. There is a pervasive hunger for trustworthy, responsible, and competent leaders. Paralleling this is an increasing intolerance, even outrage, toward tyrannically unfeeling, exploitative leaders who function in both large and small groups.

This book honors Alexander Wolf, whose psychoanalytic skills and warm human relatedness can almost characterize him as being close to an ideal leader. It celebrates thirty-five years of his work as the most recognized and influential leader in the field of psychoanalysis in groups. He is a man who has strived to cultivate and elevate others to be not only their own leaders, but benevolent leaders in their own groups and families as well. His clinical practice, brilliant teaching, supervising, and writing have deeply affected the professional and personal lives of thousands of his students and patients.

The role and effectiveness of the leader have been an overriding concern of Alexander Wolf for many years. He has been particularly interested in the motivation and training of the leader in group treatment; the leader's conception of his different functions; types and styles of leadership; the comparative effects of regular sessions, alternate sessions and co-therapy; and the relevance to culture and society of the knowledge of leadership gained in treatment.

In response to invitations to colleagues throughout the world, eighteen original contributions have been selected for this volume. They have been organized around the leader's psychoanalytic functions and objectives; his use of newer psychoanalytic applications in groups; and his role outside the psychoanalytic group.

Emanuel K. Schwartz, Alexander Wolf's long-time friend, colleague, and co-author, began the original editorial efforts for the book, and worked on it until his death in January, 1973. Mrs. Reta Schwartz and several of the contributors asked me to complete the project.

Having been a student and colleague of both Doctors Wolf and Schwartz, it was a privilege for me to carry out the editorial responsibilities.

A special section of this book is dedicated to Dr. Schwartz for his role in initiating the project, as well as for his close collaboration with Dr. Wolf. This section contains a reprint of his article "Leadership and the Psychotherapist."

Much gratitude is hereby expressed to all the contributors who have honored Alexander Wolf with their original papers. Special appreciation is also given to Deborah Jerome, Barbara Hults, and Edith Jacobs for their editorial help and to Maureen McInerney and Ann Kochanske for their secretarial assistance. Finally, I warmly acknowledge the encouragement and support of my wife Sylvia and my daughters Sharon and Janet.

Foreword

Alexander Wolf recently commented that we have always lived in times of leadership crisis, but the contemporary loss of leadership confidence, credibility, and respect seems worse than ever. The world is in desperate need of strong but flexible guidance, yet there are few individuals who possess both the necessary qualities and the desire to fill the leader's role successfully.

The type of leadership we are considering in this book, that of psychoanalysts within and outside therapy groups, is epitomized by Alexander Wolf himself. He represents the kind of group leader who communicates the most informed psychoanalytic understanding while at the same time offering warm, tender support and acceptance, so essential for human growth. He is an active, accurate and empathic interpreter of evolving transferences, resistances, fantasies, dreams, and other unconscious derivatives. But the profound trust he inspires is due not only to his professional expertise. It is due as well to his genuine personal attributes, especially his deep feeling for people and the sense of equality he conveys to all those around him.

In addition to the significance of the leader's role, functions and objectives, Alexander Wolf has recognized the equivalent if not greater importance of peer interaction in groups. He has focused on peer structures—how they may serve to loosen pathological bonds between children and parents and, more widely, between subordinates and authoritarian figures. He has recognized the value of group membership in breaking toxic symbiotic attachments. This neutralization of sado-masochistic interlocking was one of his pioneering advances in the use of the group setting for psychoanalytic work. His observation that peers tend to diminish the influences of malignant, internalized authorities is the basis for huge achievements in reconstructive group analysis.

It was fortuitous that in 1938 Alexander Wolf turned to his professional peers in an attempt to organize his first analytic group. He was moved to do so in the midst of his formal training in psychoanalysis because he was having difficulty in overcoming a certain hierarchical heaviness experienced in his own personal analysis.

In addition, his family background had exemplified a top-heavy leadership structure; he had an older brother and sister who served as a second set of parents. Due to this historical factor, he developed a disaffection, even a distrust, for some forms of leadership, especially in the political world. Thus he became sharply sensitive to the organization of interpersonal relationships along vertical lines of authority where dominant leadership demanded subordination. He sponsored peer relationships as more congenial and growth promoting.

Wolf tried to work toward an egalitarian ideal through his psychoanalytic group practice. Early in his group career he noticed that many patients tended to devalue their peers and chose either to idealize or to deride him. His goal became the distribution of authority, leadership, and power among members of his groups and the concomitant diminution of his own leadership role. In addition he made structural contributions to individual psychoanalysis through the introduction of the analysis of the individual in interaction. Because of his reluctance to turn away low-income patients, he made treatment available to a much larger population.

It took eleven years for the first full report on his accomplishments in analytic groups to appear (Wolf, 1949). After that there was a wave of his writings in this area, much of them in collaboration with myself. At that time Wolf started the first supervisory training workshop. His influence spread so widely that a recent questionnaire survey by Max Rosenbaum showed him to have had more influence over the last generation of psychoanalytic group therapists than any other single person in the field.

Alexander Wolf considers himself to be a nonretaliative, nonjudgmental, nonauthoritarian leader who invites patients to challenge and question his actions in the group. His mature, facilitative approach seems the one that best promotes the separate autonomous development of the patient.

This book is a testimonial to Alexander Wolf as a creative innovator of psychoanalysis in groups. It is a gesture of appreciation from his students and colleagues and an attempt to know him from his original contributions that taught and inspired us. With this volume, we celebrate Alexander Wolf's thirty-five years as an outstanding teacher, supervisor, and practitioner of psychoanalysis in groups.

EMANUEL K. SCHWARTZ

THE LEADER IN THE GROUP

Part I

SELECTED WRITINGS BY ALEXANDER WOLF
ON THE LEADER OF THE GROUP

Introduction

ZANVEL A. LIFF

Other than knowing Alexander Wolf personally, there is no better way of introducing the man we honor with this volume than by a thematic sampling of his writings.

Parts of nineteen articles have been chosen on the group leadership topic to give the reader a glimpse into the twenty-five-year unfolding of his rich, sensitive thinking. Much of these contributions have evolved with the creative collaboration of Emanuel Schwartz.

The selections portray the scope and depth of his interests—from specific technical problems on different phases of treatment, on countertransference and on working through, to social philosophical concerns. The latter focuses on values, creativity, uncertainty, roles of the leader in large-group conflicts, and finally on the human aspects of leadership—the use of discriminating affect, sense of responsibility, and the deeper qualities of being human and having loving capacities.

3

1. An Early View of the Role of the Group Leader

A. WOLF

The analyst does what he can to prolong the informality. When the meeting opens, he seats his patients in a circle which he has joined himself. No activity is urged upon anyone during the first meeting. It gives the patients a chance to relax in the knowledge that they will not immediately be called upon to participate. They also take this time to appraise one another secretly in sidelong glances. A part of the session may be spent in answering patients' questions with regard to details of procedure that are still unclear to them. The therapist assures them that, without permission, he will not expose a specific historical event disclosed to him in confidence during prior individual sessions. He insists, however, on his right to introduce, as often as necessary, the underlying psychodynamics which led to this particular historical event, so long as the psychic process is identifiable as resistance or transference.

In the exposition of the theory and practice of group analysis, the therapist would do well to sound a note of warning with regard to sudden infatuations and their potential involvements. Not that patients will all act out their incestuous wishes, but the record suggests that some of them will. The fact that the analyst knows that neither advice nor edict will rule out seductions should not prevent him from trying to keep group relations as uncomplicated as possible. The analyst neither forbids nor encourages sexual intimacy within the group. Were he categorically to deny sexual freedom to the group, he would duplicate the parents' castrating role. If he gave his assent to it, he would obscure transference phenomena, which must be worked through before such a relationship is freed of destructive neurotic elements. Here, as elsewhere, he cautions against neurotic ties, sexual or otherwise, which obscure the full significance and realization of what should become a healthy relationship.

Each patient is warned that if he exposes mutual confidences heard within the group to outsiders, he may be dropped from treatment if the problem cannot be worked through. Anonymity must be preserved in the unavoidable discussions that take place between patients and friends and relatives.

In recent years we have recommended that newly formed groups begin analytic work with the very first session. A good topic for starting is the anxiety each felt in anticipation of the first group meeting.

2. On the Irrelevance of Group Psychotherapeutic Leadership in Group Conflict

A. WOLF

I would like to take this opportunity to deplore the increasing application of psychiatric concepts to larger national and international relations. In some respects psychiatrists extend their interests to these immense social problems with the best intentions. We see all about us confused and troubled people and try to apply the psychodynamic formulations of the consulting room to the whole complex world. Our good intentions cannot, however, conceal the irrelevance of our proposals. In other respects our suggestions betray a grandiosity that impresses the listener less with the validity of our vast therapeutic overtures than with the fact that we are ourselves diseased.

It was bad enough in recent years to hear our urgent recommendations that national and international conflicts could be avoided, if only political leaders, hell-bent for neurotic, personal aggrandizement, would submit to psychoanalytic treatment. But now, _group therapists are out to save the world_. We have either regressed to the point where we are reliving our infantile omnipotence or we have been deluded by the illusory insistence of our patients that we are, in fact, "gods." If it required any further demonstration of the failure in many instances of psychoanalysis to resolve social conflict, we need only examine our relationships to one another. I know of no group that is

Reprinted from "On the Irrelevance of Group Psychotherapy in Mass Conflict." _Group Psychotherapy_ 5, 1-3 (April, July, and November 1952):78-79. Paper read at the Round Table Meeting on Group Psychotherapy and Psychodrama, May 10, 1951, at the 107th Annual Meeting of the American Psychiatric Association, Cincinnati, Ohio.

as torn with rivalry and dissension as psychiatric and psychoanalytic factions. We, who cannot get together, would promote group relations! We, who prescribe treatment for political leaders, have each our almighty devices for solving the world's ills. We are then not always the therapists. We, too, are tainted by the sick social process. We forget the dictum: "physician, heal thyself." Until we can demonstrate a capacity for better group relations within our own house, our counsels to larger segments of the body politic seem out of place.

But my objection to our treating the masses and their leaders is more fundamentally based on other grounds. I believe we are unscientifically extending the province of psychiatry to the category of economics. The laws that govern organic chemistry do not necessarily apply to inorganic chemistry. And the formulations of organic interaction do not of necessity cover the principles that determine the chemistry of colloids. This is not to say that each science is unrelated to the next. They are related. But a loose application of the laws governing one body of knowledge tends to obscure rather than clarify important details. In the same way the categories that explain the behavior of rats may throw some *general* light on human psychodynamics. But *we* have a feature distinct from any lower animal—consciousness—which makes us so qualitatively unique in the animal kingdom, that an entirely different set of guiding laws determine our behavior. Therefore, an easy movement from the conduct of rats, or monkeys, to that of man is more often confusing than clarifying. In the same way a facile interpretation of the motivation of political leaders and the masses is downright silly when projected from the group psychotherapeutic treatment room.

This does not mean that I do not think Truman and MacArthur, the Pentagon generals and the President's Cabinet, should not be individually or group analyzed. They and we might all profit thereby. But such recommendations are impractical, impossible, and will go unheeded anyway. They expose our own irrational aspirations. No doubt neurotic leaders and led would profit from psychotherapy. I am an individual and group analyst because I am scientifically convinced of the therapeutically socializing value of analysis. Let it be understood, also, that I know that psychotherapy would enable them to face and deal with realities that are obscured by destructive compulsion. I have no objection to everyone's getting psychotherapeutic help who needs it. But there are more urgent material and human needs than psychoanalysis, that are better met by nonpsychotherapeutic methods. The laws that govern the denial and gratification of these needs are economic, not psychological. And the resolution of these problems will not be accomplished by applying our prescriptions. Our "recommendations" are erudite but irrelevant, emotional but misplaced, well-intentioned but unscientific. We are beating our breasts in vain. The material and emotional needs of humanity will be met on a national and world scale by nonpsychiatric approaches. They will be and are being met by masses of people and political leaders who are increasingly aware of their real needs.

Let us not then in our enthusiasm for psychotherapy irrationally expand our effective roles. We now hold we can do more than treat the mere individual alone. We can treat groups of people. But taking on the whole world is maniacal and messianic, if not paranoid. I would like to suggest that in the category of economics, the economists and the laws of economics will dictate ways and means, rather than our proposals.

Finally, we experts in group relations, who would like to make the nation and society a harmonious and complementary whole, have assembled in congenial conclave. Let us see if any two of us can agree.

3. The Role of the Leader in the Advanced and Terminal Phases of Group Psychotherapy

A. WOLF

According to two group therapists, the leader is somewhat more active in the terminal phase than he was during the middle phase of group psychotherapy. Here again, I believe a discriminative view of the therapist's activity, passivity or neutrality must be taken and, if he is any of these, consideration should be given to the timing of his interventions as well as to the kind of engagement he chooses to serve the patient's positive evolution at this moment or in the future. With a member who is initially silent, the therapist may choose to be active or passive depending on which maneuver he believes will best call forth a response. With an initially verbally monopolistic member, the therapist may have at first to intervene very actively in analyzing his narcissism and, in the terminal phase, just as actively in esteeming his allocentrism. With a shy, withdrawn patient the therapist may in the beginning be quite active in encouraging him to participate, in a middle phase be just as energetic in appreciating his more vigorous communication and in a terminal phase more passive as the patient appears to be doing well enough on his own. These differences in patient requirements, depending on what stage of development each one is in, point up once more why a nondiscriminative, stereotyped prescription for the therapist's role at so-called group phases can no more be appropriate to the needs of all than to the needs of one patient in different periods of his progress.

One of the most fundamental roles of the therapist in all phases of treatment, but particularly in the advanced and terminal stages, is concerned with his traditional neutrality. In individual therapy, it is

10

easier to maintain for the most part a consistent regard for the interests of the patient, and thereby not to jeopardize his confidence in the therapist as a dependable ally. Even in those instances where the therapist is at variance with the patient, subtle and gentle means may be used to guide him to a more reasonable adjustment. In the group, however, where irrational contention so commonly arises between two members, it is more difficult for the leader to maintain neutrality without abdicating his therapeutic functions entirely and losing the regard not only of the contestants but of the whole group.

A word is in order here with reference to the doubtful value of pursuing such a course of abstention which in time may assume the countertransferential character of indifference with all the hazards in patient responses that such an attitude entails. For the therapist to assume an absolutely impartial position suggests that he has no values, no judgment, no appreciation, no discrimination, which he can exercise in resolving the seeming impasse between two patients. And if he does not step in with an attempt to heal the breach, he begins to lose the affection and respect which his position demands, if he is to go on securely in his role as therapist. So he cannot continue, under these circumstances, to maintain a nondiscriminative detachment without alienation. Yet, how can he take sides in an issue between two patients without hurting one or the other? Here again, if the therapist keeps in mind the particular, constructive, evolutionary needs of each contestant at this particular time, it is unlikely that he will go wrong. If the patients' differences have arisen from the one's acting out his compulsive intellectuality and the other's acting out his irrational affect, the therapist may analyze the bilateral intrapsychic pathology without taking sides. If, however the contesting patient is just beginning to break through his defenses to express an unreasonable feeling, he needs at this moment the leader's unqualified support. It is only when these emotional outbursts threaten to become entrenched in pathological repetition that the therapist can begin to take issue with them and point the way to more reasonable alternatives. The excessively rational member will need the leader's support as resistance begins to give way before emotional needs pressing for release.

While the therapist's aim is for ultimate reasonable interaction, he must, therefore, be guided in taking sides, by the principle of working through for each contestant the special psychopathology of the individual. In the advanced and terminal stages, the therapist will find himself sharing more and more the increasingly sound reactions of the recovering patient. While at first the latter may require the leader's endorsement of his behavior, in time he becomes able to pursue his own judgments without affirmation from the authority figure.

4. The Role of the Leader's Values

A. WOLF and E. K. SCHWARTZ

We shall now attempt to specify some of the general human values, some of those related to psychoanalysis, and more especially those that are specific to doing psychoanalysis in groups. No claim is made that we have thoroughly explored any of them or that our list is exhaustive.

1. The therapist's choice to do therapy in an individual or group situation is an expression of his values. The way the therapist perceives what is good and what is bad in himself and in the group affects the quality of the therapy. A dominating or authoritarian therapist, for instance, who sees the group as one person or who will not let the group meet as peers without him, may not do therapy as well as the individual therapist. He may demand extraordinary superego controls. But the patient stands a better chance of achieving a wholesome set of democratic and constructive attitudes toward his peers and the therapist in a group situation than with an authoritarian analyst alone.

A therapist can influence patients to become very much like himself, extensions of himself, or submissive borderline egos who act out his schizoid or conflictual demands, or who act out their own id forces. Whatever the therapist's attitude—whether he is too detached, or too aggressive, too overbearing or too compliant, too rational or too irrational——his problems can be better coped with by a group of patients than by the isolated patient. This is not to say that we go along with the belief that the therapist's problems are treated by the group.

The resources of patients can be better mobilized by their inter-

Reprinted from "Psychoanalysis in Groups: The Role of Values." *American Journal of Psychoanalysis* 19, 1 (1959):38-51.

action in a group setting than when having to deal with the therapist's problems in an exclusive, dyadic relationship. Patients working together in a group are likely to be better able to resist the therapist's irrational demands or his emphasis on pathology than patients who work with the therapist alone. The choice of a group as the medium for therapy by the therapist as well as the patient is recognition of how the group setting can be a factor in moving the patient as well as the therapist toward more wholesome values.

2. The group is a radical departure from the position of the patient on the couch, with the analyst seated behind. It is a geographic setup in which the patient is seated facing not only the therapist but also his co-patients. He is forced into interpersonal interaction and intrapsychic exploration. The value of forced interaction already has been demonstrated for the dependent, passive, detached, and isolated patient. Most people in our society, though seemingly interactive, in many respects are really very isolated. In the group, patients have to look at one another and at the therapist. Out of forced interaction, we move toward intrapsychic exploration.

When a patient sits in a group and does not look at the people around, when he sits gazing at the floor, group members soon complain that he is not looking at them, that he is not involved with them, that they want to see his eyes, they want him to talk to them. If he starts speaking to one member and the whole group does not hear, they demand that he be heard. If he addresses himself exclusively to the therapist, the group protests. The group forces interaction.

How different this is from the traditional analytic arrangement. An individual analyst, for example, came to his supervisor and complained that for the past months the patient on the couch had spoken so softly that he did not hear her. What should he do about it? He was very surprised when the supervisor said, "Why not ask her to talk a little more loudly?" This could never happen in a group. Another instance is that of the patient on the couch who would fall asleep early in each session. The therapist took the position that if the patient felt like going to sleep, this was all right with him. Then there is the therapist who writes his letters, papers, and books while the patient is on the couch.

Some analysts seem too ready to permit the patient to isolate himself in intrapsychic fantasy, pathology, or sleep. Such a therapist permits— and sometimes encourages—no interaction. He rationalizes this behavior by saying that he must encourage, teach, or develop frustration tolerance in the patient. Supposedly, one learns better to tolerate frustration by experiencing more frustration. We feel that one may be better able to tolerate frustration by being secure, by being less anxious, rather than by experiencing continuing frustration.

The principle of forced interaction is an important therapeutic process in the group. From the inception of psychoanalysis in groups, patients have been asked to "go around," to involve evrybody in interaction. From the interpersonal transactions we then can examine the behavior in terms of what stands in the way of more wholesome interaction. This is an important and constructive principle which both the patient and the therapist in the dyadic relationship often abandon.

We wish to warn against the practice of some therapists compulsively to impose pathologic interaction between patients and therapist and among patients. This is a seeming, pseudointeraction which is really noncommunicative, fragmented and fragmenting, transference and counter-transference. Our concept is quite different from that kind of forced, pathologic noninteraction in isolation. For us, the individual also must be given the opportunity to explore his own intrapsychic processes on a reasonable, healthy basis. In addition, he must have an opportunity for genuine, appropriate, and realistic intercommunication.

3. In choosing to do psychoanalysis in groups, the therapist is expressing a belief that out of conflict and controversy come gains. In the group, patients become more aware of their differences and disagreements. They learn to reach compromises, a more harmonious balance. They learn to sublimate some of their wishes, make concessions to one another, and be more flexible with each other. The therapist necessarily must examine conflict, difference, disharmony, disagreement and help patients to reach some sort of harmonious, relative agreement in compromise. What the therapist values in this scheme is not conflict for itself but compromise, sublimation, the necessity to reach some partial fulfillment for the contestants.

4. The analyst who works in groups accepts the fact that the patient must examine critically not only himself but also others. The group therapist believes that it is socially, psychologically, politically, humanly valuable for the therapist, too, to put himself in the position of being examined, criticized, challenged, questioned, that this is a valuable experience for the patient and an important value in life. We do not mean to foster rebellion which may already be a problem

of the patient. We distinguish between rebellion and the wholesome necessity to examine leaders or persons in authority positions. Patients often need to learn that they can have the right and the courage to examine leadership critically. The critical reactions of the individual patient to the individual analyst is not always rebellious and resistive.

The patient in individual analysis has no feedback except the analyst. There can be little or no consensual validation of his critical view of the analyst, who can irrationally maintain his position of omnipotence. The group, on the other hand, provides opportunity for sharing and comparing experiences, for confirming or denying whether the reaction to the therapist was transferential or appropriate.

By virtue of the fact that he puts himself before a group, the group analyst exposes himself consciously to the possibility of criticism and the confirmation of its legitimacy. The therapist is not so different from other human beings that he can never be wrong. This makes him much more human and leads to the possibility of greater equalization.

An individual analyst once said, "You know, if any patient of mine called me by my first name, I would throw him out of analysis." It is not calling the analyst by the first name that we are proposing. What we are pointing out is the attitude that I, the therapist, must never be perceived as a human being, as having a first name, as having any name but "The Analyst," in the orthodox sense. The classic anonymity of the analyst prohibits his exposure to consensually validated, realistic criticism.

Distinction must be made, however, between our position and the concept of status denial where the analyst not only subjects himself to criticism, but becomes more of a patient than the patients themselves. This is not what we mean by the therapist being subject to critical examination by group members. We mean appropriate, critical reaction. We do not mean sponsoring or acceding to patients' or therapists' demands to establish a co-pathology, co-delinquency, or co-psychosis.

Implicit here is the right to criticize authority and the need of support for that right. Experimental and social psychologic studies of the authoritarian personality support the value of being legitimately critical of authority, and also of the therapist making a legitimate mistake without having to hide behind the mask of anonymity, omnipotence, and omniscience. There are objectivity, critical value, and positive potentials also in patients, in peers, in the child, in subordinates.

5. We believe in the importance or the value of democracy. By democracy we mean not the absence of leadership or the absence of differences, but the value of each person in the interpersonal experience. A person has value in and of and for himself. Psychoanalysis in groups tends to encourage a more democratic way of relating. It rejects the absolutism of authority, the noncritical view of the therapist, and, at the same time, recognizes the value of peers. Not only parents, but also children have values; not only therapists but also patients. The one does not exist without the other; together they constitute a reciprocal unit.

Interaction between therapist and patient is valuable, but so is the interaction among patients in the group. The interaction among peers is not only, always and exclusively negative, destructive, and pathologic. The nature of a relationship to a co-patient is different from a relationship with the therapist, but nevertheless of value. Peers permit the possibility of a patient not only to be helped but also to help; not only to be supported but also to support; not only to depend upon but also to be depended upon. It attenuates the fiction of the benevolent giving by one person, the therapist.

The fact that a therapist chooses to apply therapy in the group situation says something about his valuing and his wish to explore a patient's relationship to peers as well as to authority figures. He is interested in providing a medium for the exploration of horizontal as well as vertical relationships, and the necessity to work these through. Moreover, problems with the authority figure can be more readily worked through with the support the individual receives from peers. The group facilitates the working through of authority and peer problems because both vectors are simultaneously present. The interplay of authority and peer vectors is present also in the relation of one patient to another.

The patient in individual treatment often feels that he has no value, no position, no status, no consideration, no ego, no adequacy, unless he is alone with the therapist. Alone with the therapist he has value, he is regarded, he is felt, he is considered, he is a person, but once he is with another person or a group of persons, he is lost, he is inadequate, he is inferior, he has no position, no status. Psychoanalysis in groups mitigates against the preservation of such an irrational attitude, which must be worked through whether it is considered in the therapy group, in the family, in society, or in a democratic community. Such a patient needs to learn that he has position, status, equality, an ego;

that he is a person who is valued, valuable to others and to himself; that his contributions are important; that we value him in the community and the therapeutic group.

A common problem of patients is the difficulty they have in viewing themselves as peers, as equals. For example, whenever one man in a group was asked whether he was anybody's equal, he characteristically said, "No! I'm either superior to the next fellow or I'm inferior. I am never equal." He sees himself compulsively in this hierarchical position. We all suffer from this attitude in some degree. Perhaps, in some respects, it is also a true perception; in other respects, it is a distorted perception. The reality is that we are different. The question is whether this difference really makes us unequal. The group permits one to explore and understand differences.

6. Differences are not to be ignored. The demand of society, of parents and even of psychoanalysts for conformity, adjustment, and sameness contains a denial of the value of difference. The preference among some group therapists for homogeneity is, in our opinion, the less valuable choice for the organization of therapy groups, for it reflects an attitude that tends to deny individual differences.

Differences can have equal value, but difference and equality are not on the same continuum. One can be equal in difference, because differences can have equal usefulness, acceptability, and validity. In psychoanalysis in groups it is possible to lose the sense of uniqueness without losing the sense of difference. The feeling of being unique is very often involved in pathologic formations and can be worked through. A sense of uniqueness can be given up and yet the validity of being different can be accepted. One can have a private life as well as a public life; one-to-one relationships as well as relationships to groups. One can have an individual and a group relationship. These can and should be integrated. It is possible to integrate a difference and a sameness without having to take either extreme, in uniqueness or loss of difference.

In individual analysis the therapist says, "I am the analyst, you are the patient. You may be superior to me as a philosopher, as a technician, as a teacher, as a butcher, as an athlete, or in many other ways, but here, as *analyst*, I am superior to you." In psychoanalysis in groups, by providing a different atmosphere of peers, the patient is able to work out this problem more readily. In the group, the patient experiences the difference between patient and therapist, but simultaneously the sameness of his status with regard to other patients;

they are peers. Yet each one is different, even though in the status structure of the group therapeutic situation they all are on an equal level. They all are equal before the therapist. They all are equally valuable and equally important to the therapist. The structure and difference is conjointly present. They are men and women with different histories and different problems, and in the group they can experience directly the possibility of being equal in the difference. This cannot be experienced first hand in the individual therapeutic situation.

The patient who feels he has no equals assumes that all human beings are hierarchically related. As long as he rigidly holds to this assumption he can never resolve the problem of equality and difference. Only when he accepts the fact that human beings can be horizontally related is the perception of equality in difference possible. There is no less value in the human quality of the person who is able to fulfill himself in his role in society as a mechanic than in that of the banker, or philosopher, or scientist. The difference in their contributions may be very great, and we may regard them differently, but without the mechanic the others cannot fulfill themselves in terms of their own life's plan. The fulfillment of the one is as necessary as of the other in order for humanity to progress. They have equality of necessity, of value, of responsibility, if you wish, in terms of the larger human picture. This does not mean that they are equal in the sense of no difference. But they are equal in the sense that they have value, and we can hold the recognition of differences as being valuable in itself. The difference between male and female, between illness and health, between therapist and patient must not be obscured.

W are aware of the compulsive quest for diversity, which may then become the pathologic addiction to divisiveness and diversion. On the other hand, science seeks to simplify in order to lead to clarification, but it does not deny diversity as a state of nature. The one-sided pursuit of sameness or difference can be equally pathologic and misleading.

7. We hold that there is an appropriate place for differences of opinion, even between analyst and patient; that controversy in itself and of itself is not bad, and that one can be critical, argue, and disagree and still be friends. We are opposed to those who believe it is base to think independently, to get into criticism and controversy. Conformity and submission can be the only end products of such an attitude.

This value is often neglected in the experience with the individual therapist because the patient does not really fight with the therapist, unless the therapist is counterattacking. But in the peer situation of co-patients, it is possible for attack and counterattack to occur and for the patients still to know that they can be friends. They can work together, despite the fact that they have attacked one another or even acted out with regard to one another. It is a striking admission on the part of new members of a therapy group when they indicate their amazement of how the others can express considerable ambivalence and hostility toward one another and yet walk out of a group meeting in the friendliest way and continue to work together. A new patient often feels startled by the way in which group members can dispute one another and still maintain a working relationship.

We are aware of the patient who must compulsively fight every individual before he can show any affection. This is the only way in which he can relate. There are also patients who compulsively emphasize only their feelings of being different. To be able to relate to only one kind of person, to be able to relate or function in only one way, is limiting and limited.

8. We reject absolutism, totalism, and exclusivism. The principle of multiple reactivity and complementation represents an important value of psychoanalysis in groups. It leads each patient to question the particular nature of his compulsive activity. It demands of him an examination of his prior and present modes of living. It helps him explore the possibilities of functioning in different ways. Group members question each other about the particular ways their competitive patterns limit them. Patients are forced in their exchanges with one another to seek compromises, to find a golden mean, to give up a totally isolated and egocentric position. They learn to recognize the distortion in total potency or total impotency, and to struggle for the acceptance of partial human capacities in their interaction.

The therapist and the patient must learn to accept their similarity with other individuals and their difference, as well as the different roles each single individual is called upon to play in different situations and relationships.

In individual analysis there is generally only one kind of activity the patient can perform. He, the taker, is dependent upon the therapist, the giver. What the patient gives are his "free associations." This is his work, his giving. Theoretically, the role of listener is the therapist's; the patient does not have to listen. There is no real alteration of roles, in part due to the fact that the analyst has no right to seek fulfillment from the patient. When the patient becomes healthier and attempts to alter the nature of the roles, the therapist may interpret this as resistance and not permit the change.

Psychoanalysis in groups sponsors the recognition of the necessity in all human relations to assume different roles. In the group, the patient can now, this moment, be helped; but it demands also that within a short space of time he be a helper, that while he is listened to now, shortly he must listen to the other. It demands of him now that he pay attention to his own feelings, but that the next moment he attend the feelings of the other; or even that in the moment of expressing his feelings, he must consider their impact upon the feeling of the other. Now he can be attentive to his own affect; in the next moment he must be reasonable about the feelings he has expressed. While he can give vent to his feelings, he must apply some reasonable attention to the needs of other people. While this moment he may be impulsive, the next he must be more considerate. This shifting of roles makes a healthy demand on him to be responsible and to relinquish the resistive and rigid pattern of an exclusive way of relating.

We have already suggested that an exclusive way of relating is limited, whether only with authority figures or only with peers, only in the one-to-one relationship or only in the group. Even in the group therapeutic situation, if the patient is always the giver, always the helper, this can be resistance. The occasional assumption of such a role is healthy, but always to be in the role of helper is just as unhealthy as always to be in the role of being helped. It is part of totalism.

We believe it is good that peers and authorities can be examined in the variety of their aspects because of the multiplicity of interactivity and stimulation. A person can relate to, be stimulated by, and interact with many kinds of persons. In individual therapy, the patient must relate in a complementary way only to the therapist. In the group, the uniqueness of resources in the therapist is complemented by a multiple set of other persons. In the group, the patient has greater freedom to choose with whom to react, to what degree, and in what way. In individual analysis, the patient has no such choice except in reporting outside experience or in fantasy.

9. In psychoanalysis in groups the patient learns to understand that he has no right to expect from all people the same kind of detached, objective understanding that he gets from the therapist; that the therapist's position is, in some respects, artificial. The therapist does not

behave this way in his relationships outside of the therapeutic situation. If the therapist is attacked outside of therapy, he may withdraw or counterattack, or he may be hurt, or have a variety of human responses. If the therapist is always nonreactive to the patient's provocative role, then the patient never really learns to perceive his provocative role except insofar as the individual therapist wishes to interpret it as transferential. The patient may, however, have a provocative role which is not always transferential, but related to how he functions and what kind of person he is. With the therapist alone he may never become aware of how other people feel about him and how they see him. This benefit arises only in the therapeutic group.

The patient also needs to learn about how his peers in the group react to him. In this way he comes to recognize the effects his rational and irrational expressions have produced in his peers in the group, as well as in society; in this way he gets to know his provocative roles, both positive and negative, with regard to peers as well as authorities. He becomes aware also of the difference between his peers in the therapeutic group and those in the community.

The patient has no right to the exclusive possession of the therapist or the other person. This misconception exists even in marital situations where one partner will demand the total and exclusive possession of the other. Exclusive possessiveness is mitigated by the group. However, there may be patients, as for example, the severely orally dependent type, who need a period alone with the therapist, perhaps projected as mother, before they can make a more wholesome transition to siblings, to peers, to the group, and relinquish the exclusive possession of the therapist. It would be unreasonable to refuse to perceive the patient's irrational needs for exclusive possession and to demand that he forego them at the moment. For this reason, individual sessions where they are really needed are appropriate. It is bad, in our estimation, for a group therapist to say, "I never hold an individual session."

10. Just as relationship is important, we believe relationship cannot occur unless there is communication. Good communication is nonambiguous, open, direct, a free expression of feelings, thoughts and attitudes. One of the aims of any psychotherapy is to establish communication, for without verbal intercourse we cannot achieve real understanding.

We think it is good if people have relatively uninhibited conversation with one another. Social intercourse can be relatively uninhibited.

If one is as honest as is realistically appropriate to the relationship, this is a desirable kind of communication. We think that inter-communication, even in psychoanalysis, is as important as intracommunication, that is, communication with oneself or one's own unconscious processes.

We believe that to interpret to patients that they have experienced telepathic communication and that this is the "real," the unconscious-to-unconscious communication, is destructive. We reject, moreover, the value some therapists put upon inappropriate or irrational means of communication, namely, in sleep, in dreams, in telepathy, in non-verbal contact. Their emphasis upon irrational and isolating pseudo-communication is a preoccupation with destructive values. We wonder how much they try, in their working through, to get the patient in therapy to communicate in a more appropriate way.

There are some people who can communicate in a one-to-one, private, secret relationship, whether good or bad. But the moment they are exposed to the more public situation of a group, they remain separated, withdrawn, detached, depressed, hesitant, and uncommunicative. Other people seem to be able to communicate only in the public relationship; in the group they seem related and interactive. In the intimacy of the one-to-one situation, they become isolated, hostile, anxious, uncommunicative. The presence or absence of the authority, the therapist, seems similarly to affect communication in some patients. Psychoanalysis in groups attempts, then, to provide a harmonious balance of individual and group experiences.

11. In contrast to some analysts who prize isolation, we hold that relating, interacting with other human beings, in and of itself is good. We hope that in the therapeutic situation we shall be able to examine the nature of that relationship and to help make the relationship more constructive by working through the destructive elements and distortions and by fostering positive relatednesses. But relating to other human beings, as such, is valuable, as opposed to insulation and separation, as such. Aloneness, the absence of social interaction, is dehumanizing.

The group provides a happier medium for the evocation of problems in social living and the possibilities of a struggle toward their resolution. In its emphasis upon the interactive, the possibility of increased relatedness is offered by the group. If striving for equalization of parent and child, of teacher and student, of analyst and patient, is an objective in therapy, the attainment of this socialization is facilitated in the group by providing peers who can help the individual work through his tendency to attach himself to or overinvest in the authority figure, and finally come to a more wholesome approximation of equality.

Socialization is vital to the development and preservation of man. A human being is a socialized, human animal. It seems to us valuable for him to be placed in a social context to humanize him further. The good therapist, whether he works with individuals or with groups, accepts the concept that man needs about him other human beings in order to mature, to be able to live adequately with other human beings. The analytic group is an excellent matrix in which to reconstruct the family, to provide an extrafamilial group in which to make the transition from the projected family to nonfamilial wholesome associations, and to enable the patient to return more positively to his original family, once his projections have been worked through. Through his contact with other patients in the course of his struggle for growth, the patient learns to cooperate for the continuity and gratification of self and the group.

It is true that the patient in individual analysis may work out his problem with the family as reanimated in successive transference projections on the therapist. The group, however, facilitates the resolution of these problems because the whole canvas emerges more quickly and is, therefore, available for more lucid examination and working through. One gets a better picture of the multiple transferences operating in the family at the same time.

12. We believe that the group has value in, and of, and for itself. This does not mean that we do not value individual experience in therapy and in life. Living in a group, experiencing interaction in a group, is a maturing, fostering, and broadening experience for human beings. The individual exists only by virtue of the fact that there are groups, and the group by virtue of the fact that there are individuals.

The purpose of being in a therapeutic group, however, is not so much to live as to learn. Therapy and the therapeutic group exist to provide a learning experience. This objective must be clear to both patient and therapist. Here patients are learning how to live, but the living takes place not in the group, although it is a living experience, but outside the therapy group, outside of the function of therapy. It is in the therapeutic group that one learns to live better, to live with more fulfillment, to live more constructively with other individuals and groups.

The group therapist, however, must not be misled and allow the group interaction to become the patient's substitute for social living and socialization. The individual analyst, aware of the aloneness of his patient, may encourage him to interact with other people and to socialize. The group therapist, providing a situation in which interaction with other people, the other patients, takes place, may tend to overlook the fact that this can be an isolating experience. Patients before they come into a therapy group may have relations with friends and family. They may give up these contacts and seemingly regress into the group and react exclusively with members of the group.

The ultimate objective of the therapeutic group, like the individual therapeutic experience, is that the patient will find social and sexual life and fulfillment outside of the relationship with the therapist and the other patients. This pitfall must be kept firmly in mind by the group therapist or he can become seduced by the apparency of interaction into encouraging the aloneness and isolation of the patients. Patients may misuse the therapy group as the invested experience of socializing and thereby isolate themselves as some patients isolate themselves within the individual therapy situation. This possibility must be consciously pursued by the group analyst, especially if he uses the alternate session, one of the benefits of which is socializing. By providing patients with such an opportunity, further isolation from the larger social group can occur.

Moreover, it is an error of psychoanalysis in groups to allow patients to see the subculture of the therapeutic group as a microcosm of the total society, to see all of society as a generalization of the therapeutic experience. As the patient gets better, he should want to slough off his more pathologic associates. It is, therefore, not only resistance when, after improvement, a patient wants to leave the group. To view this development only as resistance is to miss its positive implications. Furthermore, it is resistance to change for a patient not to want to leave the group, to resist getting well, because here is a controlled social life, a provided social life. Just as the family may be used as a means of not relating to people who are different, so the therapy group may be a way of relating to or avoiding relationships with those who are different, those who are not members of the therapeutic group.

13. Although we see value in real belonging, we recognize a current, phony concept of belonging. It is often a pseudo-belonging as, for example, in the group patient's inability to attach himself posi-

tively to someone outside the group. It is an apparent, transferential, pseudobelonging that isolates him in therapeutic relationships.

This happens even in life. We are reminded of the case of a young woman whose father said, "You can belong to me and be loved by me, but only on my conditions, only on my terms." That is, only if she accepts the irrational demand of the superordinacy of the parent and the subordinacy of the child. This is a kind of transferential belonging which is different from real belonging. Transferential belonging can occur in the group, and the therapist may unwittingly encourage and accept it as if it were real. One sees pseudobelonging also in individual analytic relationships where, for example, the therapist develops an intimacy with his patient and sees her only during analytic sessions, but makes no real relationship with her outside of this fantasy one.

14. We reject the tendency among some group therapists to permit a pathologic subculture to develop where one patient will say to the next, "Well, what do you want of me, that's my neurosis." This attitude is sometimes seen in individual analysis and is even cultivated by the individual therapist, when he tries, no matter what, to understand the patient and permits him to go on acting out his pathology.

Psychoanalysis in groups recognizes that the patient must become increasingly aware not only of himself but of others. This contrasts with more orthodox individual analysis where too often the patient becomes almost exclusively preoccupied with his own intrapsychic processes. In such a case, we say, it is poor individual analysis. The group, however, by its very nature demands forced interaction and interpersonal communication. The patient must be attentive also to the problems and resources of the people around him. The group demands that he be creatively adaptive to the individuals with whom he is associating. He not only can adapt himself, but he tries to adapt the environmental situation to himself.

Psychoanalysis in groups precipitates areas of interpersonal conflict and forces the individual to scrutinize his and others' roles in creating the opposition, the impasse. The antagonists must seek means to resolve and work through the intrapsychic pathology that has led to the interpersonal conflict.

Psychotherapy has been too largely devoted to the elucidation of psychopathology and given less attention to the necessity for bringing out and developing the patient's healthy potentials. Too little attention has been paid to the problem of working through. In working with groups, one is impressed with the extent to which patients confront one another spontaneously and healthily with the demand to try constructive alternatives. Questions occur like, "Why don't you try this?" Or, "Don't you see that . . . ?" Or, "Can't you make an effort to . . . ?" It is noteworthy that the group is generally more impatient with, less tolerant of, and less interested in psychopathology than the therapist. This is a positive value in human beings who are patients, who do not have the kind of interest, sometimes obsessive, that the therapist has in psychopathology.

15. We reject the view that health rises out of pathology. We see it, in its extreme, in the form of the "therapeutic psychosis." The assumption is made that out of illness, through the expression of pathology, you rid yourself of the demon that possesses you. Then you will be healthy. It is true that healthy potentials will be freer if the psychopathology is worked through. But we have the feeling that if we work more with the constructive potentials in patients, the freedom to use those potentials is increased and pathologic barriers to freedom will atrophy. But it is a misconception to believe that the source of what is health giving, of what is constructive and creative, is the pathology. Some therapists value pathology more than health.

We do not hold that catharsis results in health. Indeed, catharsis is valuable, but like pathology it is not the *via regia* to mental health. Merely to cathart, to express pathology, is not in itself curative. Something has to be done with it. To insist that it is healthy if one can express unconscious material directly is a mistaken value. It overemphasizes intrapsychic material. Nor are psychodynamics equal to therapy. Psychodynamic knowledge, like diagnostic information, provides material for therapeutic work, but together they do not constitute the therapeutic process. This is *pars pro toto* reasoning. To view therapy and dynamics as one is to misconceive the analysis of the dynamics as the cure. Moreover, psychodynamics and psychopathology are not the same. A good psychodynamic understanding of the patient includes all of his functioning, positive as well as negative. We want to know his motivations for health as well as unhealth.

With regard to psychoanalysis in groups, it is true that the group stimulates psychodynamics and that the alternate meeting in particular stimulates psychodynamics, but not only the psychodynamic pathology but also the psychodynamic healthy potentials in the patient are stimulated. What happens reconstructively depends on how the therapist uses the pathologic and healthy psychodynamics.

16. We feel it is valuable to understand that in all situations, in-

cluding psychoanalysis in groups, there is structure, process, and content, and that each is related to the others. Values are implicit in which of these we stress and how we use each of these. Those who stress content, for example, generally miss the unconscious, the psychodynamic material. They miss also status and interaction problems which arise out of the nature of the structure. The structuring of the therapeutic process also implies values. To emphasize the structure as opposed to process or content, namely, in what setting, as opposed to how and with what material you choose to therapeutize, is also one-sided and nondiscriminative. It leads to limited therapeutic results.

17. Psychoanalysis in groups provides an excellent opportunity to evaluate old values and learn new ones. As one experiences through interaction and intercommunication, and shares values, convictions, and attitudes with other members of the group, one learns to evaluate one's own traditional, familial values and, at the same time, to learn new values. Values arise in the interaction between individual and individual, group and group, and between the individual and the group. In the individual analytic situation only one of these three sources for the derivation of values is provided by the therapy. In psychoanalysis in groups, all three exist.

The values we have discussed so far are those that have specificity with regard to psychoanalysis in groups. We feel that they have application to all therapy as well as to the individual in society. Nevertheless, we have omitted a number of genuine values, some of which we must list, no matter how briefly. We are not elaborating even those we include here, but we recognize that they lie *au fond* and provide the substructure for the values of psychoanalysis in groups.

1. We have reached an unfortunate point in psychology, as well as in the culture in general, where it is believed that experiencing and expressing affect are more enlightening than logic or reason. The value of intelligence and reason is often neglected. We are not advocating an exclusive view of human function. Affect and action also are valuable. Thinking, feeling, and doing must be integrated, and the compulsive pursuit of any one of them to the exclusion of the others is not good. Nevertheless, we wish to state our belief that human desires may be directed by reason. "The voice of the intellect is a soft one, but it does not rest until it has gained a hearing," Freud said. "Ultimately, after endlessly repeated rebuffs, it succeeds. This is one of the

few points in which one may be optimistic about the future of mankind, but in itself it signifies not a little."

2. We believe that there is value in the funded wisdom of human experience. Culture, training, human interaction, and exchange are valuable. History and context must not be pursued in and for themselves, but they are useful.

3. We believe that flexibility and judgment are good.

4. We esteem educability and change. One of the ordeals of the psychotherapist is the patient's enduring resistance to change. Yet a patient with no resistance would be psychotic or the totally passive and dulled instrument of the therapist. In many ways it is overcoming the patient's resistance that makes psychoanalysis such a fascinating experience for the therapist. The patient's tempering his rigidity in the face of insight is an endlessly exciting and wonderful experience. It is intriguing to observe his opposition begin to defer to reality. The patient whose resistance takes the form of utter compliance is not nearly so interesting, until his passivity yields to self-assertive claims. But the possibility of change is one of the most stimulating, rational gratifications available to both patient and therapist.

5. A comprehensive view of human behavior includes not only the manifest act but also the motivation. Behavior and motivation may be consciously and/or unconsciously determined.

6. It is necessary for human beings to learn in the family, in therapy, and also in life the difference between right and wrong. In therapy the analyst must refuse to yield to a patient's pathology and in so doing strengthen the patient's sense of values. The sense of what is right and what is wrong is a consequence of human interaction, never of mystic, intuitive inheritance.

7. Freedom is good. It implies a rejection of false necessity, of fate. We mean the concept of choice, selectivity, discrimination, parity, and spontaneity. In freedom one can survey, understand, and accept the possibility of multiple alternatives and make a choice within those. It implies, too, an awareness of responsibility in anticipating the consequences of the decision for the self and for others. We do not mean the encouragement of the illusion that limitlessness and license represent freedom. Liberty is not derived from acting on impulse or in compulsion. Too often the patient's and the therapist's insistence upon the "right" to have every kind of experience is simply a rationalization for acting in pathology. Their freedom is lost unless they discriminate sufficiently to choose reality as more valuable than oceanic fantasy.

8. Mutual aid and cooperation are good. Not only does the human being need to be supported, but also to support others; to protect and to be protected; to help and to be helped; to love and to be loved.

9. Since problem solving is one of the characteristics of the human being, what facilitates this capacity is good. Psychoanalysis, science, rationality propose that problem solving be based upon scrutiny, causality, observation, comparison, and reason rather than upon authority and revelation.

10. Finally, we hold as bad the growing tendency in current psychotherapy to reject training, clinical experience, social interaction, and rationality. Speculation and philosophizing need more than subjective confirmation. They must be based upon human experience and tested in clinical and life situations. The present withdrawal into mysticism among certain psychotherapists as a more adequate substitute for reason reflects a bewilderment and a sense of inadequacy before the inexorable logic of science. An irrational school of therapists is regressing to magical notions of treatment while announcing them as an advance. For the idolatry of the past they are substituting glorified illusions that security lies only in the momentary satisfaction of pathologic strivings. But our experience shows that whenever we build a structure on unreasonable foundations, no good can come of it. We cannot gain more understanding by resigning our rational responsibilities or by resurrecting antiquated and cabalistic devices when sounder means are available. To relinquish our hard-won victories over mystification is to submit once again to a despotism of unreason and the destruction of values.

5. The Absent Leader

A. WOLF and E. K. SCHWARTZ

The group therapist needs to be flexible enough to allow the group to meet without him. The group analyst who never permits any alternate session says, in effect, there must be no communication among patients, except under his supervision. In forbidding the alternate meeting he denies those who are able to express themselves more freely primarily in his absence. His authoritarianism may be in the superego-dominated vector, so that all intense feeling is forbidden or regarded as acting out. Or his control may be in the id-dominated vector, so that only extravagant affect is cultivated. In either case the group therapist rejects the constructive use of the alternate session. Very repressive and very permissive treatment equally subvert the essence of what a group therapeutic experience has to offer.

Some authoritarian therapists not only reject the alternate meeting but also take the position that the patient must suffer to get well. This is a medieval, prepsychotherapeutic, preanalytic point of view. It would beat the psychopathology out of patients and beat sense into them. Such an approach makes a grand inquisitor of the therapist who sadistically submits patients to purification by ordeal.

The overdirective group therapist who views patients as dominated or as running wild without his supervision, who commands them not to function without his direction, fosters their infantilization. His domination discourages them from making contact with one another, from establishing a coexistence and community which build a positive climate in which growth can take place. It is our belief that the restrictive analyst who will not permit the alternate session is, in general, acting out his own need to dictate. In this respect, he subjects the patient again to what may have been traumatic in his earlier family experience, the denial of the right to some activity independent of absolute parental control. An indiscriminate emphasis by the therapist upon those activities he approves results in a pathologic adaptation which resists the resolution of basic authority problems.

Is therapy enhanced by an experience without the therapist? Would it be better if all sessions were with him? For some few, treatment might be improved if all meetings took place with the analyst, should such an arrangement be economically possible. But for most, therapy is moved forward by the alternate session. Patients who have a rich, interactive life outside of therapy and who can bring their reactions into sessions, who can play, who are impulsive but need more discipline, who are disorganized and cannot get down to work, who behave inappropriately, for these perhaps, only regular sessions are necessary. But such patients are less common. Even for them, to see that they can play and yet learn discipline without giving up the play is an important experience. For the isolated, lonely, hard-working, compulsive, over-disciplined person the alternate meeting is useful if not vital.

6. The Leader in Uncertainty

A. WOLF and E. K. SCHWARTZ

What certainties can the analyst offer the patient in the therapeutic relationship? He can offer the security that he is one person who consistently will be trying to understand him, be sympathetic toward him, help him resolve his conflict, lead him from confusion, delusion, and his dilemmas into reality, where realistic solutions can be achieved. The therapist can offer the patient objectivity. He will not punish or blame the patient for what he reveals and for what he expresses, nor will he act again in the traumatic way the parent did in the past. Among the legitimate expectations of the patient is not only that the therapist will have more footholds in reality and have some conviction as to the goodness of the results of therapy, but also that he will not retraumatize the patient. In addition to not being omniscient and omnipotent, the therapist, at the same time, must not be helpless, because this, too, may be a repetition of early parental situations.

Erich Fromm throws some light on the constructive role of parents which has bearing on the therapist's readiness to allow the patient a fuller group life, as against the overprotective seclusion with the authority figures and with consequent helplessness of the individual himself. He says:

> In the ideal case, mother's love does not try to prevent the child from growing up and does not try to put a premium on helplessness. Mothers should have faith in life, hence not be overanxious and thus not infect the child with her anxiety. Part of her love should be the wish that her child become independent, eventually separate from her.

This is related to the certainty that the therapist will not be overprotective or put a premium on the helplessness and dependence of the

33

patient. It means, also, that the therapist does not present himself as helpless and, therefore, increase the uncertainty of the patient. To present himself as helpless, as being a greater patient than the patient, offers the patient no sense of certainty or conviction that he, too, can grow up and be mature, like the model upon which he models himself, but that disillusionment and despair are the only outcomes possible for him.

Moreover, the therapist can offer the patient the certainty of the persistency and consistency of the relationship—namely, no abandonment, but routine, regularity, kindness, and devotion. The therapist will make no demand on the patient other than the payment of a fee. The therapist can offer the patient the certainty that he will make no irrational demands on him, and, if he does, he will be ready to admit and explore the unreasonableness of his position.

The therapist offers to the patient a decent and wholesome set of values. He offers the patient the certainty of trying at all times to do the best he can. The patient, to the extent that he is realistic, has a right to expect all the aforementioned forms of certainty in the therapist. However, the patient, in his quest for certainty, may make unrealistic demands on the therapist—namely, that he be omnipotent, omniscient—and the patient will test reality to see whether the therapist will be co-delinquent, co-neurotic, or co-psychotic. He may irrationally demand that the therapist love him sexually because only in this way will he feel certain that the therapist really loves him.

It may be of some interest to speculate whether the fact that the analyst remains a more remote, detached, and unidentified figure, a figure whose pattern responses are not so clearly visible to the patient, does not give the patient in individual analysis less certainty. In the therapeutic group, the patient discovers much more quickly and readily the various pattern responses of the group members, which may give him more security in knowing with what he has to cope. The individual analyst may seem like one of the gods on Olympus whom the patient cannot see. The patient often feels this way about the therapist. This vague, undefinable figure is really throwing the dice, gambling with his life. It is perhaps a question to understand in therapy, whether this state of affairs does not make for more anxiety in the patient than he would want to experience, or need be subjected to, or than is necessary for good therapeutic outcomes.

It may be useful to the psychoanalyst, in exploring the dynamics of each patient, to think in terms of certainty and uncertainty, or of realistic and unrealistic efforts to achieve certainty, and how this concept plays a role in affecting therapeutic results. Our system of education, as well as psychoanalysis, seems to give the impression that for every question there is a single, definite answer. This is unfortunate, because the problems encountered in later life and their solution generally have an indefinite character. So, too, in psychoanalysis. The nature of the origins of one's neurotic development does not have a pat, sure answer, such as a single traumatic experience, which, when recaptured, will cause a sudden change in the patient.

Some analysts seem to be seeking certainty in their work and in their relationship to the patient by holding strongly to the conviction that if the therapist can discover or uncover this one childhood experience, he will have *the* answer to the total problem. This figment is shared not only by patients who go to the films and see miracle cures seemingly brought about by the recapture of some pathogenic or traumatic memory, but also by some analysts who, too, in their need for certainty about the work they do, believe that *the* answer is to be found by digging deeper and deeper into the recesses of the pathologic past. And this may be true of various analytic schools, too, which, in order to deal with their anxieties and doubts concerning their theoretic and practical position, must become convinced that there is a particular answer, only one answer, whether it is birth trauma, or culture, or some other generalization representing *the* answer to the poor development of the personality.

We are not suggesting that generalizations should not be made. But a monodimensional view of the nature of the human personality, of human functioning, is antianalytic and must result in therapeutic failure. One of Freud's important contributions to psychoanalytic thinking was pointing out the multidimensional origination and development of human thought and personality, in its health and in its illness. Knowing with certainty, even for the analyst, is something that cannot be achieved. Uncertainty will always be in the nature of the work that we do, not only in the patient but also in the analyst and his activities. Man must foster the ability to accept uncertainty and recognize that there is no monodimensional, single answer, except perhaps in the mathematical and in the precise sciences. Is it not true, then, that, while we are always looking for more realistic, appropriate mathematical answers, we are questing certainty, but the capacity to tolerate and to try to understand the unknown and to face uncertainty is part of a more secure and certain approach to one's environment? So one aim of psychoanalysis is to interpret and become master of our own uncertainties, both as patients and as analysts.

7. The Mystique of Group Dynamics in Psychoanalytic Leadership

A. WOLF and E. K. SCHWARTZ

A sharp distinction must be made between the therapist's recognition of group trends, the enrichment of his knowledge of the group as a group, and his activity as a therapist for patients who constitute the group. In some way, hidden behind the group psychodynamicist's position is a rejection of therapy. There are various kinds of groups, therapy groups as well as other sorts of groups. One may then use the group in order to study group dynamics or to accomplish other purposes such as education. Or one may use the group therapeutically. The tendency to use group dynamics in the therapeutic situation is a way of anthropomorphizing the group and looking for group dynamic laws as if the interpretation of these to the group would be therapeutic in some way.

The field of group psychotherapy is already crowded with conductors, leaders, and counselors inadequately trained in psychoanalytic psychotherapy. To these ranks are now being added the group psychodynamicists who are attempting to do therapy with inadequate means. What is even more startling is to discover how many psychoanalytically trained therapists are trying to make indiscriminate use of group dynamics in treatment. Such emphasis suggests either a disregard for or a lack of knowledge of the principles of psychoanalytic therapy. If we focus our attention on group dynamic processes, we cannot also at the same time easily attend diagnosis, psychopathology, individual psychodynamics, dream analysis, resistance, transference and countertransference reactions, provocative roles, multiple reactivities, and other relevant parameters. Concentration on group dynamics can become an avoidance of the necessity for good analytic training in psychotherapy and a rationalization that treatment equates with the elaboration of group dynamic processes.

While group dynamics may apply to all groups and have usefulness in understanding groups, the interest and preoccupation with group dynamics in therapy groups may be a reflection of resistance and countertransference in the therapist. Scheidlinger notes that Bion and Ezriel "suggest some useful hypotheses regarding the utilization of group dynamic elements in the service of resistance." Frank states that "the universal tendency of members to continue interacting outside of the regular group meetings may be viewed as a manifestation of their efforts to become cohesive." Such seeking one another out after regular group meetings may be less a search for cohesion than a compulsion to act out.

The therapist is involved in a process of levelling, when he demands a group function as if it were a uniform group. Such obscuring of disparity applied to the family group would repudiate the reality of the difference between parent and child, between older child and younger child, between girls and boys, between father and mother. Although the family may seem to function as a unit, it is unreal to view it as if it were constituted of mirror images within the family structure. These unlikenesses are rejected in the implication that there is a basic family dynamic, a family unity, which contains within it no place for independent motivation, personal history, variance in one's own reaction even to the same family traditions, structure, and heritage. The second child is not entering the same family as the first child or the third child. With each birth into the family it becomes a new one where a new fragment of history is added and a new generalized structure is developed. Each succeeding child must deal with the family as a changing family. Its structure changes as distinguishable children are added to it.

Group dynamics in psychotherapy is based on the assumption that by changing the environment, you change the intrapsychic pathology. This may be possible. But it is not psychoanalytic therapy. It is a concept of a world utopia where everyone does good things, where everyone is good, kind, and homogeneous, where there is no conflict, no transference, no resistance, no ambivalence. This is a brave new world of undifferentiated, homogenized nonindividuals.

8. The Role of the Leader As Psychoanalyst

A. WOLF and E. K. SCHWARTZ

What, it is pertinent to ask, are the particular qualifications and functions of a successful group analyst? At present, since he is working with a technic that is relatively new, the answer will, of course, be tentative.

As Foulkes has pointed out, psychoanalysts are not *ipso facto* good group analysts, and, he goes on to say, it in no way impugns the former to emphasize that special attributes are required of the group analyst. He must first of all be a psychoanalyst. He must have adequate training, intuitive insight, a capacity for empathy, and an ability to dispose of countertransference attitudes. He must expect concerted efforts to deflate him. He must have the capacity to withstand neurotic attacks on him with composure. He must not be discouraged or thrown off balance by the intensity of interpersonal enmity which occasionally develops in early meetings. Such outbursts are largely projective in character, and his function is jeopardized if he fails to react to them with appropriate analysis. Even the most timid will assail him from the vantage point among the group, and destructive patients will test his tolerance of neurotic frustration and aggression to the utmost. In spite of the therapist's attempt to create a new, more benevolent, and permissive family, the old one with all its rivalry, aggression, dictatorship may assert itself and tax the new parent in the extreme.

He ought to be able patiently to welcome the manifold variety of transferences with which he is invested and not be misled to accept them as real by inappropriate reaction. To be sure, the analyst is afforded the same group protection as his patients. If he is unreasonably attacked, some of them will come to his rescue and support him when

38

the occasion seems to demand it. For, acting upon his injunction, they are continually engaged in reacting spontaneously to everyone present including the analyst. He, too, must expect both blame and praise according to their changing concepts of his desserts.

The function of the group analyst is to guide his patients to fuller awareness and social integration. He can best accomplish this by avoiding conceited and compulsive leadership. He can more surely achieve such a goal by attentive regard to what group members can teach him. The therapist alone need not know all to provide adequate leadership. His nuclear, professional, and leading position is not by itself enough to provide his patients with the full insight they need.

Experience with him is not comprehensive enough to insure healthy, social restoration. Therefore, it is necessary that he supplement his clinical knowledge with an understanding of the interaction of the various group members. This means that he must constantly maintain an alert and intimate connection with the rich reservoirs of understanding which are potential in the group, catalytically interplaying their intuitive insight with his own. He must attend the least small voice as well as the loudest. It will not do for him to detach himself at his desk and hand down well prepared instructions. While he seeks solutions to neurotic problems, the proper answers cannot be found without vigilant regard to group experience which is continually testing his leadership. While he plans operations for the resolution of conflict, he cannot achieve his objectives without the help of the patients. The patient members are an essential and final check on the extent to which therapeutic aims are being fulfilled. The patients' interactivity with each other and with the therapist guarantees status to each individual and finally enables him to utilize his own resources and those of the other members.

The group analyst's view of things tends to be one-sided. He sees patients and their behavior from above. Accordingly, his impression of what is happening is limited by his paternalistic, relatively non-participant position. While he engages in group activity, the quality of his participation is different and modifies his perception of events. The group, on the other hand, appreciates interpersonal forces at work from another side. Its awareness is likewise limited by its position and function in the group. To accomplish that harmony which will lead to integrated group activity, the analyst and patients must interweave their complementary roles. Leadership which achieves this is therapeutic.

The successful analyst learns never to underestimate the significance of the contribution that can be made by the members to mutual insight and social integration. Patients sometimes show themselves to be close to the unconscious truth. If the therapist is wise, he consults them and often supplements his experience with theirs. It may be said that neurotic conflict in part develops in the child out of contradictory influences imposed on him by his parents, who are exploitative, dictatorial, selfish, and at the same time cooperative, democratic, and supportive of the child's developing resources. In the new, permissive family of the group, to the extent that the therapist is authoritarian and detached from the group, he duplicates the destructive role played by the original parents. In this way he may reinforce the patients' difficulties and undermine their actual effectiveness. To the degree that he is continually attentive to the emerging intuitive potentials in the various members, he helps to create a new family unit of the group, in which each participant can realize increasingly gratifying levels of adjustment.

The analyst who regards himself as the most active, critical thinker in the group and the patients as a relatively inert mass is likely to be led far astray. With such a misconception, he tends to overestimate himself and look down on the group; he has the illusion that success or failure depends pretty much on him and that the group is lacking in creative, contributory power. He believes that his acuteness alone determines the successful outcome of treatment. Such a view condemns the group to passivity and excludes the membership from the active participation essential to its recovery. It also reduces the group activity to a series of dictated or accidental psychodynamics whose ebb and flow are determined by the prescriptions, needs and fantasies of the authoritarian therapist. The fact is that the therapeutic process in the group proceeds in accordance with definite laws. While the development of the group moves on according to certain principles, the therapist and each patient are constantly modifying its progress. The therapist can play a most significant catalytic part in facilitating patient movement by seeing further ahead than his patients. He can do this also by desiring and struggling to accomplish healthy integration more vigorously than they. His effectiveness lies in his deep contact with each member, in his ability to understand them, in his skill in foreseeing the historical course the individual takes, and in his confidence in the potential resources of the various members.

The course a group takes is primarily determined by the various character structures of the participant members, itself a product of their previous history. The personal qualities of the analyst modify this course. This does not mean that the contributions the analyst can make should be ignored. Nor does it mean that group progress is exactly predetermined by the constitution of the patients in it. If this were so, it would make no difference whatsoever on the movement of the group, if one therapist were substituted for another. And the role of the group analyst would be a passive one in the face of the group's fatalistic course. But the influence of the therapist cannot be reduced to this kind of insignificance. He must possess skills which make him most capable of resolving intragroup conflict; of interpreting the problems presented by the patients' previous history; of pointing up the new needs created by the preceding development of the group's interactivity, of taking the initiative in satisfying these needs.

In this relatively new field of group analysis the therapist must be a person who is venturesome, for there are many new, experimental areas to explore. He should, therefore, avoid assuming dogmatic attitudes in the group's interest as well as his own. If he is authoritarian, he prevents the group's full emergence and contribution, which may enlighten him also. He seeks to be capable of admitting his own mistakes openly, of examining the reasons for them, and of analyzing the conditions which gave rise to them in order to correct them. He needs to be able to show his own shortcomings, if necessary, and so be an example to the others.

The psychoanalyst cannot encourage an inspirational atmosphere which represses unconscious factors and creates unstable illusions of success which are bound to be shortlived. He promotes a spirit of deep, mutual examination and review of personal strengths and weaknesses. Such a procedure does not destroy the patient but explores his neurotic character structure.

At times when the group falters, the analyst must remain firmly and consistently optimistic. He takes a stand against any one patient's exploitation of another. He must avoid in himself and discourage in the members the intellectual cliché that obscures the simple, richer, and more elemental meaning for which the patient is groping. A calculated, scholastic approach leads to an evasion of affective contact indispensable for rehabilitation. Here, as elsewhere, he can turn to the group for the naive phrase which is poetic, refreshing, and apropos in order to escape the compulsive use of the more restricted language of professional associates. He should set an example in simplicity, honesty, and straightforwardness to encourage those patients who underestimate their large ability to make meaningful contributions. He does not always emphasize what is said, but rather how it is said. He tries to treat complicated questions without complexity. He should not strive for the eloquent phrase. His thoughts need to be clear and distinct—their intent plain. While he plays a leading role, he strives to help the members feel he is one of them—not apart. He ought not to teach too much, for if he does, he will find himself governing rather than liberating. In this regard it would pay him to lend an attentive ear to what is said of him in the group. There he will find his severest critics as well as his staunchest defenders. Regard for what they say will help him to enlarge his understanding of himself. Again, he should not hesitate to show his appropriate feelings in the group. In doing this, he sets an example of freedom and emotional contact that is infectious. If he hides affect, the group will respond in kind. His sadness or gaiety will strike healthy reactive chords in the others. But, if he is well, he will be realistically optimistic.

The analyst is on guard against alliances in the group which conceal deeper, unrealized, and unspoken attitudes, which should be ventilated. Two patients, both fearful of criticism, may evolve a superficial and precarious neurotic amity, which undermines the therapeutic process. Their fraudulent harmony is resistance and works to prevent the exposure of facets of character structure. Patient progress cannot take place in an atmosphere of insecure and evasive peace and good will. It can move on if the analyst presses for mutual exertion and cross exposure, which develops contradictory positions. Then, when intra- and interpersonal conflict is exposed, the group can proceed to overcome these seemingly irreconcilable attitudes. The neurotic character structure must sooner or later be exposed, not coddled. Otherwise it fights for its existence and defends an outlived cause. At the same time the new and healthier personality is also struggling to emerge. The analyst must ally himself with the healthy and make himself the implacable opponent of the outmoded pathology. He can do this by openly and honestly exploring unconscious conflict and screened attitudes and encouraging the group to do likewise. In examining the neurotic framework of the personality, he must concentrate his analysis on oppressive or prohibitive trends, on overprotective and exploitative tendencies, and on ever-present penility, whether it shows itself in men or women.

Conscious and unconscious overestimation of what is generally regarded as masculine plays a part in the evolution and resolution of every neurosis. The analyst resists the obvious and insidious ways in which the masculine is overvalued. To this end, he takes every opportunity to establish the complementary equality of the sexes in difference. He exposes the devious and subtle ways in which the equivalents of masculinity are taken for granted as superior. He shows each member how, unconsciously, he has hardly progressed from the phallus worship of his ancestors. Among male patients, the analyst indicates how this may manifest itself in compulsive pursuit of women to prove sexual prowess and to relieve castration anxiety. Among female patients, he points out how male supremacy notions are reflected in what amounts to the same thing: the manifold varieties of penis envy. The analyst exposes the social counterparts of this overevaluation of the male sex organ as an incessant power drive that shows itself in diverse, antisocial efforts to establish individual dominance. He traces these sexual and social correspondents to their common cultural and personal origin. He challenges psychopathic values. In this way the therapist persists in analyzing aggressive interactions. Members must be schooled not to value each other only as men or women to be exploited as competitive sexual objects.

The analyst can foster harmonious accord if he takes pains to oppose every psychopathic alliance against healthy mutuality. He strengthens individual growth by trying to expose the destructive quality of such unwholesome compacts. He is alert to the fact that not all affinity in the group is necessarily salutary. The devils too may be in league. Under the pretext that "it is necessary to express hostility"—at times a true enough observation—patients deviously, compulsively, and sadistically attack and provoke discord and regression among others who are progressing. The analyst supports forces in the group whose interests are not partisan, but generally and reciprocally emancipating. He stands firm against and thwarts clannishness and narrow self interest. He analyzes attempts on the part of one patient to misuse another by exposing the act and its motivation. He resists appeasement of pathologic tendencies which would dominate or manipulate members. Such concessions will inevitably bridle and delay patients' progress.

The analyst constantly seeks a theoretic base to keep pace with his practical work. A flexible theoretic background, continually modified by concrete experience in the group, gives patients and therapist alike the power of orientation, clarity of perspective, faith in the work, and confidence in ultimate recovery. But he must be equally strong in practical work. Study of theory and practice will enable him to see a long way ahead and thus anticipate successes and impasses in the patients' best interest. Attention to the interplay of hypothesis and fact leads to the continuous elaboration and modification of each, establishing ever clearer insights into reality and corresponding changes in technique.

Every form of therapy is limited in what it can accomplish. While the analyst hopes to help the patient develop and realize his full possibilities, both he and the patient are partially blocked by a frustrating reality. Yet even within the present social context, certain things can be achieved. The movement of a patient from individual to group analysis is a considerable step toward his socialization. It is a vital step away from misleading glorification of individualistic acts which merely subject each of us to a compulsive competition and isolation. To this unsound emphasis on detachment and individuality, the therapist offers genuine regard and relatedness to each patient in the group, with a chance to liberate and coordinate unrealized reserves. The therapist opposes purely narcissistic interests at the expense of others. He sees that no individual really gains anything at the cost of others.

An important function of the group analyst is to make clear in the terminal phase of treatment the relation between the individual patient's freedom to act as he pleases and the needs of others in any group of which he is a part. He needs to become aware that his compulsivity demands a lack of freedom to behave in any other way. He learns that his real needs and those of others are not necessarily always in opposition. He does not feel restrained or controlled by interpersonal demands. He finds this lack of freedom to be only apparent and unreal. His seeming restraint is really an increased consciousness that roles and fulfillments are complementary. He becomes able to relinquish his detached, masturbatory egocentricity. The neurotic's compulsive insistence on personal liberty frequently masks a wish to exploit and dominate, which needs to be analyzed. When he can recognize the congruence of self realization and interpersonal fulfillment and can act accordingly, he is on the way to getting well.

An example may clarify this notion. A patient insists on his right to masturbate. It is only when he is alone that he feels free enough to enjoy an ecstatic orgasm. He is inhibited during coitus, when his penile skin feels anesthetized. As he is liberated from unconscious prohibitions, he learns how to reach new heights of personal pleasure in mutually gratifying sexual intercourse, more pleasurable to him because it also delights his partner. Rid of the illusion that contact involves demands, he realizes himself interpersonally.

9. The Leader and the Homogeneous or Heterogeneous Group

A. WOLF and E. K. SCHWARTZ

The need to generalize represents an attempt to find an overall explanation in fact or in fancy. In the face of an absolute heterogeneity, man would have no means of understanding nature, no way to cope with or control it. The therapeutic problem is how to deal with the complexity, how to cope with the group without damaging the person. A parent may regard his offspring homogeneously as children, but they need to be seen as different children. The therapist, like the parent, may become anxious or guilty that he does not feel the same way about each patient or treat all his patients in the same way. He may confuse equality with sameness. The therapist or the patient may impose a homogeneity in order to relieve his tension. The therapist may make a facile but irrelevant generalization to alleviate his anxiety.

Homogeneous structure or heterogeneous structure is a consequence of the position taken by the therapist. He may believe that mental health comes from individual submission to the group. Under these circumstances it is not the group that strives for such homogeneity, it is the therapist. For the group, given its head, even if it is originally relatively homogeneous, achieves a more wholesome heterogeneity. It is the therapist's drive for homogeneity that is the significant force. This imposition of a make-believe unity is a projection of the therapist.

The therapist may be a progressive idealist with visions that psychoanalysis, and particularly group psychotherapy, are the answer in social reform. He may believe that the democratic group will change man. But in doing so, he misinterprets parity as identity and democracy as psychotherapy. Here the unconscious aim in homogeneity is the democratic goal misconceived as subordination to group will.

The treatment of diverse patients as if they were identical helps the therapist to evade the necessity for the differentiated therapy of each one. It is quite possible that he is looking for an abbreviated form of group therapy. He may expect that the group, its climate, or its dynamics will somehow heal the patient with less need on the therapist's part to intervene. He may, like the patient, hope to evade the large number of conflicts, the struggle to resolve distortions of patients so often at cross purposes. By ignoring their disparity or levelling them in similarity he can be relieved of the differentiated necessity to work through their divergent problems. Some therapists fear subjecting the patient to alien experience, as if they would protect him from the new and unknown.

The group therapist inclined to homogeneity is essentially cynical about the constructive and realistic possibilities in patients. He seems to believe that, given the opportunity, they are more than likely to run amuck, to hurt one another, to act in pathology, to become irrational rather than more reasonable. Accordingly, he tries to establish "group precedents," a "group authority," to control an inherent tendency to misbehave. He may see the homogeneous group as a way of restricting acting out to the therapy situation. Or, he may have the clinical experience that interaction of any kind, whether appropriate or acting out, is reduced in an undiversified group. In either case, the therapist is likely to prefer homogeneity.

He may misjudge singularity as compulsive nonconformity, and uniqueness as pathological deviation. He may try to render his group homogeneously irrational with a view to establishing "therapeutic" psychoses. Here the aim is to obscure the difference between patient and therapist.

An unconscious objective in homogenizing a group may be the therapist's need to manipulate it. A group can be more readily dealt with, if it is made coalescent, if it is one mind, if the individual members have been conditioned to follow. The homogeneous group may be used by the therapist to bludgeon the patient to conform to the consensual view. The group can be more adroitly handled in the mass than in the man. But if the patient is to be lost in the group, his irrationality must be stimulated, encouraged and intensified. For he will resist his drowning in homogeneity with whatever sound reserves are still available to him.

It is quite possible that the group therapist's insistence on establishing a priority of homogeneity is an acting out of his own need authoritatively to prevail. Or, it may be that the imposition of group uniformity represents the group therapist's acting out his own submission to a suprahuman father force, invested now in a deified conventionality from which no one is exempt.

A therapist who ignores the heterogeneity of patients is likely to be authoritarian. He may think that restorative influence rests entirely with him and in extension of him, his homogeneous group. He is rejective of group therapy, of interaction among patients, of the alternate session. He may feel it necessary to dominate the patients or they will anarchically disintegrate. He feels obliged to maneuver and manipulate the group. His attitude is patronizing. He regards patients as altogether pathological with no remedial resources of their own. He acknowledges that unless he is in absolute surveillance of the group, it will fall apart. Its members are viewed as defective or entirely given over to id impulses in his absence. To be sure, both healthy and unhealthy attitudes and behavior assert themselves whether the patients are in treatment or not. It is the therapist's fancy that they become unbridled unless they are under his watchful supervision.

The pursuit of homogeneity may be in part derived from the therapist's quest for certainty. The compulsive banding together of patients who have similarities may be reassuring to the leader out of some matching necessity of his own. Or, he may feel more inappropriately secure in the presence of patients who are less anxious among their own kind. He is likely then to rationalize his preference for homogeneity in an illogical conviction that consonance is essential to the group. The projection of a homogeneous cloak over the heterogeneous qualities of patients may make the therapist feel more sure of himself but does not correspond to the realistic needs of patients.

One homogeneous aim is infallibility. In this view the therapist can be positive if the group's even tenor is unquestioned. Homogeneity then has the quality of massive conformism. It creates new problems by encouraging infectious parapraxes. The nature of psychoanalytic practice requires that we question the motivations of patients and our own as well. Otherwise we are homogeneous with their resistance. When the right to question our patients, for them to question and disagree with one another and the therapist, to be different from one another and the therapist, is disavowed, we are forced to accept homogeneity and an illusory assurance.

Often the expectation of the patient is that the members of his group share his feelings, thoughts and behavior, that they have convictions identical with his own. He experiences their differences from him as something of a shock. It is as if their not being like him represents a rejection of all he stands for. This is such a common point of view that even the therapist may be misled into attempts to cater to it by organizing as nearly homogeneous groups as possible. One function of the therapist is not to submit to the expectation that each member reflect the other's moods, values, reasoning or conduct but to analyze such a presumption as irrational and work through to the acceptance of constructive differences.

A pitfall the group therapist needs to guard against is the formation in the therapeutic group of a clique of elite patients who underline the analyst's values or manage to establish a homogeneous bias to which they demand the remaining members conform. There is a danger here of the group's becoming noxiously homogeneous, for example in its insistence that the only acceptable material for expression must be affect loaded; or in the rule that no experience of a patient outside the group is relevant; or in the dictum that historical data is immaterial and that only the here and now counts; or in the attitude that dreams are of little consequence—and a bore besides; or in the position that this or that new member is not bright enough, not up to the group level. With such a development the therapist must analyze as thoroughly as possible the psychodynamics of each patient party to this autocratically harmonizing influence, until the multiple individual and divergent aspirations in the group recover. Otherwise he caters exclusively to the majority and neglects the necessity of the individual patient.

Sometimes a therapist fosters a hierarchical setup in the group in which a ruling clique can maintain its control. In such a climate there can be little shift in participant privileges from the upper echelons to the lower and still less genuine communication between the leading and the led. Their seeming intercourse and reciprocity is counterfeit in which the dominant members govern the more passive who tend to yield to dictation, increasingly reluctant to take a first step in opposition. Not only must the therapist analyze the motivation of each member who joins the ascendant clique but he should just as carefully attend and support those patients who with some help can resist the commanding circle and develop their own initiative.

It seems to us that what often passes for concurrence in the group is itself the expression not so much of constructive cohesion as it is of diegophrenic pathology. The split ego is so characteristic of our time that many patients passively follow the more assertive leaders, lending the group the appearance of homogeneity. This manifest accordance, so liable to be sponsored by the therapist as a salutary "group climate," needs to be analyzed as it shows itself in each dominant-submissive dyad. Each group may have one or two members whose personalities strongly sway the others. They are frequently the most verbal and active, but not necessarily reparative in their insensitivity to others. In order to support weakened egos it is a function of the therapist not to be misled by an apparency of uniformity and to analyze any compulsive passivity and leadership.

Patients seem to have preferences for particular ways of being for each member. And the group tries to get the patient not to deviate from the verbalization and behavior congenial to this role. If he tries to depart from his familiar pattern, the group tends to become rejective. This is particularly true of a homogeneous group. To the extent that this tendency exists at all, the therapist should analyze it in the members.

If a therapist is inclined to foster homogeneity on the grounds that the patient's weak ego cannot tolerate the vigorous approach of a heterogeneous group which might undermine his confidence, we would say that it is the function of the therapist to analyze these judgments when they become pathologic assaults. While we, too, want the patient to believe in himself, we do not think this self-regard ought to be based on any common pathology. We would like to see each member's ego resources encouraged to grow. We do not wish to affirm and reinforce what is sick.

Each patient has different needs at different stages of his treatment. Therefore, the nature of the therapist's intervention at the beginning is not homogeneous with his intercession at a middle or terminal phase of therapy. It would be equally erroneous for the leader to apply a uniform approach to a whole group in the misconception that their needs are the same at any one moment.

An insightful observation about one patient is sometimes useful to another as well. A new awareness may be shared not only out of similar history and experience, but out of comparison, contrast and an appreciation of differences. The analyst ought to be cautious about assuming that what he says of one patient is necessarily valid for another, for his assumption that a sweeping explanation is generally applicable may play into individual resistance that would conceal personal variations. If the analyst finds one person stirred by another's probing or remembering, he is likely to find that, while one patient stimulated another out of a seemingly similar manifest content, the underlying psychodynamics have latent uniqueness for each.

There is a common misconception that individual analysis occupies itself more with genetic etiology while analysis in a group is engaged largely in the current, momentary interaction. This is a limited, one-dimensional and homogeneous notion of treatment, whether individual or group. What happens in therapy is influenced by the analyst. He can facilitate the group experience as historically oriented and the individual one as essentially current. Either approach, exclusively applied, defeats the treatment of homogeneity. More appropriate multi-dimensional therapy explores historic, present and future paths in the patient's development, regardless of the treatment structure.

There is a tendency on the part of combined therapists to be intrigued with homogeneity. They are inclined to treat the group as a single unit in group meetings and just as homogeneously to differentiate them in individual interviews. Such an approach acts as a damper on interaction at group sessions, where little or no analytic therapy is done. Deep therapy is reserved for individual sessions where the patient is distinguished from the group.

The leader discriminates between patients in order to discover their different illnesses and to be able to work through for each the specific way to enlist their cooperation and help them resolve their disorder. By this discriminating means the therapist gives each member particular insight, so that patients do not expect the analyst to approach them in a homogeneous way. Sometimes a therapist is disconcerted by patients' objections that he does not treat one member like the other. When the leader is sure that patients are heterogeneous and need to be treated differently, he ceases to feel disturbed by such complaints. And he soon discovers that patients stop insisting on identical treatment from him and instead appreciate his distinguishing their respective needs.

What is the role of the therapist in the face of a developing homogeneity, a common dynamic, a shared motif in his group? It is the analyst's function to accept and understand the manifest, but also to penetrate the resistive, generalized façade to each patient's concealed, unconscious, and differentiated interest.

It is important for the therapist to value multiformity, to appreciate diverse thoughts and feelings and to demonstrate to his patients the productive import to each of the heterogeneous organization. For, as group members discover the worth of parity in difference, they permit and encourage appropriate dissimilarity in others. Then the patients themselves cultivate a climate of mutual examination that is cordial to unlikeness. This receptivity toward divergence encourages each to unfold his particularity, which in turn enriches the group experience of all. The group's interest in the discordant view fosters a medium of friendly candor in which the patient can expose himself and have more choice in determining his destiny.

10. The Leader and the Use of Dreams

A. WOLF and E. K. SCHWARTZ

It is extremely difficult to work analytically with a patient who does not present dreams. One important function of the therapist is to try to analyze the patient's resistance to dreams because dreams do present us with understanding, insight into patients' basic and repressed conflictual material, with what is going on unconsciously. And since a primary analytic function is to make what is unconscious conscious, dreams are a basic avenue or access to what is unconscious and what needs to be made conscious.

11. The Leader and the Process of Working Through

A. WOLF and E. K. SCHWARTZ

In working through, the analyst points the way toward the diminishment of anxiety and the resolution of conflicts by constantly posing more valid, realistic, and constructive alternatives which, when chosen, confront the participants with new problems to pursue, but always on a higher level of development. Whereas, among plants and animals, sudden changes and mutations appear in the course of natural selection, in man changes are accomplished in the main by conscious planning. Having discovered the dynamics of the patient's pathology, the analyst, then, carefully maps a course of action to deal with it. Improvements the patient makes do not arise impromptu. They are the result of the cooperative effort of analyst and patient within the context of a thoughtful and flexible treatment plan. In their rational exertion the participants differ from lower forms of life which simply exploit their natural surroundings without awareness, adapting themselves and influencing their environment without consciousness. Men can change themselves by conscious effort, and direct and change external reality by forcing it to gratify their purposes. It is the struggle to reach objective and realistic common goals and to manage and control his life according to a hope, a vision, a design and a fulfillment, that distinguishes man.

The analyst, grounding himself in knowledge of the pathology that rules patients, strives to see in advance that if he treats them thus, he will imbed their pathology, but if he treats them so, he may move them to new insight and reasonable adjustment. The analyst's awareness that he will elicit a transference reaction if he countertransfers, that yielding to the temptations of acting out is bilaterally defeating, and drawing upon other generalizations, derived from clinical experi-

53

ence, enable him to attempt to predict the consequences of an act, to apply the proper timing to his interventions, and to introduce them with appropriate technical skill and consideration for the patient's needs. Instead of deluding himself that he knows patients through his own projections, he realizes that just to the extent that he counter-transfers, he knows them and himself less. He is aware of the necessity that his subjective chaff has to be sifted from the grain of true discernment. He knows that insight develops when patients can see the mutually destructive nature of projection; that understanding develops further in the exercise of learned ways and means to respond instead of yielding to obsession; and that an acute wherewithal can replace compulsion only in the light of reason. He realizes that, if he knows enough about a patient and himself, their relationship and their culture, together they will be better able to achieve a mutually constructive outcome.

Conscious, planned, and goal-directed application is essential in the analyst's endeavor to help patients. Their potential cannot be realized unless he reflectively and discriminatively follow a deliberate strategy aimed at achieving realistic solutions determined by the existing circumstances. To accomplish this purpose the analyst should be willing to use his judgment and exercise his responsibility. Instead of reducing his intervention to countertransference, to disequilibrium catalysis, or to doing nothing constructive because patients are possessed of occult, self-reparative powers, he actively demonstrates to patients that they can, in some measure, outgrow their pathologic history in the context of current and future experience. He accomplishes this, in part, by providing the possibility for a healthy interpersonal relationship as the initial healing environmental influence.

When treatment induces patients to take first steps toward establishing better human contact with the analyst, they are fortified by insight gained from a consciousness of the process and begin to make efforts to relate more appropriately. Gradually pathology withers from disuse as they function more realistically. The better the analyst understands the particular details and dynamics of this process in patients, the more accurately he can guide the course of treatment. The more the patients see that he knows what he is about, the readier they are to join him in accomplishing their ends. Only that analyst can play a decisive role in treatment whose therapeutic intervention is in the well-defined service of his patients.

These examples are sufficient to illustrate the importance of the analyst's maintaining a discriminative view of the particular pathologic dynamics of each patient, so that he can keep in mind the specially indicated means to work through. In so doing, he also makes group members aware of their uniqueness in terms of their needs as well as their potentials, so that they are not so commonly impelled to demand from the therapist that he treat them the same way. Even in the most homogeneously organized group, there are always enough differences in character structure, psychopathology and resources to call for such differentiated study and treatment. Moreover, when the analyst is thoroughly aware of these distinctions and the need to treat them differently, he no longer feels threatened by the patient's complaint that, "You don't treat me the way you treat him." But if the therapist persists in making discriminating estimate of each member, he finds before too long that group members soon follow his lead, cease demanding undifferentiated responses from him and, in their own interest, recognize the value of differences and complementation.

12. Resistances on the Part of Group Leaders

A. WOLF and E. K. SCHWARTZ

The group therapist consciously or unconsciously shares many of the resistances already described. He may do individual therapy in the group. It is difficult for him to shake off historically determined attitudes. He cannot easily give up tradition and training. In the positive move to meet the new social demand, he may continue to adhere to a commitment to individual treatment and remain basically cynical about the practice of group therapy. Perhaps some of the devotional attitudes to group therapy are reaction formations to doubts about it. For example, a group therapist's compulsive, nondiscriminative, having to know everything about each patient in the group may represent his preference for individual therapy. Or the therapist's need to organize and to persist in viewing a group of patients as homogeneous rather than heterogeneous often masks his wish to treat the group as one patient.

The varieties of group therapy and group therapists lead to confusion as to who is a group therapist. Must he be an analyst? A psychodramatist? A teacher? A discussion leader? A group dynamicist? A conductor? An orchestra leader? This confusion is sponsored by such statements as "The other man is not doing group therapy." "Psychoanalysis in a group is not possible." "The leader does not treat the patients; they treat themselves." Under attack, group therapists become defensively aggressive. Opposition among group therapists to one another is encouraged. There is fear of exposing what they do, fear of destructive criticism. If group therapists feel they are inadequately trained in individual analysis, as in fact many of them are, they will avoid clarifying the nature of the group therapy they do. They anticipate being found wanting and thus becoming an instrument for undermining their chosen field.

Some group therapists are not able sufficiently to understand individual analysis. They turn to group dynamics as an aid and use group dynamic concepts as magically therapeutic. Others have always wanted to work with patients individually, but were not accepted by analytic training institutes or were rejected before certification. Many of them turned to group therapy and subsequently added a concurrent individual session. Gradually the number of individual sessions was increased and group meetings decreased, until little by little they became more individual than group therapists. In this way group therapy has been employed as a back-door to becoming an individual analyst. A few of these therapists spend too much of their time attacking individual analysts, their father surrogates.

Some group therapists who have had adequate individual training express resistances already described by rejecting therapy in a group in different ways. For example, one therapist indicates that he uses the group as an extension of himself, by inducing the group to confirm interpretations made privately. Another analyzes group interaction only in individual sessions but not in the setting in which it occurs. Still another therapist reports that he sees the group merely as a means of breaking through defenses, but that he conducts analysis out of the group. Such therapists, although identified with group therapy, do not offer the patient treatment in the group. On the other hand, some of the rejectees from analytic training institutes have, of course, worked very hard in group therapy to prove their worth and have made constructive contributions to the development of this treatment method.

13. The Creative Leader

A. WOLF and E. K. SCHWARTZ

In providing patients with the opportunity to meet without him, the analyst indicates that he respects and trusts them, assures them that they are not regarded as certain to run wild in his absence, and that he has conviction in their ability to relate to one another within reasonable limits. From the start the analyst consciously chooses to allow them this freedom to explore thoughts, feelings, and behavior with peers and projected authority figures. He has regard for their capacity to use their own positive resources; his expectation that they will act responsibly on their own sponsors their independence.

Erikson's formulation that the growing organism's reliance and trust in himself is preconditioned by an earlier trust in another suggests the importance of developing in the patient increasing confidence in the reliability of his confidantes as a basis for wholesome ego development. The analyst, by indicating to his patients that he trusts them with one another at alternative meetings, that they can, with security, keep their distance from him, supports their learning to trust one another and themselves. Alternating closeless to and separation from the therapist enables the patient to take chances with his own resources. If he is preoedipally attached and dependent, he discovers that his survival is not ensured by closeness to the mother surrogate nor is it lost by separation.

The reality-bound analysts knows that it took time, with repeated traumata to the evolving organism, to impose the conflicts, repressions and distortions from which experience the patient emerged mentally disturbed. He knows, too, that it will take considerable time and dedication to work out the psychodynamics and work through to a new and enlarged self-understanding in reality, and that any claims to short-term cures are illusory. As a result his applications are not primarily concerned with moment-to-moment responses. While he notes

58

how the patient thinks and feels and believes now, he is equally attentive to historic developments and future possibilities. Realistic solutions require endurance and struggle, and so the analyst is generally more preoccupied with long-range rather than short-range goals.

The movement from individual analysis to psychoanalysis in a group required new ideas, new techniques, new skills, a new view of reality, a new design for the therapeutic process, and new conceptualizations. It meant going beyond the view of individuals in isolation to that of individuals in interrelation. It meant moving the patient from the passivity and detachment of the couch to a self-and-other awareness in active face-to-face contact and interaction. It meant a departure from the traditional emphasis on intrapsychic exploration to the development of interpersonal reactions, and from this back to the intrapsychic only to return again to the interpersonal. It meant the emergence of a new freedom to interact in the presence of others. It meant a movement from the idea that the patient is only a mass of sickness and that patients can only contaminate each other by their illnesses.

These leaps are creative. Those who dare make them will be initiators to some extent; but each one, if creative, will discover a new dimension, a new freedom, a new reality, a new structure, a new set of connections.

14. The Leader and Countertransference

A. WOLF and E. K. SCHWARTZ

Countertransference represents fulfillment of the fantasy of the patient with regard to the therapist, in the expectation that the therapist play a certain role. Countertransference can be seen in the excessive forms of behavior of the analyst which are repetitive and over prolonged time. Patients have needs and the analyst has needs. Transference and countertransference do occur. The question is whose real needs are central to the particular activity in duration. In group therapy, multiple transferences and, probably, countertransferences occur. The therapist is committed to being realistic and not giving in to the network of multiple transferences and transference demands with multiple countertransferences. We believe countertransference neurosis can also occur in the group, and is facilitated when, for example, the group is misperceived as one patient, or when treating the group as if it were one person. In such a distortion, it is easier to fulfill the transference demands of both patients and therapist.

As we have already pointed out, countertransference is recurrent, persistent, compulsive, repetitious, and of a continuing nature. It is obsessive, involuntary, unconscious, entrenched, manipulative and exploitive.

In the group, every therapeutic problem is exaggerated. The issues around transference and countertransference are no exception. Quantitatively and qualitatively, countertransference becomes an even more complicated matter in the group. Simply the presence of a variety of persons multiples the transference manifestations and provocations in both patients and therapist.

Following is a list of possibilities which, in our experience, need to be explored for the presence of the group therapist's transferences and countertransferences.

1. The therapist may relate to the group as if it were his own projected family.

2. He may out of his own omnipotence deny patients freedom, or demand activity out of his own depression.

3. In attending group dynamics, he may homogenize the members, see them as if they were one patient, without listening to individual voices and knowing them as persons.

4. He may not listen to projected peers or authorities.

5. The therapist may wish to be the only child in the group, or he may treat patients as only children.

6. The therapist may demand that patients shape their way of life and their values to his. The expectation that the patient fulfill the therapist's superego demands retraumatizes the patient. It is a general clinical observation that children of authoritarian parents become authoritarian, and neglected children become neglectful parents.

15. Short-Term Leadership

A. WOLF

The role of the therapist, then, in short-term treatment seems to take on even more importance. He would be wise, I think, to make it clear to all patients at the outset, and even perhaps at subsequent meetings, that the number of therapy sessions available to them is limited. From that point on his technique will be largely up to him, chosen, we hope, from a wide base of experimental work done and being done. His role will vary with his degree of commitment to therapy in general and analysis in particular; his choice of therapeutic devices; the kinds of patients he chooses to treat, in the kinds of groups he decides to organize.

If he believes he can practice analytically reconstructive treatment in a short-term therapy group, his intervention may be active, penetrating and insightful. If he believes he must avoid the development of a transference neurosis, he will stay out of the interaction except to sponsor patients' responses to one another. If he believes in eliciting strong positive transferences, which he thinks he can manipulate in the patient's interest, to effect constructive change, he will make the group leader centered, in a firm, convincing way, with the use of suggestion, guidance, counseling and even hypnosis. Only certain therapists are capable of playing the role this requires, and only certain patients are able to accept the therapist in this role.

If the therapist believes his essential responsibility is to get the patient to face and accept reality—that is, that he, the therapist, as well as the patient, have only partial powers—he will try repeatedly to confront the patient with the actualities of partipotence. In the main, what the therapist does will depend on his convictions, his experimental interests, his flexibilities, the patient's diagnosis and the therapist's impressions of the patient's needs and responsiveness to a certain kind of intervention.

Of course, this is true of all therapy, long or short, group or individual. But the short-term group therapist will have to tailor these precepts; focus them more directly and control them more in operation. He will always have to keep in mind the reality that his goals are limited, as his time with the patient is limited. He will probably find that he has to preplan the course of his responses; that he must center them mostly toward the reality needs of his patients rather than toward working out and working through their irrational, inappropriate or archaic needs.

The short-term group therapist will have to encourage group members to support one another in the adoption of constructive, sublimating alternatives to their various pathologies. He will emphasize reality not unreality; the rational not the irrational; partial rather than absolute satisfaction; compromise rather than total victory; partipotence not omnipotence; reason not unreason.

Unless the therapist is attempting to do short-term analytic group psychotherapy, he will avoid deep interpretations and unconscious material. He will tend not to emphasize history, genesis and the past as much as the present and future possibilities. He will, in all likelihood, be more inclined than in other forms of psychotherapy to set limits, to advise, teach, counsel and encourage the positive.

16. The Discriminatingly Affective Leader

A. WOLF

The question then is: Can the therapist be discriminating and reasonable enough to use certain of his feelings with certain patients at certain times and yet not be so affectively impulsive or compulsive that he has not enough conscious sensitivity and selectivity to withhold such feeling with those patients and at such times as it would be in the patient's interest to do so?

The emotion habitués among certain therapists reject thoughtfulness with the claim that insight so derived simply produces an awkward self-consciousness which interferes with the development of natural health attainable only by the unrestrained expression of feeling.

The group therapist who dares to show his feeling in a group has been described as "courageous," for making his latent affect manifest. Such a justification for a therapeutic intervention, as, say, a group leader's daring to scream out loud in the midst of a session, seems hardly a legitimate reason for using it. It is like a nonswimmer taking a job as a lifeguard merely because he is audacious.

The affect-committed therapist reacts with his subjective feelings to all the members of his group equally and indiscriminately. While it is conceivable that this might be productive for some few patients, I believe the therapist has to differentiate one patient from another and treat each one differently, because each has a personal history, a particular diagnosis, a unique psychopathology, varying kinds of healthy resources, and needs a different kind of working out and working through. Otherwise, the therapist is homogenizing the group into one patient. Therapeutic groups are heterogeneous, and the individuals in them require discriminating interventions with regard to their differentiated needs.

64

The affect-addicted group therapist claims that the patient's deepest feelings are not communicated to a therapist whose interventions are planned and technical, because the patient sees through these "tricks." The implication is that thoughtfulness on the patient's behalf is a feelingless, insincere and cunning deception played upon him. It is important for the mother to plan to feed her child, to have a time sense, to calculate in advance for the best possible future for her child. This in and of itself, is not a cold, detached attitude. It can be a considerate concern born out of love. The over-emotional group therapist counsels us to value only our immediate, instantaneous affect which seizes us in dealing with patients. But such feelings dictated by chance or compulsion may pathologically gratify the patient's transferences with countertransference.

The emotion-bent therapist protests that his expression of feeling is in itself therapeutic by engaging and involving the patient. The spontaneous component is desirable, for spontaneity is not disruptive nor inappropriate. But instantaneity is. Spontaneity is not an automatic, non-discriminative expression of one's feelings. Spontaneity requires prior struggle, searching, study, commitment and synthesis. The spontaneity of an artist does not arise out of nor is it limited to the moment.

17. The Responsible Leader

A. WOLF and E. K. SCHWARTZ

The rational therapist, contrariwise, must participate in the patient's real life decisions. He is duty bound to oppose the patient's decision to injure himself, to commit suicide or to murder someone. Yet he cannot arrogate decisions to himself apart from the patient; what he does is encourage the patient to feel free to talk things over with him and to get his help in coming to a new resolve. If the therapist helps the patient and shares responsibility with him, he need not fear the creation of inevitable dependency. Moreover, the therapist can help the patient to become independent. But if the therapist compulsively demands patient initiative, he often forces the patient to take actions prematurely and against his best developmental interests.

The therapist, we believe, has no right to exempt himself from obligation to the patient. He has the right only to be responsible, to take the most considered action on the patient's behalf. No one would deprive him of the privilege of examining his own psychodynamics, but in so doing he cannot neglect his role as representative of superego and ego influences on the patient. How else can he help a patient whose deficient reality testing and limited freedom need reinforcement? The therapist's self-control, planfulness, sense of responsibility, judgment and leadership become ideals for such a patient to identify with and to incorporate. Without leadership, we believe, there can be no insight, no reorganization, no integration.

18. The Leader As Human Being

A. WOLF, E. K. SCHWARTZ,
G. McCARTY and I. GOLDBERG

After many years of working analytically with patients in individual and group settings, we have come to the conclusion that therapy is more than a series of hypotheses concerning the development and functioning of personality, the nature and origination of psychopathology, the cause of anxiety and the defense mechanisms used to deal with it, and the ways in which the patient relates to illusion and reality. We have come to the conviction that in addition to these theoretical and technical constructs, which are applicable to doing psychoanalytic treatment with a patient, the therapist as a person, as a human being, enters into the treatment situation as an important factor. The development of psychoanalysis in which emphasis has shifted from focus upon the patient to focus upon the relationship, and more currently to focus upon the person of the therapist, is in part what we are talking about here. It is more than theoretical persuasion and the technical know-how of the psychoanalyst that effect changes in the persons who come for treatment. There is more communicated in an analysis than the historical origin of a patient's intercurrent behavior or a consciousness of unconscious processes within the self.

These additional facets have sometimes been called the educational aspects of psychoanalysis, but we feel that this is a derogatory label. We are, rather, committed to the idea that the psychoanalyst as a person enters into the analytic relationship. This does not mean that he gives up his objectivity, his neutrality, his commitment to listening and exploring the patient or making the patient's needs central to the therapeutic experience. What it does mean is that the personality of the psychoanalyst enters globally into the relationship and that there are transtherapeutic experiences that the patient has in the interaction

67

with the person of the analyst. We should like briefly to describe these para-analytic experiences—coming into contact with another person and being privy to his values, his approach to the human condition—as an exposure to a philosophy of life.

It is not only necessary for the therapist to have a philosophy of life, a set of values; whether he knows it or not, he surely has a point of view, a style of life. His way of functioning communicates itself to the patient regardless of any manifest commitment. His attitude toward life may be reflected in the way he decorates his office, how his desk looks, the clothes he wears, the kind of art he has around him, the color of the paint on his walls, the tone of his voice, the way he answers the telephone, even whether or not he answers the telephone during sessions. Certainly it is to be experienced in the kinds of things he chooses to interpret and what he chooses to ignore, whether he "thinks big" or is petty, whether he opens the door, shakes hands with a patient, says "Good morning" or "Goodbye." His value system is exposed by his optimism or pessimism, by whether he concentrates on what the patient says or follows his own inclinations and associations, and by whether he writes letters or books while the patient is talking. His commitments are manifested in whether he puts the patient on the couch or has him sit up, whether he sees patients individually or in a group, whether he sees other members of the same family or not.

The therapist communicates to the patient willy nilly what he thinks is right and wrong, what he thinks is appropriate and inappropriate. Like the parent, he conveys this to the patient not so much by what he says as by the way he acts. The therapist should encourage the patient to participate in his group, but he should also be dedicated to each member's developing his own style of life so long as it is reality oriented. The therapist is not a dictator. He does not consciously plan or unconsciously hope to direct or control the patient. He is more interested in opening doors and helping patients to open doors for themselves to the recovery and development of their own egos. He does not believe that there is only one way of living. He appreciates the healthy, creative differences among his patients and supports their imaginative and realistic differentiation one from another. In this respect he is a promoter of diverse and individual freedom. Every good analyst is a promoter of freedom so long as he analyzes resistances and transferences, and obsessive-compulsive behavior.

Does the therapist have any influence over and above analyzing psychodynamics and psychopathology? Yes, he does. Where does this extra-analytic influence come from? It comes from the therapist's philosophy, his value system. For example, do we see in the average psychoanalytic textbook any discussion of patience on the part of the therapist? Yet the therapist needs to be patient, he needs to listen, he needs not to lose his temper, he needs to hear the patient out. His patience cannot be limitless. Limitless patience is impossible. Limitless patience may mean limitless therapy. He can, therefore, have patience only within limits. This does not mean that he must become impatient but that at various points in the therapy he must push the patient to take some action. He cannot sit by patiently while the patient is forever silent or forever passive. If the therapist does, he is probably an angry man, or indifferent or hostile to the patient.

Another important influence on the patient is the therapist's acting as if he knows everything. The therapist needs to accept as realistic that he has uncertainty, that he does not have all the answers, that no one does, that no one ever will. The patient, even though he may be alarmed or may be made anxious by the therapist's uncertainty, finally begins to accept as realistic the abandonment of his own absolute certainty or absolute uncertainty, his own omnipotence and impotence, and elects instead to accept as appropriate his partipotence.

It is important for the therapist to recognize the constructive potential in the patient, to see the positives, to make them apparent to the patient. The therapist searches for the creative, the curious, the exploratory, the expansive, the questing side of the patient. The therapist also gets glimpses of the patient's yearning for sexual fulfillment. He calls to the attention of the patient these assets so that the patient can have a better and more wholesome view of himself. He looks for the positive and the problem-solving component in the fantasy, in the dream, in the patient's dealings with another group member. He is not exclusively preoccupied with the patient's psychopathology. It is this commitment that is probably the most important therapeutic aspect of his work, the commitment to the growing edge in the patient. While a group member may say to another member only what is wrong, for example, the therapist can also see what is right, and what is right for one patient may not be right for another. It is the therapist's application of these differences in reality that enables group members also to accept one another in difference, for the male patients to accept the female patients and vice versa, for the older members to accept the younger, the younger the older. Patients experience the fact that the solution for one is not necessarily the solution for another.

It is the therapist's acceptance of his limitations that frees the patient from his compulsive search for certainty, his compulsive aspiration for perfection. The therapist's freedom from having to be perfect, right, and omnipotent helps to free the patient to give up his own absolutism. The therapist is an open-minded person; there is no final end in view for him about anything. By this we do not mean that treatment is endless, or that there is no end to life. We mean that while therapy ends, life goes on, development goes on, change goes on, improvement can take place, even without the help of the therapist. The patient can grow and develop still further. It is in this sense that we mean open-endedness.

Another aspect of partipotence is flexibility. The therapist is ready to listen, bend, and yield. He does not rigidly adhere to an original commitment. He is open-minded. He is ready to hear another's point of view. He can change his mind and his hypotheses about a patient as new evidence comes in. While he adheres to certain sacred traditions, he leaves the door open for new points of view and experience. If he is flexible, he welcomes novelty rather than dogma; and he is careful not to turn novelty into dogma. In this respect he is life affirming rather than life denying, for dogma leads to emotional, psychological, and intellectual strangulation and depression. He is optimistic about his patient's recovery as well as about himself and about life. He has hope, believes in change, in restoration. He loves life and people and experiences. He does not regard, however, everything in himself or in nature as not anxiety provoking or not fear provoking. He is not ashamed to be afraid when it is appropriate to be afraid or to weep when it is appropriate to weep, but he enjoys life as well and enjoys his patients and his family and his experiences outside of his work. He can play. He can tell a good story, a good joke, and enjoy one. He sees life as multifaceted, and while he may concentrate on certain aspects of his work, he nevertheless can appreciate other kinds of work and play.

Although we are committed not only to working with the individual patient but to helping him find his way with other human beings, to a socialization, to a gregariousness, to his commitment to working and living within a group, we are nevertheless aware of the importance of his personal growth and development and his ability to think and stand on his own two feet. In spite of the fact that this is a work on psychoanalysis in groups, we wish not to ignore the fact that for each patient his own personal development is central.

We cannot conclude with any better expression of our own position than the words of Joseph Wood Krutch in his "Epitaph for an Age": "The more we teach adjustment, group activity, getting along with a group, and so forth, the less any individual is prepared for the time, so likely to come in any man's life, when he cannot or will not call upon group support. Ultimately security for him depends upon the ability to stand alone or even just to be alone. Belonging is fine. But to belong to anything except oneself is again to give a hostage to fortune." (*The New York Times Magazine* July 30, 1967, p. 10.)

19. The Loving Leader

A. WOLF

It has been said that "love is not enough," that love and love alone will not help the patient; that, therefore, we also need analytic means to treat him. But, it has also been said that technique alone is not enough; that, if we do not find some quality in the patient we like and respect, some growing edge, we cannot help him. Asya Kadis had both of these, the capacity to sense and promote positive trends in the patient as well as great skill in therapeutic intervention. I will not dwell in this article on the expertness Asya possessed, but will instead stress the value in treatment of her engaging disposition.

Neurotic and psychotic patients have assembled in groups of one kind or another for years. In more recent times these assemblies have become pandemic, and acting out has in some of these circles been identified as healing. In more reasonably and rationally dedicated groups under the leadership of analytically trained therapists, the membership is still inclined verbally to act out their archaic longings. Patients band together all over the country to try to discover and undo their pathology. In the course of this struggle they reject their noxious parents invested now in the therapist and one another. Occasionally, members, having come to the group with the hope of renewing themselves, want to drift away from the group. For, though they hoped to find there a nourishing new reality that would open fresh and wholesome vistas, they may find instead that the membership is as sick or even sicker than their own parents were.

Isolation and alienation so prevalent in the culture may then be pursued in the therapeutic group with increasing intensity to the point where members may verbally abuse each other. They abandon the notion of a cooperative relationship and settle instead for some frustrated regard for their distress even if it is hostile. Or they are tempted simply to leave the group in anger at its failure as a therapeutic

72

medium. They may then feel more fragmented, detached, defended and depersonalized than when they joined the group.

Before such a development could take place Asya's directness moved her groups to struggle for communication. Her capacity for healthy engagement re-engaged patients on the verge of resuming their detachment. Her solicitude prevented withdrawal, and they could not maintain their disconnection. Under her influence they gradually became aware of the need for prolonged exertion to achieve a more adequate adaptation. They were impelled to try again and again to undo their isolation and to achieve the relatedness they experienced with Asya by attempts to rejoin one another in more fraternal communication. Her human decency made it difficult for them to respond to her in lesser ways. As a result they became less and less able in time to treat each other with their former resentment.

Patients may, in groups, use talk defensively to obscure and subvert communication, as a way of blame rather than as a means of understanding. Instead of using the group to work through, they misuse one another much as their parents exploited them. They talk as though they were each other's captive from whose imprisonment they would flee. Asya's frankness, her honesty, and her passion for meaningful dialogue were antidotes to this kind of pathology.

She was an artist at discovering and suggesting ways to group members to promote and restore communication among them when they were on the verge of dispersing in unforgiving anger. She was alert to the covertly expressed or unconscious needs of patients rather than attending only to those who were most manifestly demanding. She could gently frustrate the inappropriate claims of group monopolists without rejecting them. By her own example she enabled group members to exchange ideas and feelings without taking advantage of each other. By sharing herself and at the same time refusing to be exploited, her patients gradually learned to unite their efforts.

Because patients are not truly related, many can easily leave the group without a sense of loss. The group is always there for them to return to, ready to welcome back its wanderers. But neither the members who remain nor those who come and go find they can talk openly. Asya could change this by her feeling for community and for the family, by her reaching for involvement, by her refusal to remain apart. Patients could not easily walk away from her caring. Her values, her solicitude were contagious.

The current mood among some patients and therapists alike is repre-

sented by an emphasis upon one's fleeting affect. The mood of yesterday or tomorrow is of little account. Similarly with thought and
tradition. A careful examination of one's history is irrelevant in the
modern scheme of things. A plan for the future is regarded as too
traditional. Freud did not emphasize one's feelings of the moment.
He asked for associations in order to recover *repressed* experience and
affect. The emphasis upon feeling in the here and now is an encouragement to acting out with unfortunate consequences in pathologically
regressive behavior. As a result there is little continuity in patient
relationships. They move quickly from one disappointing liaison to the
next with increasing cynicism and lessening hope. The goal of each
is irrelation: of person to person, of person to his past or future, of
each member to the value of his own intellect and reason.

The patient is too unconcerned with the life, knowledge and experience of the other. The other's perception is foreign to him and
has, in his view, little to offer. The patient in a group who is mistrust-
fully groping for a relationship is turned away by the isolated and
isolating others. He becomes embarrassed by the ridicule imposed on
him when he tries to be friendly and understanding and tends soon
to submit to the prevailing insistence on nonintrusion. Knowledge,
learning, intelligence and cognition are rejected for being cold and
unfeeling. Sometimes only subjective affect in the here and now are
accepted. The seekers for understanding are rejected as parental figures who are blamed as the damaging influences that brought the
affectivists to their present impasse. These lovers of instantaneity are
nevertheless not above exploiting those who have more regard for
insight, learning and tradition. Asya would have none of this. Though
herself empathic and not merely catharting and acting out subjective
affect, in her respect for the other's thought, feeling and activity, she
managed to arouse thereby in time a responsive regard in the members
for one another by her leadership.

Her caring needs to be distinguished from the transferential "loving
care" so subjectively promoted by certain group therapists who have
little concern, in fact, for their patients. These group leaders, with
their emphasis on the inappropriate expression of their own and their
patient's subjective affect simply encourage acting out with no working
through.

She could help partly because she respected them enough to try to
understand. She strove to be aware of their *repressed* thoughts and
feelings. She did not let her long-term, ultimate plans for them get so

far ahead of where they were at the present moment of their evolution, that they would become frustrated, confused or despondent.

In some respects, though patients consider themselves more liberated than their parents, their freedom is pseudofreedom. And members of a group are often equally toxic carriers of the worst features of their forbears. They may be coldly critical of any lasting man-woman relations as bourgeois and establishment. Instead they may move too easily from one partner's bed to another with little affective commitment. The fantasies of their parents may become the patients' way of life. They may reject ongoing closeness in a relationship. They may be on the move, from one person to another, from one place to another, from one sexual partner to another, from one therapeutic group to another, from one therapist to another. Their God is often activity with little thought or feeling. Asya, with her appreciation of deep-seated emotional and reasonable contact, was able to hold these wanderers with her interest, teaching them by her devotion to appreciate her ways and intriguing them with a need to communicate more deeply with one another as well. She taught them the value of lasting relationships. In this, her wisdom and maturity were manifest. So too was her pursuit of insight and the struggle to achieve a more realistic adaptation.

Patients, like nonpatients, tend to deal with one another not as persons but as sets of formulae and abstractions. They are unable to experience one another as people. They dehumanize each other. They do not apprehend one another. In such a setting Asya's ability to perceive the patient behind his resistive projection, enabled her to make the contact that led each to yield up his distortions if only for a moment, to her enlightenment and good will. Her intuition helped her to sense the latent possibilities in the patient. She could see what he might become. Her vision of his potential helped him to struggle. Her perception of his undeveloped resources enabled him to strive for greater freedom to choose a refreshing reality rather than enforced submission to his pathology.

Among patient attitudes are noncommitment to others, not even to themselves, indulgence in fantasies of action but little considered realistic activity in fact, a readiness to yield to self- and other-destructive momentary gratification of regressive wishes and self-promotion at the expense of others. And there is difficulty in advancing the growth of group members, because the most disturbed patients tend to manipulate and dominate the group. This frustrates those who have the better potentials, who are readier to share themselves in the struggle toward health. The hostility generated by the antagonism toward parental figures prevents the group from working through toward healthier possibilities.

Asya would not let these influences prevail. She encouraged the promise in each patient, till their negative compulsions tended to wither from neglect and attrition. Her patients recognized the perceptivity in her responsiveness and were engaged by her esteem for their realistic hopes. She could be relied upon to offer emotional support to any patient in need. And the dependent could at the same time look to her for encouragement to try their own resources. She had a hearty, contagious good humor that roused the declining spirit and moved the despondent to try again. She had a third ear for the patient's need, his cry for help. Yet she never saw her patients as children. She saw them as adults. She respected them. She saw them as equals. She freely shared her understanding of intrapsychic processes and interaction in the group, but she could modestly yield to a patient's occasionally more acute perception of what was taking place in a group. This was always ego building.

Patients in groups in frustration with each other often find themselves in a *folie à dix*. They face one another in multiple antagonisms in which each wants to do his own thing until anarchy and discord prevail. They become tied to each other in bonds of love and hate with a sense of failure and irresolution. Each feels his own distress and too seldom the ordeal of the other. Each excites and agitates the next until they may become an association of sadomasochists. Asya could not for long be witness to such inhumanity. She was able to turn, with one of her intuitions, a group in mutually destructive distress into a group with some compassion for each other.

One of the stresses in growing up is the difficulty the child has in relinquishing the symbiotic tie. The complications of modern industrial and urban living touch the family and make it awkward for the mother to provide the gradual separation for the growing child that would enable him to mature steadily. He is subjected instead to sudden changes, frightening abandonments and premature tests of his maturity. There are unexpected interruptions and not enough continuity. Patients subjected to this kind of treatment have little capacity to attend one another's needs more than momentarily. They are easily diverted from one another. They need someone who listens and cares what is happening to them for an extended period before they in turn have the patience to listen to one another. Asya heard and cared.

Patients in groups are not only resistive to forming mature relationships with one another, they have inhibitions about work. If they do work, they have difficulties with their colleagues in collaborative effort. They are inclined to work in isolation. They feel misused working for others but tend in their childlike dependency to seek an exploitative relationship with another person, both financial and emotional, in which the other is a providing parental surrogate. The reverse may be true in the patient who is the "mothering" person to the infantile mother, a relationship in which the patient plays the role of working to satisfy the insatiable demands of the mother. In either operation the patient feels and is, in fact, misused. In group therapy, these psychodynamics are re-enacted, when the patient expects to be provided for by the group or compulsively takes care of the membership. Often in these instances the group is homogenized and projected as the promising, providing mother or the mother who has to be provided for.

An aspect of a patient's isolation and detachment is egotism, narcissism and self-seeking. His seeming self-interest also involves finding individuals whom he can misuse without any serious application of his own. Work is a dirty word. This is sometimes referred to as "finding oneself," which must not entail effort. The struggle to achieve gratifying reciprocal interaction over extended periods requires too much exertion. Such stress can hardly be endured. "Finding oneself" has become a bugle call—or rather taps—to promote lethargy and inertia, fantasy without activity. Asya learned that the demands of and application to work added a richness and freedom to life.

Her enjoyment of life was an invitation to others to join her in its pleasures. Though she valued cognition, she enjoyed play and affective interaction. She was an inspiring example of one who took pleasure in work and in fun. She was quite spontaneous in whatever she said and did. For Asya her patients were more stimulating than depressing. Her hopefulness gave them hope and energy to go on trying, and later on, to play and to work, as she did. Her dramatic zest for life enabled her to return day after day to confront her patients.

Because Asya herself so enjoyed her life, her work and her patients, they too gradually developed increasing freedom to enjoy sessions with her. Her vivacity and bonhomie were infectious. She sought extensive commitment: to family, to friends, to patients, to work, to play, to life. She elected to make her life and the lives of those important to her rational and loving and work fulfilled. This was her choice. And patients were inspired and then disciplined by her vision to follow her lead.

Asya had no interest in possession, in money, in status. She had no exploitative needs. She was never interested in owning things, in property. For her, life was so much more profitable. It was richer than wealth. She could become intoxicated with the wine of living. Being alive was riches enough. Her personality was a powerful instrument to neutralize patients' initial misperceptions of her as a surrogate parent. It was not easy, for example, for patients to experience her as living a life of meaningless disquiet and turbulence, as money or power mad, of destructive intention with respect to them.

The patient's weariness and discontent may finally lead him to despair. The therapist's enthusiasm and optimism may be essential to keep him going. He may at times have to rely on the therapist's confidence and assurance of a happier time ahead. He may have to lean upon the therapist's faith that all will not end in misfortune and failure. This conviction was Asya's conviction. Her therapy was an act of confidence that inspired trust. And her treatment kept alive the hope of her patients no matter how sickened they were with mental suffering.

She had no need to present herself as perfect, to maintain a false façade of perpetual happiness. She did not promise Utopia for her patients. She had a value system that allowed her to reveal imperfections in herself, to be sad when she was sad. She respected herself and her patients. These qualities gave her peace of mind and comforted her patients.

Asya was an artist, and artists are the best therapists. She was also a humane scholar, and they too make the best therapists. The combination was ideal to enable her to find solutions to discord among patients as well as to intrapsychic conflict.

She had the spark, the daring to be unorthodox. She was enterprisingly experimental. She had the security to be spontaneously enthusiastic. In this spirit she was able to convey to patients her optimism that there was a better way of life than the neurotic one.

Part II

THE GROUP LEADER: PSYCHOANALYTIC
FUNCTIONS AND OBJECTIVES

Introduction

ZANVEL A. LIFF

In this first section on the psychoanalytic functions and objectives of the group leader, the contributors offer considerable differentiations between the effective and the ineffective leader. The effective leader is viewed as helping patients work through their defenses and transferential resistances to reach mature, autonomous, and responsible relationships. The ineffective leader is one who plays out his own personal counterneeds, both historic and contemporary, which interfere with the ego strengthening and separating processes in the group.

Both Foulkes and Glatzer object to the very concept of leadership in analytic work, implying that it induces followership, which is considered a fundamental resistance. They see the group analyst as more of a follower. Foulkes often refers to his group efforts as conducting, although he acknowledges that he is a technical leader who is in charge of the group structure, i.e., implementing the rules.

Battegay describes the effective leader as a moderator or facilitator who provides the right leadership dosage. For him, this leader also encourages role changing activities as well as attempting new patterns of behavior. Christ refers to the effective leader as reflective, and as one who induces self-reliance and autonomy.

Aronson portrays the effective group leader as eliciting and working through the repetition compulsion, which he calls the core behavioral sequence. He describes the well-functioning leader as one who makes patients aware of the defensive aspects of their core behavioral sequence and trains them in how to use the group constructively. Fielding emphasizes the importance of the effective leader creating an atmosphere of acceptance and understanding in the group. He also sees the leader as both a model and a teacher with a strong credible image necessary for the patient.

A central requirement for the successful group leader is his maintaining objectivity through the careful recognition and overcoming of countertransference behavior. This is stressed by both Glatzer and Grotjahn. Grotjahn further indicates how the effective leader should constantly learn and grow in the group and gain more emotional freedom.

The process of ineffective or interfering group leadership is discussed by many authors in the book. Liff details the reciprocal interplay, the mutually inducing behavior between the charismatic leader acting out omnipotent, grandiose fantasies and the charisma-hungry patient seeking an ideal parent. This deep transference-countertransference interaction usually creates a dominant-submission pattern which blocks the separation-individuation evolution. Yet sometime transitory charismatic cures occur with peak euphoric and exhilarating experiences. More often than not, however, patients become deeply depressed as great expectations remain unfulfilled when leadership promises remain undelivered.

Christ also states that the charismatic leader induces dependency and undue loyalty, while Battegay focuses on how the dominating leader causes regression and a weakening of ego strength. In addition, he states that the leader who submerges himself into the group as the "Great Mother" symbol creates regression and dependency as well. Glatzer stresses the dangers of countertransference in working with orally regressed patients—the long suffering masochistic types who challenge the leader's omnipotent needs for quick action. This can take the form of the overzealous, critical leader and/or the overly accepting and permissive leader.

Finally, Grotjahn confronts the group leader with the potential pitfall which may occur after working for many years with unconscious psychopathalogy in groups—the leader deteriorating into a fixed pattern rather than continuing to grow and develop as a human being.

20. The Leader in the Group

S. H. FOULKES

It gives me great pleasure to make a small contribution in tribute to Alexander Wolf, one of the pioneers of group analysis in the wider sense, that is to say in the application of psychoanalytical concepts and techniques to the group setting.

I first met Dr. Wolf when S. R. Slavson invited me to give a paper to the American Group Psychotherapy Association in 1949. It was the wish of the committee organizing that meeting that the paper be devoted to leadership, specifically in group-analytic psychotherapy. I had not then met Dr. Wolf nor did I know anything of his work when he spoke during the discussion of my paper. As on an occasion some ten years later, he was quite critical of my ideas. I was under the impression that he did not talk about my paper at all, and I remember saying to my colleageus when I came back home to England: "In America discussions they are very funny, they don't talk about your paper but entirely about their own work." Samuel Hadden, who was in the chair, later called my attention to the fact that either by mistake or by intention I had referred to Dr. Wolf's contribution as "Dr. Wolf's paper." I cannot say which of the two it was.

Dr. Wolf's criticism some ten years later could be ascribed less to ignoring or not understanding what I had to say. I had been invited by The Postgraduate Center in New York to speak on the theme "The application of group concepts to the treatment of the individual in the group." (Both papers mentioned are included in my book *Therapeutic Group Analysis* and essentially I am still in complete agreement with what I then said.) Alexander Wolf again spoke in the discussion. As far as I remember, the main line he took was that group psychotherapy, and in particular group analysis, had as much as nothing to do with group dynamics; that I spoke of a mixture of two quite different disciplines which I tried unnecessarily to mix up and thus confused the issue. Another idea I think was that I advocated treating the group and not the individuals.

It took me quite a while after this experience, and after a long, friendly, and very fruitful discussion we had the following day at a New York hotel with almost all leading group analysts present, to understand where the misunderstanding lay. At that time, in the United States, the term "group dynamics" was understood to refer to Kurt Lewin's concepts. This was quite far from my meaning. Let me explain this once more. I have never used the term "dynamics" in any sense other than psychodynamics, whether these psychodynamics are in a psychoanalytical individual situation or in a group situation. I did and do maintain, however, that they take different forms with each different situation. In groups, therefore, we have to look afresh at these phenomena, some of which we know very well from individual psychoanalysis.

My whole acquaintance with Kurt Lewin and his work was when I heard him speak once at a psychotherapeutic conference in Germany. I thought he spoke well and interestingly. It was also quite clear that he was critical and to some extent adversely critical towards psychoanalysis and the psychoanalytical way of thinking, and was trying to replace it. On the other hand, I remember an interesting paper by Siegfried Bernfeld on a topographical or topological approach to certain psychoanalytic concepts. Having in mind Kurt Lewin's concepts, Bernfeld found these very useful for psychoanalysis. At this same congress I made Kurt Lewin's personal acquaintance and had the pleasure of being at the same table at tea with him and my then chief, Kurt Goldstein, and taking some part in their discussion. My understanding of the holistic approach to biology, to the human organism, or to the human group owes much to the views of Kurt Goldstein with whom I worked for over two years. Although Goldstein was not a Gestalt theorist, he was near to them in many respects. He worked closely with Adhémar Gelb, and as a result I also attended lectures and demonstrations on Gestalt psychology. Fritz Perls, by the way, was a fellow participant in part of this, but he never really understood psychoanalysis. So maybe here there is more common ground with Kurt Lewin. By the way, amusingly, I have quite recently seen my work described as being based partly on that of Cartwright and Zanders. I can only shamefacedly confess that I have never, to my knowledge, seen or looked into a book by these authors.

Since my youth and throughout my life I have always been a

convinced Freudian psychoanalyst. This does not mean that psychoanalysis is my bible. I consider Freud's work like a great work of art, the great work of one person, not easy to build on without losing the essential ground. I will, therefore, confess that for me it was an act of liberation to work in what I consider a new field, group analysis, where one could build anew without in the least losing one's psychoanalytical foundation.

I mention these episodes because they are the most impressive encounters I had with Alexander Wolf. I also mention them because in spite of many distortions, as it appeared to me, and many opinions projected upon me, Alexander Wolf seems basically a friendly and decent person, and a very honest person in his own right. To the best of my knowledge I have never felt resentment about his critical attitude as I well might have done. I have always been more interested in trying to understand scientifically what is at stake, what may be behind the apparent misunderstanding.

It is, therefore, no contradiction for me to express fullheartedly my recognition of his work and my gratitude for his contribution. With great respect and warm personal feelings I wish him a well deserved retirement and a long, happy and fruitful time to come.

I shall not attempt to repeat and elaborate the basic concepts of group analysis of my kind, more precisely called group-analytic psychotherapy. I will only try to give a few of the fundamental guidelines and viewpoints which I use in order to put the whole idea of "leader" into proper perspective.

As the name indicates, I have always stressed that group analysis is not simply an application or adaptation of psychoanalysis to groups. In many ways it is more than that. Above all it is based on the whole therapeutic situation which is established—in this case a group situation. As we introduce particular features into it and, above all, an analytic (in the sense of psychoanalytic) dimension and attitude, this particular situation is more specifically characterized as a group-analytic situation. What I will try to show is why the usual term "leader" does not seem to me to be apt in describing the therapist's function.

According to my lights, while the analyst does lead the group in certain respects, and does so even as a therapist at certain points of the process, it would for various clear reasons be wrong for him to do so as a principle; it is therefore misleading to call him "leader." Before I go further, let me make a few remarks on leadership in general—a vague and somewhat romantic notion. One of the important points regarding the leader at which we as analysts may look differently is that he is not equipped with certain mysterious personality qualifications which predestine him to be a leader, just as a hypnotist is not so equipped. We know—in fact this was Bernheim's great contribution in this field—that hypnosis and similar relationships rest on suggestion. One can also turn this around, as Freud did, and say: if you are in a certain position in relation to another person or persons, then what you say, whatever you say, is a suggestion; that is to say, it is taken in and believed firmly by those whom you address. It is the position in the group which makes a person into a leader and gives him these qualities. That some persons may be more liable to be put into such a position than others need not be questioned. However, it is the transference position in the sense of the delegation of the ego ideal to a person who probably inherits the very early or primordial authority of "the father." It is that position which makes him into a leader. (Freud's formulation.)

In contrast to many of my psychoanalytical colleagues I do not consider Freud's *direct* contribution to group psychology very important. He spoke of a totally different type of group, of highly organized groups, largely from descriptions of others and from the writing desk. What he did, in fact, was to illustrate his concept of ego ideal which then appeared new to him. The material itself is very much selected and even onesided. Moreover, the idea of the group behind all this, in the German original characteristically called "mass" psychology, has nothing to do with our idea of a group; one might say it is its opposite.

In life, in our sort of culture, there are two quite different situations. One is that in which one's rank, one's position in the professional sense, for instance, makes one into a leader. It gives one authority. The other is when people work their own way up to such power positions as, for example, in politics. Unfortunately the latter, 95 times out of 100, is achieved not by the best people, by those most desirably mature and most ethically admirable people who really could do something positive for humanity. It is achieved by rather common-type specimens who have no particular respect for truth, who think of nothing but their own advancement, advertisement, publicity, who work by insinuations and machinations, social pressures and social favors, who work their way up to this position.

I have found myself on two occasions in the first situation. In the

Army, through my rank which was a direct superior to my patients, I had complete authority over them as soldiers. At the Maudsley Hospital, as a teacher of postgraduates and as a consultant in my own department, I was the superior to my colleagues whom I taught. In both these situations I may say I proved to be a good leader, although probably in a very unorthodox way.

My authority and the respect for me and my position were never threatened by the fact that I was unassuming, friendly with everybody, unless strongly provoked to the contrary, and treated them as my equals and fellow human beings. When I say I proved a good leader I mean that the purpose which I served was by general criteria and by general consent well achieved. In one case I was running a department and later helping to run a whole hospital as a therapeutic community, and in the other I was teaching registrars who liked to work with me, who got a good deal out of it, and who learned a great deal—that was the essential factor.

In certain respects the group analyst is in this responsible position as a leader. He should in no way deny this. He is the one who calls the group together, who selects the patients, in whose hands the group is, who decides who should stop, whether the whole group should stop, when there will be holidays, and so forth. He is in charge of all the arrangements. He is, furthermore, the creator of the particular therapeutic situation which he establishes. The features are well-known, but it is essential in the classical group-analytic group that the members be subject to all the precautions we are accustomed to from the psychoanalytical transference situation. They should have no outside contact, should not meet outside the treatment situation nor establish any connections; may I add that it is also better that they should not do so after treatment, at least for a considerable time. They should refrain from vital decisions, as in any other form of analytic treatment. A condition which is taken for granted, but needs to be spelled out, is that they should meet regularly and punctually, and that the session has a precise beginning and end; it is neither prolonged nor shortened for any reason whatever. In all these features and many others, the therapist is the man in charge; he has to make the decisions in the last resort and he has the responsibility. In this sense he is the leader.

Being a dynamically minded analyst, however, he knows that he does this and *how* he does it becomes an essential part of the treatment situation and of the way in which he himself is considered. As an example, on one occasion I had been forced to confront a man and a woman patient with the choice either to continue with the group or to continue meeting outside, but not both. It was rare for me to have to do this. In this situation for several weeks I became a formidable authoritarian father figure, one might say an Old Testament image of God; the group had a terrible fear and respect, and all the deep incest taboos were reinforced. Yet I had only made clear to these people in all friendliness the importance of a technical rule. We should avoid laying down any rules where we possibly can, but let the basic rules develop in the situation by tradition and by showing the group, preferably on the very first occasion whenever behavior warrants it, of the undesirability of acting otherwise. A simple example: regularity and punctuality. I do not tell people that they are expected to be regular and punctual; I take it for granted. When anyone is late or absent, the significance of such actions is made clear to the group by purely analytical means. As a result of being very much on the spot about these conditions, I have a high degree of regularity, punctuality, and a very low number of so-called dropouts compared with the records of many other conductors. I mention this because it indicates how this leadership responsibility is inseparable from the analytical function. Now we will look more closely at the analytical function of the conductor.

The first thing I discovered was that a group can proceed under conditions of maximal freedom of expression combined with considerable restraint as regards action. The next thing I discovered was that if I listened horizontally or laterally I could perceive or, if you like, produce links between what they said. In a certain sense this makes the group into some kind of psychological entity, but I have never said that it should be approached predominantly as such an entity, at least not in the typical group-analytic group with which we are here concerned. Here the group is considered the background and the focus is on the individual. These individual exchanges and interactions must always be seen in this total context from which they are co-determined.

Much later I could say that these links are in the nature of either simple associations or reactions of all sorts to what has been going on, or else interpretations which are for the most part unconscious. I learned to orient myself in discerning the different configurations in these combinations of communications, a process which was called *location*. This was extended in depth to the level of interpretation, of mental processes, of understanding on which the group, or the majority, are moving at any given moment, which level gives the key to any contribution. I also learned that the individual, who has always been in the foreground of my interest, through his own reaction picks out of this context the particularly relevant personal meaning. This is what I mean by *resonance*. Once one has seen it this all happens quite inevitably, but it was not quite so easy to see in the perturbing richness of the material which seemed overwhelming at first.

The group acts as if it knew what we call the dynamic unconscious. It can also work its way to fully conscious awareness, to have full insight. Change, however, results from the interacting processes themselves even before they are made conscious. In this view change is, therefore, the cause of insight and not its consequence. Having verified these experiences, I felt at home in such a group, and the more I felt at home the less I felt the need to intervene, not to speak of a need to lead.

To lead would suggest that the patients present me with their troubles and I could show them the solution to these troubles and cure them. This would correspond to an attitude on the part of our patients which is one of the fundamental resistances. Their suffering likes to masquerade as an illness that has descended upon them, and somebody else must be blamed for the damage inflicted upon them. Instead of having to lead the group, I had more occasion to observe and follow the group, so that one could say that the group led me. This was the only way by which I could learn what was going on. From then on I always followed my temperamental habit to have the experience first, to be guided more or less intuitively, but by informed intuition and by considered use of this unconscious communication which came to me—and then to think a lot about what the experiences were and what I myself had been doing. I have always described the way I behave in a group as not according to a predetermined idea, but I found myself behaving in a certain way, corrected my own behavior and refined it in the light of my experience, and then formulated it.

I was eventually led to a fundamental point, namely that the mind does not originate in each individual, individually, and then interact and communicate with other people's minds. We do more justice to the situation in which we work if we take mental processes as originally group-borne, with the exception of those coming from the body. The way individuals communicate and interact, how they defend themselves, how they pick out what belongs to them in particular, how they understand each other rests on some basic common ground, and is based on what was called *foundation matrix*. To some extent this develops and refines itself and becomes more and more established as the group proceeds—the *dynamic* side of the *matrix*. By "matrix" is meant this common communicational ground which is shared. This same thing was in my mind when I said that it was a psyche-group (Helen Jenning's term); what is usually called intrapsychic is in fact shared by the members, including of course the conductor.

From these general considerations it will be clear why I did not like to call my function leading. Now why did I call it conducting? There was at first an element which made me choose that term from the point of view of the musical conductor. I often felt that my contribution was similar to that of a conductor. I was not producing; indeed I refrained from producing the group's ideas, influencing them as little as I could, but I was nevertheless doing something. I was not the composer who wrote the music but the conductor who interpreted it, the conductor who brought it to light. I remember saying to my colleagues: "I feel like a conductor, but I don't know in the least what the music is which will be played." This musical connotation should not be exaggerated, but I still think it is a useful way of describing the function of a therapist in such a group.

Another reason, of course, why one cannot lead, or should not lead, is that one allows oneself to be used as a transference figure and as a projection screen, which are two different things.

I look upon the human animal principally and seriously as a social animal, as a being who cannot live in isolation and who is shaped and forced from earliest times by the significant people with whom he lives and with whom he is in concert. More than that: he is a split-off fragment of the functional unity they form. In this light when we take the individual out of his natural group and decide to treat him under analytical conditions with strangers, we see some of the elements usually ascribed to transference and repetition compulsion. There is a basic need for the so-called individual to re-establish his usual position, and then one of the collective basic elements in such a group is that he meets different responses. The phenomenon of transference in its importance can be better understood by not being overstretched.

The conductor must be very active in his own mind. I have already indicated how he orients himself, how he has to respond, how by his own feelings he has to time his interventions, to feel when intervention is necessary and when not, when he is really called upon to respond to something either the group or some of the individuals see in him and make him into. It is also clear that he can do much of this work silently. However he follows the process, he judges and internally directs it all the time. This is quite different in my view from leading it. He does not lead the group or the individuals. He directs the procedure, watches it, decides especially about resistances and defenses, when these become too strong and need to be brought to light and analyzed in their own right. In that respect—in the analysis of resistances and defenses—he is much more active. The unconscious ego and particularly the superego in all its phases is very much in the center of attention and has to be approached as the most important part of the ongoing therapeutic process.

When communication stops or is distorted, leading into great difficulties and complications and to negative reactions, the call is on the conductor to do something about it through the group. I do not mean that the group is addressed as such as if it were an entity. "Through the group" means having in mind the context in which it happens so that all, and not only the one addressed, can in their own way participate in this process of uncovering, benefit by it, and actively help with it. A well-conducted group learns to do even that work by itself, and the more work the group does, the more that comes from inside the participants, the more effective and convincing it is, and the less authoritarian. This is important because the tendency to make the therapist into a leader is one of the great resistances. It is partly analogous with positive transference, seen as the greatest resistance.

My procedure has, at the same time, the great advantage of helping to resolve the inherent need for dependency, this desperate need for dependency which perhaps repeats the individual's original dependence on the mother. To resolve that need by not accepting this role of leader and *pari passu* by carefully weaning the group from this need helps the members to grow up, to tackle problems of all sorts which eventually will be of direct therapeutic value for their leading better and more satisfactory lives.

At the same time, by refusing to be the ego ideal or to be put into that position, one counteracts the members' tendency to learn by imitation, by identification, etc., and to make the mistake of thinking that the ideal behavior would be that of the group therapist.

Not only may his way be far from ideal, but how he behaves in his function as a therapist is certainly not a model for life. There is considerable scientific value in reducing the danger of finding what one expects to find, thus confirming one's theories and prejudices. Instead, one must be prepared to listen and listen again before one forms any judgment. Nobody can be quite free from his own prejudices or theories, but there are degrees, and I am satisfied that I can reduce this element of suggestion to a minimum.

With all this stress on the conductor following the group, another wrong conception may be fostered, wrong from the point of view of my own ideas, namely that of passivity. It is true that with the orientation which I have just outlined one is more able to be receptive, to observe, to watch, to see, to be open and patient when things seem strange, which is of particular importance. With all this there is a certain passivity, if one likes to call it that, in the sense of being more receptive than active, but it would be a very distorted idea to think I am being passive in the ordinary sense. On the contrary, I take a lively part, whether I speak or not, I am very ready to be drawn in where it seems right, where it feels right, and I am in many ways much more active than I would be as a psychoanalyst. Even in that latter situation I think to describe the attitude as one of passivity is an oversimplification and actually incorrect. This is not a question of passivity versus activity.

Now as to activity, the fashion is to think of all *interventions* as *interpretations*. This concept is also far too loosely used. Interventions may equally well be questions, confirmations, requests for information, confrontations, things I want to know for my own sake. Interpretation is too often represented as the main or almost the only activity of the analyst. This comes again partly from overexpansion of the term. Some people speak as if everything the analyst says is an interpretation. One also comes across a kind of almost magical belief in interpretation and its effects. The conductor's task is above all to listen and follow the patient, to understand what the patient's own conviction of his disturbance is, what is his own theory of improvement or cure, what he expects of the therapist, what he expects of treatment, and so on.

The therapist should not think he must understand; it is sometimes very important *not* to understand, quite apart from the strong dynamic effect this has. Understanding is often approving, or saying, "If I were you, I would act in the same way" or "One can well sympathize with you." "I do not understand" in the sense of Brecht's alienation concept says: "This need not be the reaction, you could also act quite differently." Quite apart from this, not understanding is important for the possibility of learning something new.

To come back to *interpretation,* I think it should be contrasted with *analyzing,* which is in the nature of an investigation, of finding out and of helping the patient to find out himself. If he can't, the focus shifts to what prevents him, what anxiety, what emotion of any kind is in the way, what, in short, is his unconscious resistance and defense. This is more of an active task for the conductor than interpretation because it is against the stream so to speak and something which the patient cannot as well do for himself, though the ultimate work must always be done by the patients themselves. In short, I am claiming that analyzing and all that it implies (into which we cannot go here) is the overall activity. Interpretation is a part of that which is in the service of decoding; it is sometimes necessary, but better left to the patient himself.

Now a word about countertransference. Often, the term, like transference, is used in too general a sense. There is no extra problem in the group concerning one's own person. It can happen that one has emotional reactions of one's own to an individual or even toward a group which one can only find out by thinking about oneself. The real question is how much of that concerns the patients. There I feel I am more cautious than others. I think one should never communicate such reactions to the group in order to meet one's own need. If one feels that this is the motive force, one should refrain and first look into oneself. There are situations in which there is a definite positive use for communicating one's own involvement to the group. In certain situations this is not only admissible but necessary. I think, on the whole, that the group analyst can be freer than the psychoanalyst.

In case of doubt I would rather wait and see than be too ready to think aloud in the group; in many respects this is disturbing in view of one's special position, in view of the special weight and prestige one has. Personal, private communications about oneself are best avoided on the whole, but countertransference in the sense that it arises from the treatment transactions may be relatively liberally shared with the group as long as the judgment prevails that this is a good thing to do, but not where the urge arises from personal reasons.

I am hoping that in these short and deliberately spontaneous remarks I have added a little to the idea of how I see the problem of leadership in such groups and why I see it in this way. Let me end by saying something in a deeper sense about one's own involvement. Whether we like it or not, we are very much involved, even emotionally, in such group sessions. It goes without saying that we look with sympathy and empathy and with warm interest on our patients and consider them equals not only among themselves but also between them and us. What the therapist offers is his capacity as an expert, his experience and knowledge. He is comparable to a guide on a mountain, but in foreign territory, who is expert in helping to find the best way, to avoid dangers and pitfalls. This empathy, genuine as it should be, is tempered by the group analyst feeling somewhat outside and above the group he conducts. A degree of detachment is in my opinion necessary and desirable. I hope I have made it clear that this detachment is the outcome of a certain philosophical attitude to life, and is in no way contradictory to his being warm and genuinely responsive to his patients; without such feelings he could not work at all.

Perhaps I should end by saying that the aim of a true therapy should be liberation from the resistance to change, the diminishing of this resistance to change, so that members of the group become freer to learn or unlearn. The patient should emerge better able not only to enjoy life, but also to face the inevitable trials and tribulations, the inevitable suffering of life, in a better spirit, without having to add to them with a deep need for self-inflicted suffering, punishment and self-damage. Above all, the group analyst must free himself from the tendency to create people in his own image and according to his own ideas and ideals. On the contrary he must accept them as what they are and help them to become freer and to develop in their own persons. If he feels this way, he performs a really creative task which may compensate for the many strains to which our professional activity exposes us. Seen in this light it is a highly satisfactory, creative activity, in no way, however, feeding the personal or narcissistic needs of the conductor.

REFERENCE

Foulkes, S. H., *Therapeutic Group Analysis* (London: Allen & Univin, 1964; New York: International Universities Press, 1965).

21. The Leader and Group Structure

RAYMOND BATTEGAY

The activity of the group leader is one of three factors which contribute to the structure of psychotherapy groups. The other two are the composition of the group and the room setting in which the sessions are held.

If a group is led in an authoritarian manner, it will be and will remain centered on the leader. Members of such a group will have the chance to develop themselves only as far as the leader permits. The roles of the participants are therefore very precisely defined. Because such a group activates regressive tendencies, the roles taken over by the members are mostly those of early childhood. All the members maintain these roles, which are facilitated by the dominating attitude of the leader. As an illustration, I can cite an example of a nontherapeutic group, to which the same laws can be applied:

In a supervision-group for ministers giving lectures in school classes, one of the members reported about his failure in a class of 13-year-old boys. When he entered the classroom, he saw the boys jumping from one seat to another. He told them: "You can sit wherever you want, even on the wardrobe. I shall leave the room until you have arranged your affairs. You may call me when you have finished them." Thus, the minister behaved in a very authoritarian manner. But he thought his behavior was very group-centered and democratic. Some minutes later, he was called back by one of the class members. Indeed, he found some boys sitting on the wardrobe and others sitting quietly on different benches. In tht very first moment, he felt the resistance of the class and tried to speak with them. But he could never break through that resistance and had to give up the class. When the director of this school took over, the boys told him that on the one hand the minister was behaving very dictatorially, and that on the other

95

hand they were—only apparently—allowed to behave the way they wanted.

As we can see in this example, the leader behaved very dominantly, despite his apparent use of democratic words. The schoolboys fulfilled his orders to the letter, but they did not assume any individual responsibility. They behaved in a regressive manner, in such a way that the group structure was destroyed and a chaotic state resulted. Of course, the ambivalent authoritarian attitude of the leader facilitated the disruption of the class.

In every group that is led in an authoritarian manner there is the danger that no distinct role differentiation will be developed, except the two-step hierarchy with the leader on one side and the led on the other. The led persons in this case very often tend to refuse responsible roles. They are in danger of becoming a "mass in a small frame," in which they are emotionally linked very closely but do not develop their own intellectual capacities to take over differentiated and responsible functions in a social frame. Therefore, the danger exists that they will all either behave exactly as the leader orders or, as the example shows, in a disintegrated way (Staehelin), so that even the leader no longer has any influence.

Our experience with group psychotherapy at the Basel Psychiatric University Hospital and Out-Patient Clinic since 1955 corroborates this evidence, even when we use directive methods of group psychotherapy. Alcoholics and drug dependents, for example, who are approached by group psychotherapy, initially need directive support and fulfillment of their oral needs, but they cannot be directed to such an extent that they never get over their infantile dependency needs. In purely analytical group psychotherapy with neurotics or in analytical self-experience groups with young doctors or psychologists who want to be taught to become psychotherapists, dominant leadership is entirely contraindicated. Perhaps a dominating attitude could hurt their narcissism and help to work it through, but the participants would expect the leader to do the work for them while they remained in a passive-regressive dependency. By their own self-experience we hope to make them aware of their own unconscious tendencies and of their own neurotic patterns of behavior. The participants should experience by themselves that they have the responsibility for achieving insight and change. Only if the leader renounces domination will they recognize that in this kind of group a participant may, consciously or unconsciously, temporarily also enter the role of an auxiliary therapist and help the other patients. If the leader is dominating, such a development is not possible. The members in this case are not able to develop new sides of their personalities. The dominating leader provokes, as Freud (1955) demonstrated for the archaic group, feelings of castration in the fantasies of the members. A lot of aggressions will arise which, because of the dominance of the leader, cannot be articulated. These aggressions which cannot come out will finally be directed toward the members themselves.

Those members who like to be led in a very directive way in the group are always in danger of remaining regressive and fulfilling obediently what the leader wants them to do. This total obedience is dangerous, as the experiments of Milgram at Yale University (1966) showed, when 62% of the persons tested administered electroshocks up to 450 volts on the order of a leader. It can never be therapeutic to seek total identification with the leader from the group members. Such unlimited identification is dangerous not only because of unthinking obedience but also because of the associated weakening of the ego. Such identification can bring about a partial or total loss of individuality and ego boundaries. In a group of schizophrenics we have studied since 1963, we can see that some of the patients with very weak egos very often identify to such an extent with the leader that it results in the loss of still more ego-strength. Dominant therapists facilitate this development toward further weakening of the ego.

It is not easy to determine the right dosage of leadership in a group of schizophrenics. On the one hand, they need this identification with the leader, because, as Etzioni has shown, for all groups, it is easier to identify with the group through identification with the leader, since he is always the participant who is seen most clearly. Ego-weak schizophrenics, therefore, tend to find support from a strong leader. They cannot get the same feeling of ego-strengthening from the other members because, especially in the early stages of a therapeutic group, the other members are not experienced as distinctly as the leader. On the other hand, the therapist should seek to minimize his importance bit by bit and to be slowly replaced by the other participants. In a group of schizophrenics, we have been treating for years and which is a slow-open group (Foulkes: new members are only taken when others have left the group), we recognize that the newcomers very often direct themselves only toward the therapist. Later on, after they have participated for a longer time and have gotten sure of the attention of the therapist, they direct themselves more to the group. For these groups it is especially important that the therapist does not take too dominant a role; otherwise, he would suppress the members in their development. He should help the group members to find their own ways and to contribute to the activation and strengthening of their egos. He should support the originality and creative differences of his patients and not direct them in a way that he thinks is good for them (Wolf and Schwartz).

THE LEADER TOTALLY INCORPORATED INTO THE GROUP:
WE-GROUP OR THE GROUP AS A GREAT MOTHER

Especially with alcoholics, but also with other kinds of participants, we have observed groups in which the therapist undergoes a common regression with the other participants. The collective becomes, therefore what we would like to call a We-group or a group that acts as a Great Mother (Neumann). We observe a tendency of the individuals to hand their individual responsibility entirely over to the group. A group in which only collectivity is felt leads to a state in which the members do not develop their own role differentiation and activities. Therefore, the danger arises that they may lose ego strength.

If the group is treated as a whole and not as individuals, we can assume, as Argelander, Bion, Stierlin and others have described, that the individuality of the participants is weakened. If the therapist is also entirely included in the group, the participants may experience themselves in their fantasies as part of a whole and the group as so all-mighty that they wish to remain in it always. In a doctors' self-experience group, which met for 7 years at a 10-hour weekend session four times a year, one of the participants said half-seriously, half-joking: "So let us be together until death separates us." In this group the therapist was no longer experienced in a special role; the participants integrated him entirely into the group. Perhaps, in his counter-transference, the therapist also identified too closely with the group and saw himself only as part of a whole. He did not seek to maintain a differentiated role as a therapist and perhaps needed the group for his own purposes as a nutritive and strengthening milieu. The attitude of the "therapist" and his countertransference may be decisive in the development of an entirely closed entity which is experienced more or less unconsciously as a Great Mother (Neumann).

It is not difficult to understand that the group easily undergoes a regression toward an entirely we-centered collectivity, when the therapist experiences himself only as a part of a whole, in which he feels protected. But in this case, the therapist does not see the group as a therapeutic milieu for the participants. He rather abuses the group for his own purposes and holds it in its regressive tendency toward a Great Mother, without giving feedback of their behavior to the members. The participants will not become responsible for themselves and may even lay down the responsibility they had before. Since the unconscious expectations of the leader toward the group as a comprehensive mother may provoke prolonged regression in the members, we urge that each therapist undergo a training analysis. The group, with its reinforcement effect on the emotions, activates unconscious needs in the therapist, as well as the other participants.

If a group, mostly by the regressive attitude of the leader, acts as an undifferentiated collective, the participants are no longer interested in what goes on outside of its frame. They are totally centered on the group. The collective is experienced as an enlarged ego on which all libido of the members is fixed. In such a group, laws may develop which are not suitable for human beings outside the group. The participants live in a system representing the pleasure principle more than the reality principle (Freud, 1963). Whereas a therapeutic group should give the possibilties for both insight and social learning, such a group does not give opportunity for either. Such a group activates only unreflected pleasure. A totally we-centered group can, therefore, not be therapeutically useful. On the contrary, its purpose is only its own existence. In Switzerland we studied a religious sect in which each participant lived a totally we-centered existence. Some years ago it happened that a young girl of this group was beaten to death by the other members, who were trying to beat the devil out of her. In this entirely we-centered group, the sense of outside reality was totally lost, and the members had lost sight of the limits of what a young human body is able to suffer. They were all shocked by the death of their member and entirely unprepared for it. Such groups, being totally centered on themselves, in which the leader has undergone the same regressive development as the members, have a weakened capacity for insight, conceptualization, and even the laws of outside reality. Therefore, if a group leader has the tendency to create strong cohesion among the participants, we are always skeptical about his countertransference and of the "therapeutic" aim of the group.

In an analytic self-experience group with doctors, a woman participant who had attended sensitivity-training sessions for 10 days, from morning to evening, said that during that time she became, together with the leaders, entirely part of the group, but that afterwards when she was separated from the others, she started to be depressive to an almost unbearable extent. In reporting about the pleasure during the sensitivity-training period, she complained initially about the frustrations within the analytic group and said that the sensitivity-trainng group had much more integrated her into the collectivity. To the other members of the analytic group and slowly also to herself, it became clear that in the sensitivity-training group in which she had participated before, she, and probably the others, including the trainer, got more or less totally dependent on the group. This group dependence, after the cessation of the training period, provoked her depression. It happened, as Richter (1972) states, that a group dependence appeared.

This danger is especially strong when the group is experienced by the members as a comprehensive totality, as a Great Mother. In a sensitivity-training group which is only directed toward the interactional level, such a development is much more possible than in an analytically oriented group. In an analytic group which deals with deep psychological motivations as well as interactions it is possible to work through the dependency needs which may appear in the participating individuals. An analytically trained leader will not let the group come so far that all the members will at the same time acquire such a deep oral dependency on the group that they lose every possibility of self-reflection. A well-trained analyst will never abandon his position as a critical observer, maintaining the distance necessary for conceptualization.

THE LEADER AS MODERATOR

Only those groups in which the therapist is attentive to the group process and the individual tendencies of the members, while at the same time remaining in the background as moderator and facilitator of the group, are really therapeutically effective. Group psychotherapists who allow the group the possibility of being group centered rather than leader centered give the members the opportunity to take over different roles and to thereby discover sides of their personalities undetected until then. As Wolf and Schwartz underline, the therapist should not try to dominate the patients within the therapeutic group. He should help the members to find their ways and contribute to the enrichment and revival of their egos. The therapist should not, as Wolf and Schwartz say, think that there is only one path toward human fulfillment. They state that the originality and the creative differences in each patient should be supported. It is, therefore, necessary that the leader know his own unconscious tendencies and countertransferences. Only then can he protect the group from developing an unconscious dependence on him.

By maintaining an analytical attitude, the leader gives the participants an opportunity to develop new perspectives on their existence. The therapist will participate actively in such a group only at moments when none of the other members is giving feedback or interpretations, asking questions when there are problems to be worked through. In therapeutic groups, it is not the task of the therapist alone to do the analytic work. The participants themselves should be encouraged to enter temporarily into positions of auxiliary therapists. The leader cannot accelerate the group process by being dominant. He can only help the group if he gives the individual participants the opportunity of undergoing by themselves the different steps of group psychotherapy. Whereas Freud (1963) identified the three factors "remembering, repeating, working through" as the essence of individual analysis, we have observed in our group-therapy experience since 1955 at the Basel Psychiatric In- and Out-Patient Clinic, that the following three factors are of special importance: Repeating, insight and social learning. The therapist cannot do this work for his patients. He is only able to provide feedback or interpretations which may help the patients to find which motives are behind the repetition of neurotic patterns of behavior they demonstrate in the group repeatedly. He may also encourage them to try new ways of communication and by this facilitate social learning.

In principle the group members must have time to undergo the process of regression and maturation by themselves. Certainly it is possible, as Goulding (1972) has shown in developing Berne's transactional analysis, to develop short-term methods—e.g., by formulating early injunctions of the different participants and afterward trying to bring the patients to redecisions within the frame of the therapeutic group. But when we help the participants in that active manner to attain insight into their early hindrances, and to come to a redecision for developing new, enlarged patterns of life, we are doing only focal-group psychotherapy, short-term group psychotherapy in which focal conflicts may be resolved. But with neurotics who suffer from disturbances of very early drive-development phases and from very complex pathological behavior patterns, we cannot use such focal methods. Besides, we have to consider that the leader has to be very active in these focally directed group psychotherapies. In so doing, he attains a very dominant position. If the patients should really develop different sides of their personalities, they should have the opportunity to grow slowly and to take over different roles, different activities within the group. Only the group with changing roles allows the the members to recognize their real possibilities and limitations. The dominating leader would endanger the patients by further weakening their egos. With Goulding's method of formulating injunctions and a redecision, there is also the disadvantage that only one member is focused on at a time. It is then no longer group psychotherapy in the sense that more than one participant is treated by means of the group. We could almost say that it becomes a treatment of one member in a group-setting. I think that the whole group as well as individual members should always be kept in mind by the therapist.

If the therapist prevents himself from being dominating, the group process can develop slowly. After an initial phase of *explorative contact* of the members, a stage of regression will come, in which the members are confronted with a regressive *reactivation of their infantile needs*. They will ask the therapist to give them a theme to lead them. Only when he refuses to fulfill these reactivated early wishes of the participants can they become aware of the multiple and multidemensional transferences linked with these unconscious needs (Slavson, 1951). After this phase of *insight*, they will recognize that they have *to change and to develop new patterns of behavior* if they want to be considered as contributing members of the group. Only by recognizing step by step which behavior really belongs to him, will the patient or the member be able to grow. The participants must have the opportunity to try different roles without being driven by a leader, until they see by themselves what their personal ways of life are.

A doctor who belonged to an analytical self-experience group of general practitioners and psychiatrists complained about the fact that he had always been neglected, especially by his mother who dominated the family. He now tried repeatedly in many sessions to get the attention of the others by claiming rejection by the group. The other group members kept silent in the face of this repetitive and compulsive pattern of behavior. Only after recognizing the significance of the silent feedback of the group, first more unconsciously than consciously, then with more clear consciousness, could he get insight into the early influence of his parents and his consequent inhibitions. Only then was he motivated to change and to learn through the social interaction of the group with its normative potence.

REFERENCES

Argelander, H. "Gruppenanalyse unter Anwendung des Struktur-modells." *Psyche* 22 (1968):913.

Berne, E. *Principles of Group Treatment* (New York: Oxford University Press, 1966).

Bion, W. R. *Experiences in Groups* (London, England: Tavistock Publications, 1961).

Etzioni, A. *Soziologie der Organisationen* (Munich: Juventa, 1967), trans. by Lepenies, R. and Nolte, H. from *Modern Organizations* (Englewood Cliffs, N. J.: Prentice-Hall, 1964).

Freud, S. "Formulierungen über die zwei Prinzipien des psychischen Geschehens," *Gesammelte Werke, Bd. VIII* (London: Imago, 1955), p. 103.

Freud, S. "Massenpsychologie und Ich-Analyse." *Gesammelte Werke, Bd. XIII* (Frankfurt: S. Fischer, 1963), 4th ed., p. 71.

Freud, S. "Erinnern, Wiederholen und Durcharbeiten." *Gesammelte Werke, Bd. X* (Frankfurt: S. Fischer, 1963), 3rd ed., p. 125.

Goulding, R. "New Directions in Transactional Analysis: Creating an Environment for Redecision and Change" in Sager, C. J. and Kaplan, H. S. *Progress in Group and Family Therapy* (New York: Brunner/Mazel, 1972).

Milgram, S. "Personality Characteristics Associated with Obedience and Defiance towards Authoritative Command." *Journal of Experimental Research in Personality* 1 (1966): 282.

Neumann, E. *Die grosse Mutter* (Zürich: Rhein, 1956).

Richter, H. *Die Gruppe* (Rheinbek-near-Hamburg: Rowohlt, 1972).

Slavson, S. R. *Analytic Group Psychotherapy* (New York: Columbia University Press, 1951).

Staehelin, J. E. "Massenpsychologie und klinische Psychiatrie." *Swiss Archives of Neurological Psychiatry* 60 (1947):269.

Stierlin, H. "Uebertragung und Widerstand" in Preuss, H. G. *Analytische Gruppenprozesse* (Munich-Berlin-Cologne: Urban u. Schwarzenberg, 1966).

Wolf, A. and Schwartz, E. K. "Psychoanalysis in Groups" in Kaplan, H. I. and Sadock, B. J. *Comprehensive Group Psychotherapy* (Baltimore: Williams & Wilkins, 1971), p. 241.

22. Contrasting the Charismatic and Reflective Leader

JACOB CHRIST

This paper contrasts the charismatic leadership style with that of the reflective psychotherapist. The charismatic leader tends to create a group that is dependent on him. He will often produce much emotional discharge and will leave people with a feeling of emotional support. The reflective leader by contrast fits into an already existing group and tries to affiliate himself with his co-participants. He tends to create a cohesive group that will foster attitudes of self-reliance and autonomy. The consequences of these two styles both in group psychotherapy and larger groups will be outlined.

The theme of *leadership* is much in the public eye at present. Much controversy is transacted in general terms and pertains to a variety of issues from the political to the intellectual. More specifically, even in the helping professions and especially in the field of group therapy, "leadership" is often poorly defined though beset with emotionality. At times it is hard, therefore, to find one's way with the many statements that are made about leadership.

As a first point I would like to go back to ideas stated by an early investigator into the matter of small-group dynamics—Cecil Gibb. He says, in essence, that leadership is not an attribute of the person of the leader but is *a relationship which one individual makes with a collective*. It is clear that a leader is only a leader when there are people ready to be led. In one situation a leader may prevail, whereas in another situation, with a different collective, that same person will become a follower. Leadership therefore is a *role* which is determined by the individual and the collective existing at this moment. True, certain individuals have a propensity to handle a number of situations in a leadership role and might, therefore, be called habitual leaders.

But the term "leadership qualities" should be understood to mean only a habitual *role* in a given situation and not an innate personality characteristic. The best way to find out about leadership qualities in patients or trainees is to put the person in question in an experimental group setting and see how he behaves. Propensity for the leadership role is much easier to discern in this way than in a one-to-one interview situation.

It is very useful to recognize not only one but a variety of leadership models. Fritz Redl, in his paper of 1942, considerably enlarged the theoretical framework of psychoanalytically oriented group therapy when he described ten types of group formation around a "central person." The central person is not always the leader in the conventional sense, and leadership or "becoming the central person" is not determined necessarily by the leader's personality but by a number of circumstances related to the needs of the group and the situation at hand. The supplier of forbidden drugs, for instance, has a leadership function among certain groups not because of his personality but simply because he has available what is wanted or desired by others.

From the many varieties and types of leadership situations I would like to contrast two characteristic styles as particularly relevant for the field of group therapy, or for that matter for all functions related to mental health. One style might be characterized by the capacity to become a *charismatic leader,* engendering loyalty in the followers and bringing to them a feeling of being "supported." The other style might be characterized by the leader's capacity for *affiliation,* where he can make himself one among his fellow members and bring about a feeling on their part of being understood, strengthened and "an equal to the leader." Both the charismatic style of leadership and the affiliative type of leadership have their advantages and disadvantages in clinical situations. It is not that one is good and the other bad. Both types of leadership can be exercised for the good, and with great skill; and both can be misused or be totally ineffective. More often than not a leader's style is mixed and has characteristics of both types. Let me describe both styles in their pure form with the help of some observations from group psychotherapy.

In a beginning group psychotherapy session or training session, the members are all new, unknown to one another, and there is tension in the air. The group leader appears, the session is to begin and all eyes are focused on the leader who is to "make things happen." This situation of infinite expectation of the leader and potentially infinite power on his part does not last very long. For soon it will appear that the leader cannot fulfill all the expectations placed on him. Yet this situation with the leader in an uncontested position of power will return time and again, especially in crisis situations. It is not unattractive in its less extreme forms, both to a charismatic leader and to some group members. When a leader succeeds in keeping alive the great expectation that people have of him, when he fulfills people's needs and stays in power, when finally he can create the impression that he is freely giving of himself to the group members, then he will become the charismatic leader.

The characteristics of this leader in group therapy are rather well known. He is usually a nice guy. He is helpful, giving, warm, most of the time intelligent, articulate, and outspoken. He is usually not the silent type, and will intervene frequently and overtly in the conversation, giving it guidance and direction toward the goals recognized to be therapeutic. It is this type of leader who often can hold onto his patients very well, he has fewer dropouts than others, and it is this leader who will create an intense loyalty among his group members, primarily to himself and only secondarily to one another. If we can say one negative thing about him, it is that he tends to keep his group members dependent on him and he dominates the group interaction often to an undue extent, thus depriving some of the less gifted members from getting a fair and full hearing. He will often not tolerate outright antagonism to himself. He is not inclined to share his work with colleagues or transfer his group to some other leader on occasions when he has to be away or if he should have to terminate. If a co-leader is present he or she has to be clearly subordinate as his leadership is highly personal. Patients who participate in such groups will often extol the competence and the knowledge of their group leader and state in a vague or general way that they have been helped by him. Quite usually patients will talk about the leader first and foremost and attribute only secondary importance to whatever help they may have received from other group members.

In therapeutic practice or supervision one would, of course, have to admonish such a charismatic leader to put himself somewhat more in the background, to be silent, to allow the members to help one another, and to become more a participant in the group rather than its leader. Nevertheless the charismatic leader is the one who "gets things done," who can mobilize difficult patients into some activity, and who often can, so to say, treat the untreatable. The field of group psychotherapy has its charismatic leaders and they have often been the great *innovators* and movers in the discipline.

I would describe the charismatic leader's counterpart, the *affiliative leader*, as perhaps a rather inconspicuous person. He does not, on the surface, have characteristics which make him outstanding, striking, or particularly attractive to people. He does not impress at first as specially competent, nor does he seem to be beset by a desire to change the world around him. He does not shine in the initial contacts, but he gains when one gets to know him more closely. His talents are not needed by a complacent or dependent group which is ready to welcome a great leader, but he is the man to look for when one deals with an angry or unresponsive group. An example may be a group of delinquent adolescents, a streetcorner gang or, on the other hand, chronic hospital-hardened psychotics. None of these types of patients will respond well to a self-assured charismatic leader. The more inconspicuously a group therapist can work his way into some of these difficult patient groups the better he will do. Streetcorner gangs or delinquents usually have their own more or less charismatic leaders, who often do not care to be displaced by someone coming in from the outside. Therapeutic success here will not depend on the leader's taking power or meeting expectations, but rather on developing a place for himself *within* the communications network of the group. He may in time pursue a variety of acts or interchanges with individual members and become important in a personal way to several of them. By becoming himself involved in what goes on in the group, he may help effectively. Unlike the charismatic leader who forms or structures his group to his own needs, the affiliative leader accepts the existing group structure and finds a place for himself within it. What he loses in terms of leadership quality proper, he may gain in closeness and intimacy with the members.

The question may arise of which style is best in group psychotherapy. The answer is not one or the other; of necessity group therapy contains ingredients of both. In the beginning stages of a psychotherapy group it is necessary to form and structure a group, and this takes some talent for making relationships, arousing expectations, and creating loyalties. However, if a group stays on that level, structured by the leader, something is missing. Sooner or later the group therapist will affiliate more closely with his members, rather than leading them. If he, however, only affiliates he may lose an important aspect of his therapeutic leverage, for time and again informed decisions or guidance are necessary in order to insure the group's progress in therapy.

In the following analogy I will present something that resembles a natural experiment where we have the opportunity to watch two group leaders of opposite styles substitute for one another with their respective groups. The reactions of the groups to a change in leadership will be very telling.

Dr. Able and Dr. Baker, as I shall call them, were both psychiatric residents and each had a group of eight outpatients in treatment. The two were friendly competitors with each other, and they had agreed to cover each other's group during their vacations. Dr. Able had an outgoing, supportive and free-wheeling style of doing therapy, while Dr. Baker tended toward a more reflective listening and less "giving" attitude in therapy. Both enjoyed an excellent reputation within the hospital and were generally considered equal in their overall performance, even though their styles were sharply contrasting. Both were having their first experience as group leaders under supervision, both had attended a hospital-sponsored training group experience, and each of them had a group supervisor who shared some of his own characteristics and style of doing therapy.

Dr. Baker's group had been rather solidly established and ran relatively uneventfully at the time that he was to go on vacation, leaving Dr. Able to cover for him. When Dr. Able entered the group room he found only the co-therapist present. He asked: "Where is everybody?" And eventually the co-therapist went out to the waiting area to bring the group members in. They were in a habit of waiting outside and filing in in orderly fashion, something that was alien to Dr. Able's rather informal style. Dr. Able felt relatively little discomfort in the new situation. He perceived in the first few minutes of the group experience that Dr. Baker had been considered something of an outsider in the group and had been leading from a distance. The group readily took to the contrasting style of Dr. Able with something nearing delight. Within a short time they were "throwing bouquets" to him and with this he was able to get away with a comment that much of the dialogue in the group appeared to be social chatter. The group was able to accept this because they felt that the new leader was willing to share feelings and informality. In the following two sessions there was more easy discourse among the group members and with the leader, and some heretofore silent members were included in the group procedures and talked a great deal more. It was a foregone conclusion that Dr. Baker would return to resume leadership of his group.

After his return, however, Dr. Baker was given a hard time by his group. The interim therapist had been seen as much more giving and much more likable. In particular, group members appreciated and reported repetitively that Dr. Able had given straight answers to their questions. The answers could hardly be called profound, but the fact that they were given had meaning. One patient had asked about phobic symptoms, and Dr. Able had answered that they were due to anxiety. In subsequent sessions the group remembered repeatedly the emotional experience with Dr. Able, who was so different, and they had high praise for his work with the group. Dr. Baker noted in later sequence that whenever he used his own characteristic interpretative and distant manner the group would comment on Dr. Able's more emotional and individually styled remarks.

The reverse experience was indeed quite different. When Dr. Baker entered the room where Dr. Able's group was meeting, he found the members already present and engaged in friendly talk with one another. They did not spontaneously introduce themselves but complied somewhat reluctantly after Dr. Baker had introduced himself and asked them to inform him of their names. All group members displayed the same attitude toward Dr. Baker, best characterized as disinterest. Dr. Baker himself felt considerable anxiety about this unstructured situation and did not take an active part in the meeting for some considerable time. After several members had exposed some personal issues that they were presently concerned with, Dr. Baker in his typical way expressed his opinion to the effect that it might be better to discuss the "here and now" situation of the total group rather than a number of individual and external problems. His participation was seen as disturbing the group's usual way of proceeding. Yet his crucial intervention, encouraging the group to concern itself with the here and now situation, had a strong impact on the following meetings. Some of the group members liked the new approach so well that they felt that perhaps they should continue group therapy with Dr. Baker rather than return to Dr. Able. Dr. Baker did not immediately intervene to state that Dr. Able would of course take the group back; thus a heated discussion ensued where members seemed to compete with one another vigorously for the attention of the new leader. This brought out in turn the fact that they had been competing for Dr. Able's attention beforehand rather than becoming a cohesive group. This was painful for some to realize.

Upon Dr. Able's return no anger was expressed at all. His return was greeted with a sigh of relief, and Dr. Baker was never held up to Dr. Able as a better therapist. Yet the consequences on the future of this group were profound. For from then on they always considered the group as a whole as the last authority. In the long run it appeared that the experience of "coming together" which the reflective therapist had brought about was a far more lasting change in the group than the feeling of emotional support or of "being given to" that the charismatic therapist had brought to the other group.

DISCUSSION

The introduction of a person of opposite style creates in each instance an additional challenge to the group. In the example, this was resolved in quite different ways. The *short-range* effect of a charismatic leader will be a great deal of *emotional intensity*, and he will thereafter remain a good memory for the people he has met. The long-range effect does not seem to be considerable. Upon return of the regular therapist there is a great deal of turmoil and anger at the regular therapist, but that will subside. It is quite different with a reflective, interpretative therapist who may enter a group led by a charismatic leader. He will be considered a stranger, an outsider, will not be welcome, and his departure will be greeted with a sigh of relief. The charismatic therapist once again is in the saddle, memories of the other therapist will not be reproduced often, but the group may have changed dynamically into a *more coherent group*. A charismatic leader usually does not produce a very coherent group. It is only his presence that holds the group together.

We may thus add to the description of the charismatic leader and his group by stating that his group is likely to be dependent on his presence, will not take kindly to substitutes, and will resist efforts at becoming a more cohesive group. A reflective and affiliative leader, by contrast, will have a cohesive group which will, however, be vulnerable to a person who radiates much emotionality. For the affiliative leader will be always overshadowed by the charismatic leader. He well have to bear angry responses if his group is temporarily taken over by a charismatic leader, but the long-term effect will be slight as his group has built-in cohesiveness and reliance on the group itself.

It would seem that different leadership attitudes can have far-reaching consequences above and beyond the scope of the therapeutic group. Innovators or creative people sometimes also have charismatic ways of operating. The effect that an innovation of any kind will have will depend in part on the style of the founder or principal figure in a new movement or new organization. With the present rapidity of communication through the printed word or radio and television, much leadership effect which was formally restricted to face to face encounters can now be felt over long distances. Moreover, airplane travel has made it possible for charismatic leaders to be seen and heard in person in various parts of the country. The group effect that they may have on an audience will become predictable, repetitive, and occasionally stereotyped.

The noncharismatic leader—for instance, a good researcher or a person with high credentials, but not a good speaker—will often find the initial impact of his work negligible. He moreover may not care too much about mass effectiveness, but would rather be recognized and accepted in a small but selected group of peers. He might be the societal or academic analogue to the reflective or affiliative group leader. He is interested in becoming meaningfully involved in a relatively small interpersonal network. Some group therapists often are researchers, at least researchers in the sense that they give precedence to careful observation of the inner workings of the group or an individual, rather than dramatic external action. The reception such a research-innovator gets in any given area is to a large extent determined by the preexisting climate in the place where he speaks. If people with common interests are around and carry prestige he will be well received. The nature of the message is then more important than the person who carries it.

It is very different with the charismatic innovator who might be the leader of a school, a strong proponent of a new movement, or in some other way a person defined as outstanding. In this case, frequently the person is the message rather than the content or the thought behind him. Reception of such a person depends less on the existing climate than on the charismatic person himself. In time it tends to become repetitive and the performance expected from that person will be known in advance by those having been exposed to him previously. It is usually necessary for an audience to be at least mildly in favor of the point of view of the innovator. The tendency of the charismatic person is to support those who agree with him and bring around those who may have some doubts. He will be out to create followers and often application or enrollment forms for his society are available. The experience that the listener takes home with him is that of having received something new and different from a great person, which will enrich him and change his ways from now on. The emotionality created and experienced is quite regularly strong and has a vaguely tension-releasing, emotionally liberating or even cathartic effect. Suppressed emotions come to the fore, inhibitions vanish, and feelings are flowing freely for the followers of the new movement. It is perhaps this tension-releasing and emotion-freeing activity of the charismatic leader that constitutes his highest asset and his most treacherous danger, for groups or movements patterned after the charismatic model tend to unleash forces both for good and for evil. It is no surprise that group movements such as encounter and sensitivity groups have found widespread success among our inhibited, tension-ridden middle class. They are largely of the charismatic variety rather than of the investigative reflective type. The prevailing ideology of most encounter-group movements centers around release of emotions, free flow of affection, and the like. We may say that Sigmund Freud's early hydraulic model of the mind as a sort of pump system with valves and blocks has been revived to the exclusion of all else. Leader-centered groups become the medium by which freeing up of the emotional flow is accomplished. A degree of dependency on the leader ensues regularly in the group. In the main people tend to become "followers" rather than independent searchers. They tend to become "committed" rather than discriminating. They gain a sometimes lifelong contact with a movement and are henceforth identified with the cause. The cause is really a derivative of the leader under whose spell they have been.

Many causes would likely never have come to fruition without their important charismatic leaders. The world in general and our discipline specifically would be much poorer had it not been for the innovations of influential people presented with a quasi-religious conviction. Yet there must be relief from causes and ideologies, as they become oppressive for the mind, just as there must be relief from tensions. A reflective group therapist, who will carefully search the feelings and doings of his group members, might help them to grow up in their own way rather than enlisting them in the service of his cause. While leaders for worthy causes will always be with us and will continue to be effective, we might in a discriminating fashion find that the reflective or affiliative group therapist or researcher will prove to be a much more needed resource when matters of consequence such as neuroses and psychoses are to be discussed.

SUMMARY

The following sketches may be given of two contrasting leadership styles as observed in psychotherapeutic groups and to some extent in larger formations.

1. The so-called charismatic leader tends to create a group which is dependent on him, will see in his person the focus of their interaction, and will experience a feeling of support, release of tension, and freeing up of emotions.

2. The affiliative-reflective group leader will tend to be inconspicuous, dependent on the current group interaction, and clearly not in the center of the groups interaction as a person, but rather as a helpful force. His group will tend to remain group centered, will not likely be influenced by him in any ideological direction but rather focus on the growth and well-being of its own members.

3. The effects of a charismatic leader tend to be intense, emotional, relatively short-lived, and predictable. On the other hand, the effects of the affiliative leader depend to a large extent on the situation he encounters. He may exploit the existing potential forces and direct them toward the aim of benefiting individual members or the group as a whole.

4. At a time when mass movements clearly come more readily under the influence of charismatic leaders, typical phenomena of emotionalism and dependency can be observed. The importance of unbiased and personally meaningful work with smaller or larger groups will, however, remain a major factor not only in treatment but also in research and development in the field of mental health.

REFERENCES

Gibb, Cecil A. "The Sociometry of Leadership in Temporary Groups," *Sociometry* 13 (1950):226-243. Reprinted in A. Paul Hare, Edgar F. Borgatta, and Robert F. Bales, eds., *Small Groups* (New York: Alfred Knopf, 1955), pp. 526-542.

Redl, Fritz. "Group Emotion and Leadership," *Psychiatry* 5 (1942):573-596. Reprinted in abridged form in A. Paul Hare, Edgar F. Borgatta, and Robert F. Bales, eds., *Small Groups* (New York: Alfred Knopf, 1955), pp. 71-87.

23. The Charismatic Leader

ZANVEL A. LIFF

Originally a central notion in theology, and more recently an important concept in sociology (Weber, 1947) and in political science (Tucker, 1968; Lacouture, 1970), the concept of charisma (derived from the Greek, meaning "gift") has now begun to appear in group psychotherapeutic literature.

Rogers (1970) has indicated that "groups focused on personal growth are losing enrollment to those where the drawing card is the charisma of the leader." Yalom and Lieberman (1971) use the term "charisma" in referring to a quality of emotionally stimulating leaders; and they differentiate high, moderate, and low charisma. They indicate that high charisma leaders are unsuccessful and contribute to high casualty rates. Christ (1972) has contrasted the charismatic leader with the reflective, affiliative leader.

This paper will explore some basic issues related to the concept of charisma in group psychotherapy, focusing on both the needs of the leader and of the patient.

THE SOCIOCULTURAL CONTEXT

More and more writers are referring to the spirit of our times as one of unsureness, of feeling helplessly adrift and threatened. In his book *Souls on Fire*, which is essentially about charismatic leaders, Wiesel (1972) writes that "all the conditions that existed when Hasidism came into being prevail again today. Emotional and physical insecurity, fallen idols, and the scourge of violence."

With accelerated social and cultural change and highly transient living (Toffler, 1970) there is a search for leadership which provides firm, credible guidelines and directions. We are living in a "turn-on" society, and an age of boredom in which people are desperately

114

searching for excitement. There is an appalling lack of continuity, a pervasive lack of confidence in our personal ability to change objective reality. There is great impatience—a sense of urgency even in one-to-one relationships. At social gatherings, for instance, there is a constant search for that charismatic person or conversation.

People move from apartment to apartment, from city to city, from job to job, from divorce to divorce, at an unprecedented rate. There is a widespread feeling of dislocation, disconnection, a sort of rootlessness stemming from the high mobility of our time. Packard (1972) refers to our country as "a nation of strangers."

Because of these conditions, I feel that we are moving into an age of charismatic hunger. The most profound evidence for this is the upsurge of the small-group movement, including both psychotherapeutic and psychoeducational groups in the United States. In this connection, Christ (1972) comments:

> It is no surprise that the group movements such as encounter and sensitivity groups have found widespread success among our inhibited, tension-ridden middle class.

The extraordinary growth of demand for "encounters," for group experiences of all kinds, and for charismatic leaders in these experiences seems to be a reflection of a sociocultural condition in which people are experiencing apathy, uncertainty, and powerlessness.

Some additional conditions which also give rise to charisma hunger are the waning of religion, the drug culture, the sudden collapse of established authority, the profound but vague, unclassified feeling of threat to the welfare of the human group.

> . . . And when man in the more affluent industrialized parts of the world lives not only with the terrors and anxieties of the nuclear era but also, increasingly, with the deep ennui and distress of unrelatedness that life can breed in mass technological society, the outlook is rather for new messiahs and movements led by them (Tucker, 1968).

Charismatic leadership is thus a form of crisis leadership—leadership that promises, with absolute certainty, deliverance from all disasters and all distress.

Throughout the country people are flocking to all kinds of group experiences and seem to be gravitating toward the more charismatic leaders—leaders who project absolute certainty in their promises of cure. Janov (1972), for example, makes the absolute claim that he has now found a cure for neurosis. Casriel (1972), in his book *A Scream Away from Happiness,* similarly and simplistically sells happiness through the cathartic-abreaction approach, while other leaders also make comparable claims for delivery into the promised land.

The search for the strong, supportive, and protective figure who conveys absolute sureness fits into the magical thinking and messianic wishes of hundreds of thousands of people. The high charismatic leader promises miracles, if his followers will only submit to his dominance. His leadership is based largely on feelings of faith, hope, and belief, almost on the salvation qualities experienced in certain heroic personalities, and it has its origins in hero worship and the personality cult.

Most of the followers are in states of distress and depression and are searching for idealized leaders to rescue them from their helpless, despairing state. They approach these group experiences with great expectations and become very devoted, loyal members of the "following"; but underneath this magical search are intense feelings of sensitivity to attack, hurt, and rejection by the group as well as by the leader—and there is a basic fear of loss and abandonment.

THE CHARISMATIC LEADER

The early sociological literature on charisma (Weber, 1947) described the charismatic leader as one who scoffs at fixed rules, routine, and tradition, who scorns predictable regularity and rejects old ideas. His personality qualities set him apart from ordinary men, and he is treated as though endowed with supernatural, superhuman attributes. It should be noted here that the charismatic leader is perceived as such by the follower—rarely, if ever, by himself. Weber says: "It is recognition of charisma on the part of those subject to authority which is decisive for the validity of charisma."

The high charismatic leader is an activist, with a sense of the prophetic. He has a sense of mission and feels that his is a special calling, as if he has been chosen by God. He radiates a buoyant and stubborn self-confidence, an unshakable belief in success, an enthusiasm which provokes and evokes enthusiastic responses from the group participants. Again in Tucker's words:

> This indeed, may be the quality that most of all underlies their charisma and explains the extreme devotion and loyalty that they

inspire in their followers: for people in need of deliverance from one or another form of distress, being in very many instances anxiety ridden, easily respond with great emotional fervor to a leader who can kindle or strengthen in them a faith in the possibility of deliverance.

In the small-group movement, many such leaders, responding to the charisma seekers, tend to act out a grandiose, omnipotent fantasy in which they play the role of saviors with divine power to heal, or inspirational revivalists. The vacuum created by the impossibly high expectations of the "followers" fits into the leader's own unconscious fantasy images. More often than not, he experiences himself as a missionary in a mass rescue effort to save our sinking society. Extremely high charismatic leaders with strong religious-savior orientation, such as Billy Graham, convey an unusual presence, an aura which dominates the group. They convey extraordinary promise and thus appeal to the deep passive dependence needs of the group members.

> The charismatic leader tends to create a group that is dependent on him. He will often produce much emotional discharge and will leave people with a feeling of emotional support (Christ, 1972).

In this respect they greatly resemble the leaders of charismatic movements of the past. They are reminiscent of the faith-healing revivalists, of prophets of doom, who admonish their followers to give up sin, alcohol, or any of a myriad of vices. And "oftentimes, the relationship of the followers to the charismatic leader is that of disciples to a master, and . . . he is revered by them" (Tucker). As Anthony Storr puts it in his evaluation of Janov's newest book, *The Primal Revolution*:

> I am quite sure that Janov has made a lot of neurotics feel better. So did Mary Baker Eddy, Frank Buchman, Mesmer and any number of other prophetic characters who had complete confidence that they were right and that everyone else was wrong.

INTERPLAY: TRANSFERENCE AND COUNTERTRANSFERENCE

With the intense charisma craving in our population and the equally strong charismatic leadership needs, we begin to see in these group relationships and interactions a deeply rooted transference-counter-transference interplay with origins at the earliest levels of human development.

In an article on group transference in psychotherapy, Schwartz and Wolf (1964) write: "Countertransference represents fulfillment of the fantasy of the patient with regard to the therapist, in the expectation that the therapist play a certain role." In the plethora of charismatically oriented groups mushrooming in our society today, this transferential charisma-hunger can thus be easily translated as the infantile search for the ideal parent who is all-nurturant and all-protective, who will deliver his children from the oppressive predicament of their lives manifested in chronic boredom, depression, and apathy.

The countertransferential need may be viewed as twofold. First, as an overidentification with the deprived, helpless group members who have to be healed and cured; thus the leader indirectly acts out his own self-restitutional fantasies. Secondly, with countertransference toward the group as a whole, as his own idealized parent figure who will feed back adoring love (translated into high fees and continual referrals). This charisma hunger, one of the multiplicity of needs of an apathetic public, in turn provides for the leaders an extraordinary avenue of fulfillment of their own personal counterneeds for impact and even omnipotence—perhaps to overcome and compensate for deep feelings of inadequacy. The followers, feeling a tremendous sense of uncertainty, are in search of certainty. And

> . . . transference itself is a maneuver to increase certainty. What characterizes the neurotic is that he gravitates toward the trans-ference figure, toward the father, mother, or sibling figure that is familiar to him. . . . He is trying to reconvert them into ever more gratifying familial figures (Schwartz and Wolf, 1959).

In our contemporary culture many people are feeling a sense of life-lessness, a sense of numbness within. Time and again they describe feeling "dead inside"; they are searching for action, for excitation, to be "turned on" by authorities who have absolute conviction. These feelings are the carrying over of infantile needs to be passive, to have everything done for them without having any responsibilities in return (unqualified, undemanding love), to avoid adult responsibility for themselves and society. Here in the charismatic group their trans-ference is defined as being "turned on" by the leader, whom they can then blindly follow *en masse*.

The countertransference is the translation of the leader's opposite need: to "turn on," to be their savior, to lead them, by performing wonders, out of distress into joy, safety, etc. It is the acting out with grandiose goals of his own manic antidepressive needs. The predominant style of these leaders is to "turn on" those who have defensively "turned off," who have organized their lives around the guiding principle of maintaining safety and security.

Charisma hunger is a *super*transference and countertransference with magical overtones, including the Lazarus complex: the group member who is depressed and turned off (dead, lifeless) is turned on, ignited, brought back to life by the charismatic leader. Clearly in such a group situation, it is not the *real* needs of the patient which are central, but the illusory needs of the leader. Christ (1972) says, in fact, that the charismatic leader "forms or structures his group to his own needs. . . ."

CONCLUSIONS

I am concerned that these group leaders, in their eagerness to heal and cure, tend to violate the dignity as well as the privacy of the person—his right not to participate, to be quiet, to withdraw without the ridicule, humiliation, reprisal, or rejection of the leader himself or of other group members.

Schwartz and Wolf (1964) observe that "in the group, every therapeutic problem is exaggerated. The issues around transference and countertransference are no exception. Quantitatively and qualitatively, countertransference becomes an even more complicated matter for the group." They also list seventeen possibilities which, in their experience, "need to be explored for the presence of the group thrapist's transferences and countertransferences." Of these, we find four that have particular relevance for charismatic-leader groups:

> The therapist may out of his own omnipotence deny patients freedom, or demand activity out of his own depression.
> In attending group dynamics, he may homogenize the members, see them as if they were one patient, without listening to individual voices and knowing them as persons.
> The therapist may wish to be the only child in the group, or he may treat patients as only children.
> He may demand that patients shape their way of life and their values to his. The expectation that the patient fulfill the thera-

pist's superego demands retraumatizes the patient. It is a general clinical observation that children of authoritarian parents become authoritarian, and neglected children become neglectful parents.

The high charismatic leaders are the ones who contribute to the high casualty rate of group members because they are extremely intrusive, confronting, challenging, and authoritarian. In this connection, Christ (1972) observes:

> . . . he (the charismatic leader) tends to keep his group members dependent on him and he dominates the group interaction often to an undue extent, thus depriving some of the less gifted members from getting a fair and full hearing. He will often not tolerate outright antagonism to himself.

He is aggressive and coercive and provides a high stimulus input. The patients, who are of course the casualties, come with great expectations and fail to attain their unrealistic goals. In fact, Christ says that "a charismatic leader usually does not produce a very coherent group. It is only *his presence* that holds the group together."

Part of the apparent improvement sometimes observed with charismatic leaders might be called a charismatic cure, similar to the transference cure which takes place because the patient temporarily identifies with and incorporates the healing attitudes of the leader. Although this does affect the surface structures of the patient, it does *not* reach the deeper structures; it is largely a transfusive improvement, and since such improvements do not work through the problem of loss and separation, they have a tendency to fade out with time.

The first research making reference to charismatic qualities of group leadership was by Yalom and Lieberman (1971). Their study of group leaders from various theoretical persuasions tends to bear out my hypothesis that the type of group may be less important to the client than the leadership style. Eighteen encounter groups of ten varieties were involved. The group participants were students at Stanford University. The leaders were considered highly experienced and each group continued for 30 hours. Casualties, defined as those who "as a result of their encounter experience, suffered considerable and persistent psychological distress," were given as 16 out of 170 (10%) and were evaluated by other group members rather than by the leaders.

To my mind the most important finding for purposes of the present discussion is that of the sixteen casualties seven had been in groups led by four of the leaders. Yalom called these leaders *"aggressive stimulators."* They were *"intrusive, confrontive, challenging,* while at the same time demonstrating *high positive caring;* they revealed a great deal of themselves . . . they were the most *charismatic, authoritarian* (and they) focused upon the individual rather than upon the group." They had a *"religious aura"* that apparently led them to "imbue the individual with a system of beliefs and values . . . rather than to encourage the individual to change according to his own needs and potential."

Such leaders are *selling;* they are not tuned in to the individuals in the group, who are, of course, all at different psychological levels and in different psychological places.

Indeed, the high charismatic leader strives initially to *accentuate* rather than alleviate the followers' sense of distress, their sense of being in a desperate predicament from which only *he* can rescue them. Obviously such an approach tends to encourage the group into passive dependence, and totally precludes differentiated perceptions of group patients or non-patients, perceptions related to "where they are at." Without the leader's awareness of the very urgent need on his part for such perceptions, group members as a matter of course become "homogenized"—they cease to be individual persons with individual problems.

Thus, the high charismatic leader is actually counterproductive: he is not a good leader and is, therefore, antitherapeutic. The basic bond is interacting out, which does not help anybody to grow up, but rather *perpetuates* the infantile delusional state. It may make the group members feel better, but it does not help them work through toward autonomy, toward becoming responsible, independent human being. Finally, the focus here on the negative impact of the high charismatic leader should not cause us to neglect the value of moderate charisma among group leaders. Moderate charisma can be considered as an expression of enthusiastic dedication and caring which does not oppress the individual patient nor obscure the conveyance of understanding and acceptance.

REFERENCES

Casriel, D. *A Scream Away from Happiness* (New York: Grosset and Dunlap, 1972).

Christ, J. *Whither Group Therapy: Charisma or Affliction?* Paper presented at
49th Annual Meeting of American Orthopsychiatric Association, 1972
(mimeo).

Janov, A. *The Primal Revolution* (New York: Simon & Schuster, 1972).

Lacouture, J. *The Demigods* (New York: Alfred A. Knopf, 1970).

May, R. *Power and Innocence* (New York: W. W. Norton & Co., 1972).

Packard, V. *A Nation of Strangers* (New York: David McKay Co., 1972).

Rogers, C. *Carl Rogers on Encounter Groups* (New York: Harper & Row, 1970).

Schwartz, E. K., and Wolf, A. "On Countertransference in Group Psychotherapy." *The Journal of Psychology* 57 (1964):131-142.

Schwartz, E. K., and Wolf, A. "The Quest for Certainty." *A.M.A. Archives of
Neurology & Psychiatry* 81 (1959):69-84.

Storr, A. "An Instant Cure for Mental Illness." *New York Times Book Review*,
December 5, 1972.

Toffler, A. *Future Shock* (New York: Random House, 1970).

Tucker, R. C. "The Theory of Charismatic Leadership." *Daedalus* (Summer
1968):731-756.

Weber, M. *The Theory of Social and Economic Organization* (New York:
Oxford University Press, 1947).

Wiesel, E. *Souls on Fire* (New York: Random House, 1972).

Yalom, I. D., and Lieberman, M. A. "A Study of Encounter Group Casualties."
Archives of General Psychiatry, 25, 1 (July 1971):16-30.

24. The Leader and Change

BENJAMIN FIELDING

The role and effectiveness of the group therapist has never been thoroughly or satisfactorily studied and researched, nor does our literature claim any great knowledge on the subject. For this reason, the attempt to determine who does what in group, or what produces changes, presents considerable difficulty. Similarly, previously used techniques, as well as the budding and flourishing new ones, have not been investigated thoroughly enough to show with any clarity that any one approach is "better than" another. And if asked for concrete specifics, most group therapists would more or less reply, "I do pretty well with my patients; they show significant changes; the group process works relatively well with what I know; but I don't know specifically how and in what way my patients have changed."

I do not by any means wish to intimate that we work entirely in the dark, for experience has shown us that changes most certainly do occur in group therapy. Thus far, however, neither the specificity nor the accuracy of prediction are easily attainable. But however difficult it may be to research criteria for changes in human behavior, and especially through group therapy, there is nevertheless a need to explore the idea of such criteria. This article is an attempt to examine the dynamics, the participation of the group therapist, his own impact on his patients, and what equipment he brings to the leadership of a group therapy situation.

The pursuit of more effective group therapeutic approaches has mushroomed tremendously since the beginning of the 1960's. This search for revolutionary methods for change parallels the restlessness during the past decade in all areas of human activity—the headlong rush for better and faster answers. Obviously dissatisfied with the slow movement toward change of the older theories and techniques, group therapists have been creating and introducing more active approaches in an upsurge without parallel in the past. Exponents of the encounter, the gestalt, the transactional, and many other new group methods have indicated in one way or another that they can produce better and faster personality changes and remedy neurotic behavior.

In these new approaches, the therapist is more "active" in introducing a variety of techniques which have intensified the participation in the group to achieve certain "knowledgeable objectives." In fact, each therapist appears to believe strongly that what he wants each particular patient to relate to, and the manner in which that patient does so, will in each case facilitate that patient toward the objective of change.

But *why* and *how* do these patients improve? Is it the dynamics of the therapist's personality? Is it his personal philosophy—or his theoretical point of view; his skills in utilizing the group?

All indications, both from experiments and from the reports of psychologists and psychiatrists experienced with group therapy, confirm the importance of the therapist's role to the success of the group, although only a few articles have been written dealing with this role and its effect. And from my own various observations of therapists practicing group psychotherapy, there does seem to be a direct relationship between the viewpoint of the therapist and the outcomes—i.e., the therapist mobilizes the group and brings it into the position where it can be the avenue through which changes can be produced—i.e., the way the group functions reflects the functioning of the therapist. His belief in what he has decided will "work" will be communicated to the group.

Some therapists, for example, have demonstrated in practice and described in the literature that their group members communicate with each other solely—or primarily—about their reactions to each other. Others present to their groups incidents experienced outside the group so that members will react to these outside experiences. Still others utilize the analysis of patients' dreams in group as the primary avenue toward insight gaining for each patient.

Some therapists will have a patient or a number of patients "act out" in a given fashion some situation from one patient's childhood experiences. They believe that re-experiencing the situation under the patient's present emotional conditions will elicit vivid observation, experience, and awareness, which will in turn produce some insight of great relevance for that patient in effecting change. Certainly, other patients, particularly by observing and/or by helping that patient to act out, to re-experience an incident, will also learn from that experience, if only to better understand that particular patient.

Then there are therapists who focus primarily on the underlying reasons for the expressed (verbal and nonverbal) behavior of group members. In these therapists' words, "awareness, insight, working through of defenses, of transferences, etc.," are the objectives to be achieved by this "technique."

Each of these therapeutic modalities implicitly indicates that the process of change will follow from the therapist's belief in how the basic objective—patient's knowledge effecting changes in himself—is to be achieved by one particular mode of group interaction. And patients will follow what the therapist believes, what he practices, and above all *how* he practices. It is not uncommon to observe, during special workshops, a group that has functioned in a specific fashion with one therapist suddenly change (different group member interaction) when another group therapist takes over. In short, the therapist brings about a kind of atmosphere and participation that reflects his own belief in his way as the best way to produce change.

THE LEADER AS THE GROUP MODEL

Studies and research on individual therapy suggest that the therapist who relates to his patients with warmth and high personal regard effects greater changes than the therapist possessing other equally positive characteristics including, among others, intelligence and creativity. We can thus assume that the successful therapist provides for the patient an atmosphere of acceptance, liking, and understanding—one in which emotional contact has been achieved.

The literature on group therapy indicates that a variety of therapists with different therapy modalities, with different approaches to the working-through process, achieved successful results. But the first important element in any discussion of the therapist must be his relationship with his patients. The significance of this relationship seems undeniable. M. B. Parloff (1961) found in an experiment that a better therapist relationship leads to an increase of patient objectivity and effectiveness (the two factors, plus comfort, that were used as criteria for improvement). The experiment's results also suggest an association between therapist relationship and the dropout rate in group therapy. Parloff reports that those who dropped out had poor therapist relationship "ratings" as compared with the rest of the group. In addition, those patients who in the estimation of the raters had formed a better relationship with the therapist perceived other group members as being socially attractive.

Certainly a crucial aspect of therapist relationship is the personality of the therapist. Several articles seem to point toward preferable behaviors. In a general manner, Mullan (1955) suggested that the therapist needs more than just experience and knowledge to achieve success. As evidence, he cites the fruitful efforts in therapy of some psychiatric residents. For him, the therapist is more an artist than a scientist, for a scientist is inclined to fall in with his patients' desire for scientific formulae for "cures" and/or proper living. Furthermore, the therapist, according to Mullan, must dissociate himself and the group from the confines of culture. He feels that some qualities needed in a therapist are interest, enthusiasm, devotion, activity, togetherness, love, and sympathy. That's a rather long list, but fortunately the question of therapist personality has been approached more directly and scientifically.

Betz (1963) has used Strong's Vocational Interest Inventory in an attempt to quantify the relative success of lawyer-type versus math-physics-science-teacher-type therapists. Although the application of her findings is limited since she uses only hospital records of schizophrenic patients, she reports that in these cases, at least, the lawyer-type therapist shows a better record of improvement (60% as compared to 40% for the science-type). Betz speculates that therapists who fall into the lawyer category show greater spontaneity and freedom in their leadership, while the science-teacher-types are more didactic and impersonal.

Truax (1966) has reported a study (one of several of this type) testing the relation of therapist empathy, genuineness and warmth to therapeutic outcome. The findings support the contention that patients of psychiatrists offering high levels of therapeutic conditions (warmth, empathy, and genuineness) tend to show greater improvement than those of therapists providing relatively lower conditions.

Grosz and Wright (1967), in an experiment concerning the effect on the tempo of verbal interaction of rotating the therapist, found that neither changes in therapist nor in patient composition made much of a difference. They concluded that the most reasonable explanation for the steady gain in the communicational transactions within the group was the development, and its transfer from session to session, of an understanding of how the group was meant to behave, learned from the behavior of the therapist. Thus a change in therapists is not disruptive as long as each one continues to "teach" his group how to interact.

More conclusive proof of the therapist's teaching-model role comes from an experiment performed by Astrachan et al (1967). They found that the therapist helps his patients define their relationships to one another and sets up the standard of behavior that is accepted in the group. Indeed, the core groups in the experiment reflected their therapist's inclinations and philosophy in their interactions.

It is interesting to note also that even though six to ten patients comprise a group over a long period of time, the tone and manner of what happens in the group depend mostly on the therapist. This may appear to be a naive statement, but there is such great emphasis, in articles on group therapy, on the influence of the *group* on individual patients and on the healing aspect of the dynamics of interaction within the group, that one could easily bypass the role of the therapist himself in bringing about this type of dynamic interaction and the manner in which patients will communicate with and relate to each other.

THERAPIST INFLUENCE ON THE GROUP

The influence of the therapist on his group needs to be emphasized again and again. It can pass unnoticed by the therapist unless he is at all times aware of, and sensitive to, the group's reactions to him.

For example, a few months after one of my groups got together after summer vacation—with three new members and five from the previous year—they began talking about skiing. From my knowledge of this group, I knew of only two who had gone skiing before this discussion. When a new member asked me where to go this winter, I asked how he knew I was a skiier. I soon found that one of the older group members knew this from last year, the new ones learned it from him, and very soon six of the eight group members had taken up skiing. The way the therapist expresses himself in the group, the way he interacts with its members, is of utmost concern; and the effects are immediately visible and can produce lasting and dominant changes in his patients.

To emphasize this point, let us take the group therapist who believes it is necessary for the health of an individual to fully express rage in the group. He is thus generating a collective group experience which in turn will result in a sense of relief and well-being. This therapist's group members are taking into themselves (absorbing) the (model) attitude and preoccupation of the therapist and are expressing what they perceive from him as the avenue toward help and health. These patients will help, coerce, pressure, persuade others that they *must* express their rage; and reacting to the authority approval and the consensus validation of the group, the newcomers will eventually express themselves similarly. What is the atmosphere in such a group? There is a feeling of acceptance and encouragement—and of achievement when a group member attains the results aimed for in the group. And for members who have permitted themselves to bask in the self-expression sanctioned by the group and directed by the leader, there is also the feeling of warmth and satisfaction.

The objective of the therapist (expression of rage) has been achieved. Some patients may in fact have benefitted by the cathartic effect of this expression. Some, however, may have had to produce "rage" to satisfy the therapist and to reduce the possibility of disapproval from group members. The implications for change with this procedure, however, still need to be researched and uncovered. But we can easily see that the manner in which the therapist relates to a patient is taken up by the other patients, resulting in critical attitudes toward certain kinds of behavior. The same result (interest in the other patient and his behavior) can also be achieved with another kind of "interpersonal interaction" between therapist and patients. For example, the difference between saying, "Why were you not here at the beginning of the session?" and "I feel left out when you don't come at the beginning of the session" is not just a difference in "technique"—it is a difference in interpersonal relationship which stems from the therapist's interest in the patient and his willingness to be something more than just an observer and a seemingly critical questioner.

Obviously, the manner and the focus of interest of the group therapist profoundly affect the group atmosphere and how the members interact with one another, and this cannot be reduced simply to which techniques are being utilized. To ask the group to react to a fight between two members by saying "Why don't you relate to what's going on?" is altogether different from "Can you, Janet, understand what Joe is trying to say to David?" which begins to work through one aspect of their interpersonal relationship via an understanding of the intrapsychic meaning of each other's communication.

The point I am making here is that when I relate to the group as a challenger, the interpersonal relationship will be different from those in a group where I am an involved, supportive, understanding, member who knows that the influence I engender is going to produce corresponding affects.

A major goal for the therapist is, of course, to elicit participation which may be more difficult than it would appear. Becker (1968) has reported that the mere presence of a leader lowers the activity level of a group. As compared with unled and patient-family sessions, there were significantly more seconds of silence in the therapist-led sessions, less activity, and fewer instances of two people speaking simultaneously. In another study, Harrow, Astrachan, and Becker (1967) decided that while there was no simple relationship between group emotion and therapist presence, depression and tension were markedly higher in therapist-led sessions.

The importance of verbal participation is in itself open to question. Sechrest and Barger (1961) have found that patients *value* most highly those sessions where their own participation is high, primarily in terms of help received, contributions made, and relevance of the session to their own personal problems. This is not to say that the sessions most highly valued by the patients are necessarily the most beneficial to them (see Snortum and Myers, 1971). Active participants found the discussions more interesting, but did not necessarily gain greater understanding or feel more "catharted." Since elicited participation was found by the experimenters to be just as relevant as spontaneous participation, it might be a good idea for the therapist to set as one of his goals a high level of participation.

In another study it appears that the selection of patients is not crucial to the success of a therapy session. Johnson and Gold (1971) designed a study to test the ramifications of different group compositions. They have concluded that the selection of patients is not of itself a crucial variable. The major task for the therapist is to match his techniques to the behavior pattern of the group and minimize the contagion effect of negative behavior. The only criterion for selection of patients is that the group be heterogeneous. Glatzer (1969) has reported that this factor is important to success in therapy. To Glatzer, heterogeneous groups are significant.

It is not my intention to present here a treatise on "how to do it better," or on which approaches and techniques are "best." My purpose is, hopefully, to encourage group therapists to become more sensitive to, and aware of, their impact on group members. In this way we might complete the cycle—what the group has learned and how it evolves and develops will in turn have a greater impact on the therapist in effecting changes in the behavior of all his patients.

"DIFFERENT PATIENTS" AND THE THERAPIST

A mother who was a caseworker once came to me for consultation about one of her children whose behavior challenged her and rendered her helpless. She had gone to workshops and had learned behavior modification approaches that had "worked wonders" for her other two children, but this "technique," so successful, so valid for the two children, did not work with the third, "difficult" child.

Similarly in group, it is not uncommon to find ourselves working well with many of the group members, with a familiar and accustomed feeling of ease and comfort. But what about that silent member who, if left to his own choice, would remain silent during many sessions and then suddenly erupt in sarcasm, or manifest depression or withdrawal, or stay away from sessions? Obviously, the therapist had encouraged and contributed to this pattern of behavior. And not only has *he* affected this patient—he has also affected the group to establish and perpetuate his own pattern of interpersonal relationship.

Can the therapist, early in the group process, relate to the patient who presents behavior that is "different" from the rest of the group? Can he relate to the dynamics of group member interaction? What particular dynamic reflected in a behavior affecting interpersonal conduct makes the *therapist* uncomfortable.

Take the patient who in almost every group session, after an entire hour and often at the very end of the session, suddenly blasted out. No type of intervention helped, nor did anything else the group members focused on with this patient. An index of how the other members related to this patient can be seen in their reactions: "Why did you wait so long before you blast us? Can't you talk earlier?"; "You are so intense when you come out, no one could satisfy this intensity"; "You want to be the center of attraction and it's getting you nowhere." Not until the therapist (after working out his problems through supervision) began to pay attention to this patient from the start of each session—and later on suggested that he come prepared to talk first—did the intensity diminish, and in a short time this patient became a constructive group participant rather than a disruptive one.

This case is by no means an example of technique; it is rather an example of a therapist not being able to work with the dynamics of a particular patient and utilizing the group to handle it instead. But the group in turn expressed the feelings of the therapist, who did not understand these dynamics.

This point of really *knowing* patients is paramount, though emphasizing it may appear naive. The patient presented above saw the group as a mountain to overcome. He saw that mountain as a symbol of his mother who could demolish him, and who could be difficult to interact with, unless he behaved as she wanted him to. The intense anxiety in this symbolism, the paralysis he experienced, could not at first be overcome by explanations or analysis, but through a different experience. The therapist's specific knowledge of this patient's experience with an important parent could be more helpful in initiating the process of change than leaving it primarily to the group members.

THE THERAPIST'S CREDIBILITY

One of the most challenging tests for the group therapist is in the area of credibility. Unless he feels at ease with his belief that change can be achieved, he will not come across with credibility.

One of the forces for health and change for any healer—and we must take the definite position that we are healers, since people come to us with their suffering—is the credibility of our own belief in our ability to help. In individual treatment this is highly important, and continuously challenged and tested by our patients. But with six to ten patients in a group, this credibility must withstand a much greater and wider range of tests. Does the therapist *believe* in group therapy? To what extent, and for whom?

This belief can be felt in the way he relates to the experiences of group patients, in which things are brought into the group and which into individual therapy. The question: "Would this patient at this point be helped more in group or in individual therapy?" could begin to get at the therapist's attitude toward, and his belief in, group therapy. We have individual therapy sessions two, three, four, and five times a week with some patients. Could we think of having group sessions that frequently?

If the therapist genuinely believes in the effectiveness of group toward facilitating change, could he accept such goals as:

—helping a group to dedicate itself to a common goal—the relief of suffering for each and all of its members;

—helping patients attain greater satisfaction in interpersonal contacts;

—helping patients to be individuals without deriding others;

—helping patients to feel and be involved with each other;

—helping patients to love and allow themselves to be loved?

Group therapy approximates a personal reality model oriented to life experience and can be called a laboratory for effective living.

CHANGE AND THE WORKING-THROUGH PROCESS

The concept of change in psychotherapy is much harder to deal with than the role of the therapist. There is a marked dearth of information, particularly specific or experimental information, on working through, perhaps the most critical aspect of the therapy process. I will deal first with some general ideas on change, then move to the specific question of working through.

Durkin (1971) believes that the analysis of transference and resistance form the crux of group psychotherapy and can be used to change character on a more or less permanent basis. According to Durkin, each member's intrapsychic conflicts are translated into his interpersonal behavior and through his relationship with the group. These relationships are modeled on the original family constellation. The shift or generalization of attitudes and reactions from early life experiences onto surrogates evoking similar attitudes can be explained by the fact that the original family constellation was a cornerstone in structuring the personality, and the transferred family constellation in the group is a cornerstone in the restructuring of the personality. With the aid of learning self-awareness, self-exposure and self-examination, the members realize that their methods of coping, developed when they were too young and helpless to deal with the outside world, are not necessary in their relationships in the group.

While patients converse on a conscious level, they give each other unconscious cues for setting up interacting neurotic patterns of behavior which would both ward off conscious infantile drives and secretly express them in a disguised form. Transference allows the therapist to see how a member's intrapsychic conflicts are translated into his interpersonal behavior.

A transcript from one of Durkin's (1969) actual sessions reveals that she considers the open interpretation and acceptance by the patient of his transference neurosis to begin the process of change. We know, however, that although transference analysis and exposure take up the earlier sessions (earlier in relation to therapy termination—transference reactions may go on for years of therapy), they are not sufficient, Durkins's thinking notwithstanding, to effect change in personality. They are only the first step toward the working-through process, the second vital aspect of group therapy, an aspect that has not received nearly enough attention in the literature.

Working through is the continuous attempt to transform intellectual insight into affective understanding by resolving resistances which impede insight from leading to significant and lasting changes. Locke (1961) reports that the mere indication by the therapist of transference is not enough to bring the neurotic process to an end because the patient continues to transfer until the *purpose* of his maneuver is brought out. Working through is not spontaneous, it is subject to therapist management. The therapist must, according to Locke, first help the patient to free himself from the obstruction of his repressed feelings; then take the patient back to the past and demonstrate the patient's purpose in distorting the present so that he can perceive his behavior, interpret himself, and test the reality of living as he meets it.

Wolf and Schwartz think that in working through the analyst points the way toward the diminishing of anxiety and the resolution of conflict by constantly posing more valid, realistic, and constructive suggestions which, when chosen, confront the patient with new problems to deal with, but always on a higher level of development.

In actuality, working through is not a "cut-and-dried" process: it requires creativity and imagination on the part of the therapist, as well as an ability to make the patient trust him and follow his lead.

There are significant blocks to working through which make the job extremely difficult and time-consuming. One complication in group therapy is suggested by Leopold (1959). He believes the group setting advantageous to therapy, partly due to the group's ability to act as a unit. The therapeutic potential comes from the members, who elicit specific transference reactions, and from the unity, which encompasses the sum of all the reactions. The patient's responses are returned by the group, often in a more purified and meaningful form.

Despite this advantage of group therapy, however, says Leopold, the fact that the group *does* form a unit creates levels of transaction. *All these transactions must be utilized therapeutically by the therapist*, since each level of transaction has a "meaning" within the context of the therapy.

Let us now discuss some of the steps essential to working through. Fried (1961) reports the importance of conduct rather than verbal expression in influencing patients to adopt new modalities of behavior. Insight often fails to reduce the tendency to repress, and by itself does not remove the character difficulties resulting from excessive re-pression. Acquisition of new strengths produces change, and this is not brought about solely by verbal expression. Fried uses examples from her own practice to illustrate the effect of therapist conduct. In one case, a break in a patient's symbiotic relationships was caused by the therapist's showing the patient that her own feelings were not dependent on those of her patients. In a second case the therapist forced a patient to use active self-experience and self-protection; when this patient focused on his own needs and feelings he felt stronger than when he concentrated on his attacking and abandoning wife.

Karush (1967) categorizes specific types of working through, and summarizes what he calls their fundamental varieties. For Karush, the most important effects of working through are new perceptions and conflict-free affects appropriate to those perceptions. The therapist must function as a teacher, a definer of reality. He motivates behavior as a representative of the superego, influencing by suggestion or even by authority and, most basically, as an idealized object who influences by example. (Here we see again in practice the therapist-model con-cept.) The relationship between the therapist and patient can be viewed as an alliance. If that alliance is malfunctioning (because, for example, the patient may be unwilling to reveal an embarrassing desire with respect to the therapist), access to the working-through process can be blocked.

I believe that the most essential requirement for effective group therapy is for the therapist to adapt his talents to the needs of his group patients. And it may be precisely because there are so many different approaches and methods that there have been so few articles detailing the working-through process. The article on encounter techniques by Rachman (1971) and that on the use of fantasy with delinquent boys by Perl (1963) are examples of specific adaptations of the therapeutic process. Perl has found that delinquents will reveal their fantasies with less resistance than they will their fears and anxieties. At the same time, these fantasies reveal a great deal about adolescents who have evaded the grasp of reality. It is this type of innovative therapy that is most commendable.

And it is important to realize, too, that patients derive different benefits from therapy sessions, just as therapists use different methods. Papanek (1960) has found in experimental study that the group members use therapy in different ways, and she compares the results to the test involving children choosing their own diets. Certainly numerous tests show that patients have very differing ideas of how they think therapy should be conducted.

Therapists, too, have found that a workable technique with one group can be an "unsuccessful" approach with another group.

CONCLUSIONS

Research in group therapy needs to become more specific, at the same time taking into account a number of issues involved in continuous interdependent interaction. When a therapist writes an article on techniques, on general theoretical positions with practical clinical applications, and does not deal with the particular way he puts his technique into practice, he is shortchanging the therapist reader, who really wants to learn whether and why one "technique" may work better than another. Translating research findings into practice could be far more fruitful if we knew something about the therapist himself, about his groups, his theories, his belief and his techniques.

We need articles on group therapy that indicate a modality of working through with a patient over a long period of time, that indicate the stages of development of this working through, how it was reflected in the group, how the therapist consistently handled it, and how the group members effected and were helped by the working through.

I believe, too, that therapists should experiment with having groups meet two to four times a week in order to determine more conclusively the effects of group therapy as an entity approach to change.

The medium of change in group therapy is the group, but its architectural composition and type of instrumentation come from the therapist. And here I should like to re-emphasize the fundamental importance of the therapist as the group architect. For it is he who must provide for the patient an atmosphere of acceptance and understanding in which emotional contact has been achieved, who must serve as a model and teacher for his patients. He must at all times be aware of, and sensitive to, the group's reactions to him. He must elicit a high level of participation; and to accomplish this he must assume the vital task of matching his techniques to the behavior pattern of the group. It is absolutely essential that the therapist understand each patient's style of communication, that he *really* know each patient in order to be able to initiate and facilitate the process of change, rather than leaving it primarily to the group members. Primary, too, is the credibility of the therapist—the clearness of his own belief in what he is doing. And, in addition to all this, he must be creative and imaginative in developing the group therapeutic process, and able to inspire trust in following his lead.

Our research should acknowledge the presence of these basic elements as well as uncovering others, and should specifically demonstrate their effectiveness and their interaction, in order to arrive at more conclusive evidence for the successful process of change in the group setting—and the role of the therapist in that process.

REFERENCES

Astrachan, Boris M.; Schwartz, E. K.; Arthur, H.; Becker, Robert; and Harrow, Martin. "The Psychiatrist's Effect on the Behavior and Interaction of Therapy Groups." *Amer. J. Psychiat.* 123 (May 1967):1379-1387.

Becker, R. E. "Influence of the Leader on the Activity Level of Group Therapy." *J. Soc. Psychol.* 74 (1968):39-51.

Betz, Barbara J. "Basis of Therapist Leadership in Psychotherapy with the Schizophrenic Patient." *Amer. J. Psychother.* 17 (April 1963):196-212.

Durkin, Helen E. "The Group in Depth." (New York: International Universities Press, 1964).

Durkin, Helen E. Lecture at Postgraduate Center for Mental Health-Group Psychotherapy Workshop, 1971.

Fried, Edrita. "Techniques of Psychotherapy Going Beyond Insight." *Int. J. Group Psychotherapy* 19 (1969):292-306.

Glatzer, Henrietta T. "Working Through in Analytic Group Therapy." *Int. J. Group Psychotherapy,* 18, 4 (October 1967):513-523.

Harrow, M.; Astrachan, B. M.; and Becker, R. "Influence of the Psychotherapist on the Emotional Climate in Group Therapy." *Human Relat.* 20 (1967): 49-64.

Johnson, Donald L., and Gold, Steven R. "An Empirical Approach to Issues of Selection and Evaluation in Group Therapy." *Int. J. Group Psychotherapy* 21, 4 (October 1971):456-469.

Karush, A. "Working Through." *Psychoanal. Quart.* 36 (1967):492-531.

Leopold, Harold S. "The Problem of Working Through in Group Psychotherapy." *Int. J. Group Psychotherapy* 9 (1959):287-292.

Lewin, Kurt, and Lippitt, Ronald. "An Experimental Approach to the Study of Autocracy and Democracy." *Sociometry* 1 (1938):292-300.

Locke, N. "Working Through." *Group Psychoanalysis* (New York: New York University Press, 1961), pp. 145-157.

MULLAN, H. "The Group Therapist's Creative Function." *Amer. J. Psychother.* 9 (1955):320-334.

Papenek, Helene. "Prospective Test Evaluation of Changes Effected by Group Psychotherapy." *Int. J. Group Psychotherapy* 10 (1960):446-455.

Parloff, M. B. "Patient Relationship and Outcome of Psychotherapy." *J. Consult. Psychol.* 25 (1961):29-38.

Perl, William R. "Use of Fantasy for a Breakthrough in Psychotherapy Groups of Hard-to-Reach Delinquent Boys." *Int. J. Group Psychotherapy* 13, 1 (January 1963):27-33.

Rachman, Arnold W. "Encounter Techniques in Analytic Group Psychotherapy with Adolescents." *Int. J. Group Psychotherapy* 21, 3 (July 1971):319-329.

Truax, Charles B. *et al.* "Therapist Empathy, Genuineness and Warmth and Patient Therapeutic Outcome." *J. Consult. Psychol.* 30 (Oct. 1966):395-402.

White, Ralph, and Lippitt, Ronald. "Leader Behavior and Member Reaction in Three 'Social Climates,'" *Group Dynamics: Research and Theory*, edited by Dorwin Cartwright, and Alvin Zander, 2nd ed. (Elmsford, N. Y.: Row, Peterson, 1960), p. 527.

25. The Leader as Supervisor and Supervisee

HENRIETTE T. GLATZER

Long experience in supervising has confirmed for me that a large proportion of the difficulties therapists have in group psychotherapy concern their countertransference. This becomes particularly evident when supervising well-trained therapists who are often impeded in their handling of group patients not so much by their lack of knowledge of individual and group psychodynamics as by their countertransferences. Since this is a highly sensitive area, I try to pave the way for an investigation of it very early in supervision. In order to help supervisees overcome their timidity and reluctance about their overinvolvements with patients and to dilute their anxiety and defensiveness, I try to create a favorable climate by telling them how important and ubiquitous a problem I consider it to be.

I define countertransference so that there is no ambiguity about what I mean. I state that when I refer to it, my reference is to all the therapist's unconscious reactions to the patients' productions as well as to all his own personal needs, neurotic projections, and distortions which affect his therapeutic technique. I tell them it is known that well-analyzed, well-trained, and experienced therapists cannot be conscious of all their attitudes toward their patients and so some form of countertransference always takes place. I explain that it has been found that multiple transferences in the group not only increase the chances for countertransferences, but make them more complex. Since the intense reality of the group situation places a greater strain on the group therapist and tends to evoke more irrational responses from him, it is a greater hazard in group psychotherapy if it is not recognized. From the beginning I try to get the trainees to observe countertransference in themselves and one another in a task-oriented way.

This can be achieved if the supervisor carries into the supervisory hour the analytic climate of empathetic neutrality. If he can tolerate his student's mistakes, limitations, and anxieties without "supertransference," that is, without undue irritations, need to censure, feelings of superiority or oversolicitude, he will be able to treat presentations of problems as valuable communications. The trainees will then experience, as their patients should, the analytic percept that all their productions are important clues. By encouraging the trainees in their evaluations of one another's problems in an inquiring manner and by responding to their ideas and opinions in an accepting way, the supervisor demonstrates in practice how reactions to fellow members can be utilized as equivalents of free associations. If a supervisee is not permitted to become an object of attack, whether he is the presenter or the critic, if case material and discussions are treated objectively, anxiety and defensiveness are reduced, permitting the supervisees to interact productively and helpfully with one another's problems.

It may seem obvious that supervisees should not be humiliated by a supervisor or fellow students, but unless the supervisor really experiences the material his students give him of their neurotic entanglements with their patients as expressions of confidence in him and as important for learning, the supervisees will tend to feel criticized and rebuffed and will refrain from sharing their material, especially any which pertains to their countertransference. An objective attitude in supervision is essential in assisting the supervisee to relate with less anxiety to his patients, his co-trainees, and his supervisor, so that he can learn better. By an objective attitude, I do not mean indifference, aloofness, or the lack of human warmth often associated with early classical analysis, but instead, an empathetic neutrality. If the supervisor can become an objective model for his students to follow, they will be more likely to absorb and transmit a similarly friendly and accepting attitude toward their patients, so that not only the supervisees but the patients themselves will experience the impartial dynamic qualities of the psychoanalytic method which is neither inflexible, rigid, nor unconcerned.

As the supervisory sessions go on, there is often opportunity for the supervisor to pick up and point out the subtle nuances of intragroup transferences in the supervisory group. Making trainees cognizant of their own preconscious reactions to one another in the super-

visory group heightens their awareness of similar uneasy feelings in
their group patients. Experiencing and perceiving their own initial
fear of exposure to the group, their own competition for and with
the supervisor, their own rivalry with one another, generates empathy
for their patients. It is to be emphasized that although analytic techniques are used to illustrate the processes of group interaction among
the supervisees, they are not employed to work out personal conflicts,
or only to the extent that they interfere in therapy. Transferences and
projections are pointed out by the supervisor to sharpen the trainees'
skills, to sensitize them to their overinvolvement with their patients,
but not to do group therapy per se. I do not deal with or encourage
Fellows in training to investigate in any depth one another's character
traits. This is for the trainee to take up in his own personal therapy.
It is enough if the supervisee becomes aware through his group
supervision that his personal style might be interfering with his
therapeutic work with patients and he frequently brings back this
problem to his own therapist or personal therapy group. Because the
atmosphere is one of inquiry, the exchange among Fellows does not
become a battleground for unresolved personality "knots" but leads
to constructive self-examination of their techniques and their countertransferential involvements and is, I believe, of eventual benefit to
their patients.

It became evident to me, while supervising, that orally regressed
patients presented the greatest technical challenge and induced the
most countertransference in group-therapy trainees. In order to understand countertransference of group psychotherapists with orally re-
gessed character patients, I will discuss briefly the psychogenesis of
the tenacious character resistances of these patients. These patients as
children experienced greater than usual difficulty in giving up the
magical fantasy of omnipotence. The inevitable frustrations in the
oral phase made them project their hatred of childhood restrictions
onto the first external thwarter of infantile delusions of grandeur, the
mother or mother substitute who became the principal target of the
child's rage and aggression. The hostility which the affront to his
narcissism evoked in the child was projected onto the mother in the
form of the preoedipal "witch fantasy." The depth of their original
narcissism made it difficult for them as children to divert and sublimate
their aggression by identifying with the parents, nor was pleasing
their parents by behaving in an approved manner a source of gratification for them. The preoedipal "witch fantasy" of the bad mother

was repressed and underwent little modification by reality. This fantasy was, therefore, incorporated into the superego and then turned against the ego in the form of guilt, depression and masochism. The aggression which is taken over by the superego is transformed into guilt and depression and used to attack the ego. The aggression which remains in the ego serves a defensive function and is employed masochistically to provoke rejection and punishment. It is the weak ego's way of attempting to preserve the infantile delusions of omnipotence. "I force parent-mother-environment to punish me." The masochistic solution is an attempt to outmaneuver the environment's effort to impose the reality principle, it is the impoverished ego's way of maintaining its illusion of omnipotence by reducing authority to absurdity. These patients unconsciously seek to reinforce the masochistic bond to the bad preoedipal image by repeating with everyone their former experience with the perceived rejecting mother. When such individuals become patients, they repeat this infantile power struggle in treatment. The masochistic victories they achieve over the therapist by keeping therapy at a standstill are unconscious sources of narcissistic gratification. This struggle is highlighted in group therapy, for the stakes are higher. Thwarting and defeating a therapist before others heightens the patient's sense of power. On the other side, the group therapist's feeling of inadequacy is deepened, the blow to his self-esteem for his inability to reach his patients is augmented in the group because there are witnesses to his felt "ineffectiveness."

This brings me now to the subject of countertransference of group therapists to orally regressed patients. The arduous task of the working-through period is intensified when dealing with such long-suffering masochistic patients. Repeated handling of their deep negative transferences and strong resistances often pall on the therapist. He may become involved in countertransference with these difficult patients and his own unconscious oral problems may become reactivated. The blow to his narcissism in not curing these patients, in having to struggle for a long time with a plateau or regressions, may make him try to push them to where he wants them to go, not to where they are able to go at that time. His own omnipotent needs may make him overzealous and overconcerned about his patients' progress and drive him to force improvement and achievement on them. A therapist's problem with narcissism may prevent him from evaluating criticisms by patients when they complain about his authoritarian attitude or whatever, when they are justified.

In the more recent years of supervising I have found that oral countertransference problems have often led to the use of various action techniques in analytic group psychotherapy. It is the task of the supervisor to determine whether the therapist's use of action methods is for the purpose of giving patients added help and when it is motivated by countertransference. In my experience, it has been employed by some group therapists to bolster up a despairing or anxious attitude toward very resistive patients, especially those who are orally regressed. Other group therapists have used action techniques as a positive magic gesture to show a bad preoedipal mother how hard she should have tried to help her child. Their therapeutic overzealousness may be a reproach to her for her neglect of them. Their decision may be still linked with the original power struggle with the all-powerful mother of the nursery years; they try to invoke magic solutions and actively "cure" patients in order to lessen their own infantile feelings of inadequacy and passivity. Oral countertransference may drive the therapist for quick impulse gratification, to get great pleasure and elation from his work. This need can seriously interfere with the repetitious hard work of the working-through period which can become tedious and deflating to the ego. Laboriously unraveling layers of resistances is a far cry from leading a group session on to exciting climaxes.

I feel that the more charismatic leader is frequently impelled by his own unresolved omnipotent wishes to be very active and lead his patients instead of following them. In well-functioning analytic groups, the therapist is more of a facilitator, intervening when the group members are locked in the impasse of transference resistance. Assiduously analyzing transference and resistance in a group brings about a dynamic interaction which leaves little time or need for action techniques. Let me give you two brief examples of my patients who decided to supplement their therapy by joining action groups.

CASE ILLUSTRATION

Bob was a borderline patient who had been a homosexual and whose individual treatment had helped him to the point of going out with women, but who could not make meaningful or sustained relationships with them or with men. Animals were the only living creatures he trusted. His analyst sent him to one of my groups. When he joined my group, he described the other members as flexible statues. Although he kept inching slowly but steadily in his relationships during his group treatment, he still could not relate easily with people and could not go out regularly with one woman. Later he wanted to be able to cut through the barrier of fear and distrust, so he could marry his girlfriend or give her up and find someone else. But he stayed in this frozen position. He had heard of marathons and asked to attend one to see if he could make a breakthrough. I sent him to a colleague because I did not see this request as a resistance but an effort to help himself further if he could.

When he returned to the group after the marathon, the group members were eager to hear of his experience. He told them that the most important thing for him was his discovery in the going-around-of-looking-in-member's-eyes that he was afraid to look them straight in the eye because of guilt and that he felt bad inside. He had to look each member eye to eye and tell him he was not bad. He cried there and felt purged. This experience of recognizing by his behavior in another group that he felt he was bad because of guilt became grist for the mill as the other members said they were glad he got something out of his experience but reminded him that he had often talked about some unknown guilt feelings. The same slow frustrating rate of progress continued, however, for two more years until, through the transference in the group, he worked and reworked on his fantasy that he had been instrumental in his brother's death and that the archaic woman (mother) would kill him in retaliation. It was after his superego accusations were finally exposed and the heretofore inaccessible core of repressed fear and guilt were revealed and repeatedly worked on in the group that the necessity for maintaining his fear of women markedly decreased and he was able to get married. It was not until a year after his marriage, which was going very well, that we felt he was ready to leave the group. Most of the members did not want him to go because he had become a valued member of the group, relating well and helpfully to them. He left expressing his love, affection, and gratitude. He kissed me and the other women goodbye, a vivid contrast from seeing us as all flexible statues.

CASE ILLUSTRATION

Another example was Larry, who came for analysis. He had been in analysis for a short period of time with a classical analyst but found that experience unsatisfactory. I felt that a group would be helpful in breaking through his highly intellectual and disdainful defenses. When he spoke he actually looked down his nose at you. I decided to put him into twice-a-week, individual analysis and once a week in a group. He worked very well in his individual sessions, but was "l'infant terrible" in the group. He criticized the use of dreams in the group as suited only for individual treatment, he wanted more interaction, called any interchanges except provocative and angry ones superficial and mind-fucking. He would not trust the group members with any of his problems or feelings but was brilliantly insightful about their conflicts and psychodynamics. He could only show negative feelings in devastating critiques.

Although they resented his intellectual keenness when he used it negatively against them, and felt dominated by his fluctuating behavior, the other members liked having him in the group. One day he decided to implement his experience with our group with gut-level groups to express his primitive anger. I tried to pick up his negative transference to me, but he denied this; he said he just thought the way I ran groups was pallid. He began to attend encounter, yoga, breathing, shouting, gymnastic, and awareness groups. It was only after several bouts with an injured back, loss of voice, and ultimately boredom with what he began to experience as superficial games, that he gave them up. At one point before this, he was so subtly disruptive in the group, using words and concepts with surgical dexterity to attack some members, that I began to consider taking him out of it. Fortunately I talked to a colleague and became aware of my negative countertransference and my wanting to punish him for not appreciating being in my good group. I was also in awe of his brilliant insightful maneuvers and this may have interfered with my effectively analyzing his resistance in the group. I also had to let him go at his own speed and find out for himself.

Later it became clear that his behavior in my group was his negative transference to me as mother, whom he felt abandoned him most of the time to maids and governesses and, above all, gave him a younger brother whom he detested. He always refered to her as superficial and silly. His unconscious purpose was to sabotage and attack me through the group by indirectly showing me up as a shallow and inept leader. This was similar to how he used to get even with his mother by attacking his brother (sibling members in the group) and thwarting her wishes in adroit ways. His transference to me was split. I was the negative oedipal mother, demoted and downgraded in the group, and the generally respected, ideal, positive, oedipal mother in individual treatment. It was after repeated analysis of his transference to me and the group that his trust and respect for them gradually developed to the point of confiding his feelings to them and letting them help him. When he had to leave the group for a year, he and most of the group members were upset. While he was away he sent a Christmas card, thanking me for having tried so hard to teach his heart.

On the other side of the coin, the group therapist who is overpassive, oversilent, and overpermissive may also be involved with oral countertransference. He may be magically acting out the role of the "good mother" to his patients. His overpermissiveness of their acting out may be an unconscious magic gesture of reproach to his own mother: "No matter what they do, I will accept them; this is how kindly I should have been treated by you; this is how a good mother should behave toward her children." No matter how negative, provocative, or self-destructive his patients are, he has to remain passive and permissive. The masochistic passivity of the therapist does little to loosen, and may often reinforce, the masochistic and insistent dependency of oral regressed patients. Analytic silence may also intensify these patient's fantasy of the "bad, nonfeeding" mother and so increase their anxiety.

26. Growth Experiences in the Leader

MARTIN GROTJAHN

Some aging therapists develop the belief that they are superior to all others. Others may become bitter and cynical about the needs of their patients, or they may become exhibitionistic and narcissistic, believing that everything is permitted and possible as long as they do it themselves. Many may simply become depressive or resigned. However, their reputation by then may be affirmed and an encounter with these great men of therapy may still be worthwhile.

Group therapists are not patients among patients, even when we allow ourselves to become members of the group-family. If we deny ourselves this alliance with our groups we become rigid or lazy or old in the worst sense of those words, meaning: "of closed mind." We would deny ourselves an opportunity for growth and maturation—and the group would miss an encounter with a responsive and human therapist.

A therapist is mature when he has learned how to deal with the inner reality and outer environment of himself and his patients. He becomes wise when he has also learned how to deal with the problem of aging, and finally with dying and death. He will have died young if he refuses to learn with his group.

There is a definite difference between therapeutic benefit and learning. Therapists must not become a burden to the group; however, we must remain students among people who all want to learn how to live honestly. Our patients can show us how weak man is and how strong in fighting his weakness. They can show us that, no matter how young they are or how old we are and how many years we have spent in our profession. As a Jewish proverb says: "If you learn ONE good word from a fool, call him a hochum."

Sometimes it seems that people with European background and upbringing have a somewhat easier time developing an effective thera-

146

peutic alliance with a patient. I am talking about a specific European attitude which I had a chance to observe in the early times of the Berlin Institute of Psychoanalysis, when we continued our discussions in the coffeehouses after the meetings and debated with enthusiasm, skill, joy, artistry and intense emotion. We did not need enemies as long as we had friends. It is this open hostility toward a friend which forms an essential part of any working alliance. A working relationship is a fighting yet still affectionate relationship; the healthy ego of the patient fights together with the therapist against the bad, the evil, the sinful, and the sick. People who believe that one should not fight with a friend will have difficulties in understanding the essence of a therapeutic alliance. One should fight only with his friends. In group psychotherapy this attitude is a necessity and the group knows that without being told. The group knows this as well as a healthy family where the natural tendency to growth and maturation is the basis of much infighting. This is a part of honest and spontaneous interaction. To exercise it can become a great lesson for the therapist.

I am often touched but also amazed when a therapist goes all out in his affection for a patient he hardly knows. I frequently need years before I get to that point—which for me heralds termination of therapy since the cutting edge of my critical attitude is the indication of my therapeutic efficiency. There are patients who do not understand this and if the therapist is not aware of it he may drive them to the drop-out point. One patient explained my behavior to a fellow patient with the words: "Grotjahn fights for your soul, not for your affection."

It seems equally true that a therapist developing that kind of honesty which is the essence of psychoanalytic group psychotherapy also has a chance to become free and spontaneous in the expression of his hostility as well as his intimacy. If he feels free in both, he becomes a truly free and existential man. Effective use of this freedom in the therapeutic relationship is a proof of his therapeutic skill.

When I compare my attitude over the years in the one-to-one relationship with my later developed attitude of "responsive spontaneity" in groups, then I realize that I have become more courageous and direct. Where I used to be diplomatic—or hesitant—I am now direct and open; where I used to ask a question, I now make a statement, anticipating that my patients will respond to it.

A frankly critical remark in the group will be heard and reacted to. The same remark in the one-to-one relationship might have been devastating and overwhelming. The person in the group feels stronger.

Emotional freedom is the great benefit a therapist may gain when he conducts groups well. His example of giving to the group and taking from it is a model for everybody. Only in this sense does he become a member of the group and participant in all interaction.

The therapist needs strength and endurance for the necessary infighting. He must have it to start with, and he will develop it further as he goes along. He must not be what a patient of mine once called a "hit and run therapist." These are therapists with a good intuitive guess for the patients' sensitive areas, which they invade with speed and accuracy, but then do not stand their ground and work on the interpretation. Instead they retreat with speed similar to that at which they advanced. They prefer an easy peace to a necessary, painful encounter. This does not give the patient time for working through, and what was intended to be a maturing experience may turn into a trauma followed by defensive measures, complicating further work. The loss is not exclusively the patients'. The therapist, too, will lose, since the process of working through moves in both directions between the antagonists. A therapist who is a veteran of such skirmishes will grow much. A therapist who cannot look straight into the eyes of his group has not yet developed enough strength.

There are, however, certain exceptions: insight, as the word implies, is inner vision and sometimes when I want to look into the unconscious meaning of interaction, I may close my eyes "to see better." In the language of the symbol, the Seer of Antiquity is blind—or like Wotan has lost at least one eye, which is now inner-directed.

The therapist may know fear but he must not retreat from it. He must learn how to use the power of sickening fear in order to ride on top of it to health.

The therapist also may know temptation toward his patients, be it feelings of intimacy or an urge to violence. He even may allow himself occasionally to show his feelings of affection and tenderness or of annoyance and outright outrage. Here again the group situation offers much greater emotional or verbal freedom to the therapist than the atmosphere of intimacy in a one-to-one relationship where an emotional encounter would be overwhelming, at times devastating.

In addition, the group is an effective supervisor for the therapist who has not forgotten how to learn. This openmindedness to feedback from the group makes group therapy a learning experience for the therapist, and an equally therapeutic one for the patient.

It would be an abuse of the therapeutic situation if the therapist presented himself as a patient, as I know some therapists do. Conversely, it would be a severe insult to the principal rule of honesty, frankness, and sincerity if the therapist were not willing to offer his unconscious for understanding by the group. He has to learn how to function between the opposite extremes of becoming a burden to the group, and trying to remain out of reach and aloof. The conductor of an orchestra plays no instrument—but it helps if he sometimes takes an instrument—or at least imitates its sounds with his voice —and shows how he wants it played at that moment.

It would be a peculiar family in which the mother or the father did not occasionally appeal for understanding. My experience with my colleagues and myself shows me that it is easier to grow old gracefully as a group therapist than in the isolation of an individual analyst. We do not need to abuse our groups as tools of treatment for ourselves, but we may accept the help of the group in the continuation of our self-analysis. Beethoven is supposed to have said: "If you understand my music you are saved." Applied to the therapeutic situation this means that when we are understood by our patients in our groups we have learned something, as they have benefitted, too. A family who understands mother or father will have freed the way to further growth, maturation and individuation. Parents, sometimes, learn and grow with their children, and so does the therapist. This apparently is given to him to a much larger extent through the group than in a one-to-one relationship, where the patient is not a member of a family, but like an only child. A family can deal with a father in doubt or rage, but an only child should not be a confidant.

There is one other theme that can be discussed and worked through to a deeper degree in groups than is usually possible in the one-to-one relationship. Not only aging and sickness, but also death and dying can be discussed more easily in groups than in individual analysis. Where there are only two people involved, it almost always sounds or feels as if each is talking, or at least intends to talk, about the death of the other one. Soon the dialogue ends in guilt and silence.

In the group the associations about death and dying are felt deeply, often painfully, but with less guilt and anxiety than in the loneliness of the analytic situation. I am more and more convinced that the analysis of death anxiety has been neglected in individual psychotherapy. It is of the greatest importance not only in psychotic conditions but quite generally. To have dealt with death as unavoidable leads the therapist to master this anxiety in himself, and helps him to take another step in becoming the existential man he ought to be.

Analytic group psychotherapy will help the therapist to accept his motherliness in the best sense of the word. He will trust his intuition, his spontaneity, and his freedom. He even will learn how to fight for his family when a "bad mother" is threatening.

There are also changes in a therapist's narcissistic orientation when he conducts analytic groups. Almost every aging analyst considers himself "the best in his profession." Perhaps that is a necessary illusion in our profession, and it may be generally true even outside of analytic work. A surgeon may have an equal need to consider himself "the best." The group therapist who is truly responsive in his work with groups must respect the sensitive intuitive, and often correct perceptions and interpretations of people for each other. Everybody is at times a good therapist, women even more than men. Women seem to be more identified with the image of the mother while men may be more identified with the image of the son. Feminine, motherly understanding is the matrix out of which the therapeutic attitude develops. What at first may feel like a blow to the therapist's narcissism later develops into confidence in the therapeutic impact of the group.

"Freedom" for the therapist means greater, more spontaneous mobility or responsiveness in the face of anxiety, fear, guilt, and depression. It means the conscious use of countertransference in the service of empathy.

It would seem logical that after lifelong experience in his work, the veteran therapist should be pretty much the Perfect Man, but he obviously is not. The character change produced by years of conducting psychoanalytic group psychotherapy as outlined here is an abstraction, a hope, perhaps even utopian. Its realization is dependent upon so many human frailties that it frequently is not realized.

The lifelong contact with one's own or other people's unconscious harbors dangers to mental health. Using them as a challenge presents the opportunity to grow with our work. Failing this challenge may lead to the pathology of the therapist, the Mother Superior complex in the young ones, conflicts about seduction and temptation in the middle aged ones, and the God complex in the senior therapists being only some choice examples. Cynicism, depression, alienation, and isolation are other possible outcomes.

It is the assignment of the therapist to work his way through the dangers, challenges and opportunities of his work, as if he were his own favorite patient.

27. The Leader's Role in Focusing

MARVIN L. ARONSON

My main tasks as an analytic therapist, as I interpret them, are to elicit and work through current manifestations of each patient's repetition compulsion. In so doing, I utilize both individual and group psychotherapy in combination.

THE CORE BEHAVIORAL SEQUENCE (CBS)

The main unit with which I work is the Core Behavioral Sequence (CBS). This term refers to the repetitive patterns employed by patients in their efforts to obtain gratifications from the therapist and other group members; it describes the sequence of events, intrapsychic as well as interpersonal, which transpire between their initial perception of stimuli in the therapeutic situation and their overt responses to them (Aronson, 1964a, 1967).

Schematically, the Core Behavioral Sequence may be rendered as follows:

$$S\text{---}>O\text{---}>R$$
$$s \quad\quad r$$

S refers to the external stimuli *gestalten* which impinge on the patient during therapeutic sessions. In individual therapy, S consists of the sum total of the patient's verbal and nonverbal communications plus the therapist's technical and countertransferential reactions to these.

S is much more complex in analytic group therapy. It comprises all of the following features, operating sequentially or simultaneously: (1) the patient's own behavior *vis à vis* the therapist, individual group members, subgroups, and the entire group; (2) the therapist's reactions to the patient, other group members, subgroups, and the entire group;

151

(3) the reactions of individual group members to the patient; (4) the reactions of subgroups to the patient; (5) the reactions of the entire group to the patient; (6) the reactions of the other group members to each other; (7) the reactions of the other group members to the therapist; (8) the reactions of the other group members to the group as a whole; (9) the reactions of the group members to common events impinging on the entire group, such as therapist's vacations, entry of new members, termination of old members, etc.; (10) the reactions of the other group members to the total setting in which the therapy takes place (especially in institutions); (11) shared thematic material in a given session; and (12) the aggregate of all interactions occurring in previous sessions.

s, the internal stimuli, refers to those repressed images, fantasies, and memories that are brought closer to consciousness by the therapeutic milieu. These symbolize unconscious conflicts between the patient's wishes and impulses, usually sexual or aggressive, and hostile introjects. When activated, they serve as internal stimuli and trigger his characteristic defense mechanisms and interpersonal maneuvers. In individual therapy they manifest themselves spontaneously in the patient's dreams and associations, or are unearthed by interviewing techniques. In group therapy they are additionally elicited whenever a given S induces a transferential projection of the introjected figures, an identification with forbidden impulses, or both.

R is the internal response of the patient's ego to the triggering ss. Its function is to hold in check the anxiety aroused by s's coming closer to consciousness. If the precipitating s is conflictive, r is synonymous with one or more of the Freudian defense mechanisms—such as repression, denial, reaction formation, and so on; if s is innocuous, r represents normal equilibratory forces within the psychic apparatus.

Whether or not to classify a transferential projection as s or r depends on the extent to which it is utilized in the service of resistance. Transferential perceptions which are amenable to analytic explorations would be classified as s; transference resistive acts would be r.

R refers to the patient's overt responses to S and to the s's and r's induced by it. It is the most manifest component of the CBS, unlike s and r, which can only be inferred from the content of the patient's communications, R is directly observable in his interactions with the therapist and other group members. It is distinguished from other actions by its compulsivity and repetitiveness. All fixed role behavior, all reiterative acts would automatically be classified as R. R is synonymous with such terms as "defensive maneuver," "security operation," and "neurotic interaction."

What are the advantages of viewing the patient's therapeutic actions in terms of the CBS?

1. It provides the therapist with a rational framework for cataloging the patient's multifaceted patterns of behavior.

2. It can be taught to patients—at least, in its broad outlines.

3. It highlights the importance of the frequently overlooked *S* situation and sensitizes the therapist to its effects on the patient's behavior.

4. It is broader than the concepts of transference and resistance; it spells out their interpersonal manifestations concretely.

5. It is conducive to a disciplined therapeutic approach; in order to use it properly, the therapist must be able to differentiate core patterns from peripheral ones.

6. It systematically links overt actions with underlying intrapsychic processes.

7. It helps avoid the error of concentrating disproportionately on either interpersonal or intrapsychic phenomena; it requires the therapist to attend to all processes intervening between therapeutic stimuli and patients' responses to them.

The therapist's goals in working with CBS's are twofold: to help the patient achieve greater ego mastery over internal (s-r) conflicts; and to aid him to develop more effective means of obtaining interpersonal (S-R) gratifications. The focus with borderline patients is primarily on the S-R components of their CBS's—how they respond to others and how they, in turn, stimulate others to respond to them. The assumption is that improving interpersonal skills within the group will lead to enhanced functioning outside of the group. With neurotics, by contrast, the primary emphasis is on intrapsychic aspects of their CBS's. Working through unconscious conflicts between introjects and impulses reduces masochistic patterns; analysis of their transferential distortions increases the likelihood of obtaining practicable interpersonal gratifications.

THE CORE BEHAVIORAL SEQUENCE IN INDIVIDUAL ANALYTIC THERAPY

Individual analytic therapy is the modality of choice for establishing a working relationship, training the patient to be a patient, motivating him toward deeper explorations of his personality, and helping him face the anxiety which is inevitably stirred up by exposure of unconscious conflicts. It is the method par excellence for investigating s's and r's in detail and for tracing their historical development (Aronson, 1964a, 1965, 1968, 1971).

The main limitation of the individual therapy format is that it does not always permit elicitation of the full range of a patient's CBS's. The orthodox analytic assumption that all parental, sibling, and other transferences will ultimately be projected onto the therapist is often not borne out clinically; the content and form of CBS's are very definitely conditioned by the therapist's personality. Consequently, many repetitive patterns are never manifested in sessions and can only be inferred indirectly from the patient's descriptions of his behavior outside of therapy.

Another drawback of individual therapy is that some patients, consciously or unconsciously, inhibit expression of negative transferential attitudes out of fear of losing the therapist's love. Others, particularly if they possess weak egos, are unable to comply with the analytic demand that they convey all of their thoughts and feelings verbally; this places too much pressure on their resources and can lead to untoward acting out (Aronson, 1964b).

I find that the effectiveness of individual therapy as a vehicle for eliciting CBS's reaches the point of diminishing returns after approximately 10-25 sessions. At this point, I usually introduce my patients into groups while continuing to see them concurrently in individual sessions, as needed.

EFFECTS OF THE GROUP THERAPY FORMAT ON ELICITATION OF CBS'S

The format of group therapy increases the number and variety of S's and allows the patient to engage in a wider range of R's—he does not have to channel all of his thoughts and feelings into direct verbal communication with the therapist. It also enables the therapist to capitalize on the spontaneous eliciting and interpreting activities of the group members, and provides him with a more varied technical armamentarium than is ordinarily available in individual therapy.

How do these features of group therapy effect the elicitation of CBS's?

To begin with, the therapist does not have to rely on patients' descriptions of their behavior patterns in the original family or with currently significant figures; he can observe these directly. Second, the group increases the richness of transferential projections. Its manifold *S*'s precipitate a wide variety of sequential and simultaneous multiple transferences, affording the therapist a rounded picture of how patients felt and acted in relation to the entire family, not just with one parent alone. Third, the cooperative communion on common thematic material that characterizes all well-functioning analytic groups, especially as they work with dreams, can be extremely helpful in unearthing idiosyncratic fantasies which might not otherwise be revealed in patients' spontaneous associations or transferential projections (1).

Finally, the group format affords patients considerably more latitude in exploring parental transferences than does individual therapy. They can express these obliquely through identification with others. For example, they can split them, viewing the therapist as the good parent and the other group members as the bad parent, or vice versa. Or, temporarily, they can avoid dealing with them until they have worked through important subsidiary transferences.

EFFECTS OF GROUP RESISTANCE ON ANALYSIS OF CBS'S

Group resistance constitutes the greatest single obstacle to analyzing CBS's in a group setting. CBS's cannot be worked with effectively unless the following conditions obtain: (1) the foreground for most patients is limited to the spontaneous productions of one or at most several group members, common thematic material, or the therapist's interventions—all else is background; and (2) the group members are motivated to work on their own and each others' CBS's.

Since neither of these conditions prevail in resistant groups, it is difficult to determine whether a given behavioral sequence truly reflects the personal psychodynamics of the presenting member or is largely reactive to, or reflective of, the group resistance itself. Even if it were possible to make these distinctions, any CBS's produced under these circumstances would receive short shrift from the group members.

To prevent this state of affairs, it is incumbent upon the therapist to detect and dissolve group resistances as expeditiously as possible. The following criteria are particularly helpful in detecting group resistances:

1. Three or more members (two or more in smaller groups) simultaneously show increased signs of anxiety and/or emotional withdrawal.

2. Transferential projections become intensified and homogenized and are directed chiefly toward the therapist or the group as a whole.

3. Most or all patients avoid direct verbal communication and spontaneous interaction with each other and with the therapist; they do not bring up emotionally meaningful material nor do they reciprocate when others attempt to do so.

4. In advanced states of group resistance, patients come late, fight compulsively, engage in long hostile silences, and, ultimately, drop out.

The presence of an entrenched, as opposed to a transitory, group resistance is *prima-facie* evidence that the therapist has not previously worked through the members' individual resistances. The best way to prevent group resistances is to delay placing patients into groups until the principal tasks of the individual phases of therapy have been adequately dealt with in prior individual sessions. These include solidifying the working relationship, arriving at a comprehensive psychodynamic formulation of the patient's nuclear conflicts, and exploring his resistances to therapy generally, as well as to group therapy specifically.

A variety of techniques for coping with entrenched group resistances have been described in previous articles (Aronson, 1967, 1970). Among these are training patients to use the group constructively, gratifying needs for contact, frustrating certain transferential needs, consulting with the group about its own resistance, varying the length and frequency of sessions and changing the group's composition.

If group resistance persists despite the implementation of these techniques, the likelihood is that the therapist's countertransferential attitudes and actions have become the primary S's for most members of the group. Investigation usually reveals that the content of group resistances is directly reactive to the therapist's countertransference, or symbolically caricatures it, or both (2).

MOBILIZING THE GROUP MEMBERS TO WORK ON CBS'S

How can the therapist blend his own expertise with the spontaneous reactions of the group members in such a way as to secure the most advantageous analyses of CBS's.

The two extreme alternatives—conducting individual analysis in the group, and letting the members treat themselves—are obviously inappropriate. The first reduces the members to the status of mere observers; the second deprives them of the therapist's professional skills. A third alternative, calling upon the members to interpret each other's behavior, is also unsuitable in that it artificially inhibits interaction and precludes exposure of their CBS's.

The therapist can best mobilize the members to work on CBS's by the following means: (1) instructing them to bring their own thoughts and feelings into the group; (2) encouraging them to respond to each other and to him as openly as they can; (3) demonstrating how such responses can be profitable to them; (4) expressing in words and attitude that he values their contributions to the group process.

In the initial phases of a group's development, the therapist and members view CBS's from entirely different perspectives. The therapist regards them as compulsive replays of core conflicts which are to be understood and eventually interpreted. The members' responses, on the other hand, are governed largely by unconscious identification with their contents and transferential attitudes toward the presenting member. However, by the middle phases of group therapy (by which point they have gotten to know each other more intimately and resolved many transferential distortions), the members' understanding of the meaning of CBS's coincides increasingly with the therapist's. Consequently, any patient who presents a CBS in the group benefits not only from the therapist's interventions but also from the valuable feedback of his informed peers.

WORKING WITH CBS'S IN THE GROUP SETTING

Following is an outline of how I work with CBS's during the middle and later phases of analytic group therapy:

1. Before the group convenes, I review the CBS's which have emerged in preceding sessions and formulate plans as to how to deal with further manifestations of these in the forthcoming session. Also, I speculate on how to reach those members who have not recently revealed CBS's.

2. At the outset of the meeting, I study the members' interaction to determine whether the group is functioning at its characteristic level of efficiency. If the group does not achieve its usual level of efficiency within ten to fifteen minutes, I assume a temporary group resistance to be operative and take immediate steps to resolve it (3).

First, I point out, as noncritically as I can, specific examples of anxiety or resistance and invite the members to comment on these. For example:

> There seems to be some tension in the group today. I noticed that John and Nancy came late. Last week, Joe and Mary were also late. The women seem to be talking mostly to me and the men are keeping themselves in the background. Recently, some of you have expressed a desire to see me individually rather than in the group. Do any of you have any thoughts or feelings about what is going on?

Often, this type of intervention suffices to dissolve the group's tension and to reinstate a normal flow of communication. If not, I further delineate the ways in which each member reveals his anxiety or resistance. Occasionally, I introduce my own reactions into the group, particularly if I feel they reflect or contribute to the group's anxiety. In the example just cited, I might say: "I've found myself having fleeting fears that the group might dissolve." Should the impasse continue beyond this point, I offer hypotheses as to which common S's, including my own countertransferential actions, might be stirring up anxiety in most or all members. Then I interpret the resistances of the more active participants and concomitantly indicate how the passive members utilize these for their own resistive purposes. Finally, I deal with the anxiety and rage which frequently erupt when defensive maneuvers are challenged.

3. As soon as the temporary group resistance abates, one or perhaps several group members will spontaneously manifest a CBS in his interactions, dreams, or associations.

4. I take note of the immediate responses of the others to the emergent CBS. Do they (a) ignore it, (b) avoid it, (c) interact transferentially or realistically with the presenting member, (d) identify with s-r or R, or (e) commune with each other on a common theme touched off by the CBS?

5. If they ignore the CBS, I do not usually intervene except, perhaps, to offer hypotheses to the presenting member as to why his CBS "fell flat" and to suggest how he can engage the others more effectively in subsequent presentations of himself.

6. In the event that the group members avoid a CBS because it induces anxiety in them or because they are preoccupied with other matters, the immediate problem is whether to give priority to their

needs or to those of the presenting member. In most cases I focus on the group's anxiety first because, unless this is resolved, neither the presenting member nor the others will be motivated to work on the CBS productively (4). Again, I specify how each member expresses his anxiety, point out some of the defenses utilized, and encourage speculation as to what intrapsychic material may have been stirred up.

7. If a CBS engages most patients, that is, if they interact transferentially or nontransferentially with the presenting member, identify with s-r or R, or commune with each other on a common theme, I let them carry the action until they have drained the CBS and their reactions to it of emotional significance. When I do intervene, it is usually to highlight some aspect of the CBS that has been ignored by the others or to relate it to similar patterns in the member's behavior outside of the group.

8. In interpreting a CBS, it is essential that the patient become aware that his behavior does in fact constitute compulsive acting out of a core conflict. Accordingly, I spell out his R's in as much detail as possible and encourage the others to supplement my observations with their own. Then, as explicitly as possible, I point out those S's in the group which repeatedly trigger the CBS. Finally, I cite examples of how his CBS corresponds to similar behavior outside of the group. For example:

> I notice, John, that each time Bob boasts of his accomplishments, you argue with him, and do so with apparent relish. You clench your fists and simultaneously smile, as if the battle were intrinsically pleasurable. You show a similar pattern with Mary, especially when she expresses confidence in her sexuality. It seems very important for you to show them and the rest of us that you are more powerful. . . . You have told us that your wife complains of your "domineering tendencies" and is afraid of losing her autonomy in the marriage. . . . My guess is that Bob, Mary, and your wife all represent the "contemptuous laughing devils" that have been appearing in your dreams recently. Also, that when you assert yourself, you are identified at least partially with whatever these "devils" represent. It seems to me we ought to examine the symbolic meaning of these dreams more closely. Do you have any further ideas about them? Does anybody else have any hunches?

NOTES

1. Ideally, groups should oscillate between interaction and communion. Too much preoccupation with either can be resistive. Overemphasis of interaction masks intrapsychic material; communion suppresses latent transferential projections.

2. For a description of procedures for dealing with countertransferences in groups, see Aronson (1967, 1971).

3. Brief blockages at the beginning of sessions do not necessarily signify group resistance. More likely they reflect normal consolidative phenomena and do not require special therapeutic handling.

4. Priority is given to the presenting member only if he is in a genuine crisis or if his actions constitute an imminent threat to the group's integrity.

REFERENCES

Aronson, Marvin L. "Technical Problems in Combined Therapy." *Int. J. Group Psychother.* 14 (1964):425-430.

——— "Acting Out in Individual and Group Psychotherapy." *J. Hillside Hospital* 13 (1964):43-48.

——— "Organization of Programs of Conjoint Psychotherapy." *Psychiat. Quart.* (suppl.), 29 (1965):299-310.

——— "Resistance in Individual and Group Psychotherapy." *Am. J. Psychother.* 21 (1967):86-95.

——— "Patient Selection in Group Therapy." *Voices* 4 (1968):93-95.

——— "Techniques to Raise Intensity in Group Psychotherapy." *Psychiat. Annal.* 2 (1971):39-51.

Part III
NEWER PSYCHOANALYTIC APPLICATIONS

Introduction

ZANVEL A. LIFF

This section widens the range and scope of the psychoanalytic group leader. Both theory and applications which go beyond the traditional group approaches are considered.

Mendell discusses the implicit leadership training goals in his group activity. He perceives himself as a leadership model to be transmitted to the patient and carried over by the patient in his marital, familial, and larger group relationships. He views the emergence of good leadership qualities and skills as almost the essence of dissolving psychopathology.

Recognizing the need for optimal flexibility, Strachstein extends psychoanalytic group principles in her work with married couples and families. She stresses the need for more actively directive leadership positions in these special groups. Her orientation focuses on the interactive system in which change in one part changes the entire system and wherein change to the system may change each part. She contributes a valuable literature review as well as an excellent case illustration.

Utilizing closed circuit TV confrontation techniques, McCarty attempts to develop and expand the more reflective, observing ego in the psychoanalytic process. He describes how this method promotes increased ego leadership in the patient.

Cohn has developed an integrative theoretical model which balances the thematic material with the patient's feelings and the collective feelings of the group. She calls this orientation a theme-centered interactional method. This approach is described as taking place in the here and now situation of the group.

Referring to the group as a transitional object, Kosseff bridges psychoanalytic object relations theory with group practice. He describes how this approach offers the group leader a way of sensitizing himself to the deepest intrapsychic implications of interpersonal behavior. By focusing on the earliest derived patient anxiety within the framework of object relations theory, the group is collectively viewed as a newer, healthier identification source which provides accepting support, absorbs destructive emotions, and encourages risk-taking separation.

28. The Leader as a Model

DAVID MENDELL

My views on the role which leadership plays in group therapy and in the family have emerged gradually. I have gained from men of considerable insight and from many isolated experiences. As the pattern becomes more coherent, I see leadership as a quality that is not absolute or fixed. It passes from "leader" to "patient" or "student." I have learned from teachers who have brought out my leadership abilities. Similarly, patients in group therapy, while submitting to the initiative of an experienced controller, will develop their own innate qualities of leadership. These qualities will in turn be applied to a group member's family. The chain of action is continuous.

Coming into the armed services as a family doctor in 1942, I worked as assistant to Sam Ross, a flight surgeon. He showed originality and initiative in the then unusual practice of giving physical examinations to several men at a time, instead of the usual time-consuming and monotonous individual examinations. If a man had anything unusual, he would be held out for a staff consultation at the end of the day. This process provided stimulation and interchange for Sam Ross and other staff members in formulating the diagnoses. As I advanced from the position of flight surgeon's assistant to that of commander of the medical department of a neighboring base, I further developed this procedure. Ultimately, a small staff and I gave physical examinations to one thousand men concurrently. Although this was a more unusual endeavor than that of Sam Ross, it was well accepted by my superiors. The morale of the doctors improved, and the examinations were more thorough and accurate.

These experiences made me aware of my leadership inclinations. The much-touted slogan in the service—"Take your pay, pass the buck, don't volunteer for anything"—had no appeal for me. As the oldest of three brothers, I was accustomed to being responsible and giving orders. Through chance, a propensity to turn adversity to advantage, and a desire to take responsibility where it seemed necessary, I gained greater authority and greater control of my environment.

As chief medical officer in 1944, although not in my province, I organized a mental health unit with limited skills and few personnel. It was evident to me that disciplinary and emotional problems were not being handled optimally. At that time I organized and counseled with small groups of soldiers who had been A.W.O.L., or who were repeaters on sick call.

In 1947, Erik Erikson, in seminars and supervisory sessions at the San Francisco Psychoanalytic Institute, introduced me to the concepts of "mode" and "facultative" functioning. Erikson used the term "facultative" to indicate the capacity or freedom to be or do, as opposed to the doing or the inhibition of doing by compulsion. In this chapter I wish to focus upon this therapeutic module. Erikson used and first established the term "mode" within the framework of his psychosexual developmental scheme, which is now universally recognized as a way of being or doing. His own mode of leadership, although unrecognized by me as such at the time, was revealed in the genuine, accepting manner in which he received our first hesitant contributions to a seminar on dream associations. I remember my disbelief that this tentative and ignorant venture of mine, lacking thought and preparation, could possibly be a useful contribution to such an outstanding authority on dreams as Erikson. I realized later that this was due also to his mastery of the large abstraction. The assurance with which I now trust my unconscious in a group can be traced back to those beginnings with Erikson.

The leader must have confidence in the validity of his unconscious. He must be able to persist in face of adversity in the group. Self confidence is intrinsic to facultative leadership. By the same token, the leader should be open to reason and not cling compulsively to past beliefs in the face of inadequate evidence.

In 1948, at the First International Congress for Mental Health in London, I made the acquaintance of Wilfred Bion. Little attention was paid at the Congress to psychotherapy groups, which were not so well known or accepted at that time. Bion, in an informal chat, related his methods of therapy for groups of hospitalized servicemen. I was struck by the individualistic qualities of leadership and initiative which became evident as he told his story. He did not apply the techniques or conclusions of individual therapy to the group, but wished to discover the dynamics of the group afresh, and to see how the group's vitality related to each individual. He began by sitting silently in front of his first group, allowing tensions to build up, and then at the end, sharing his observations and interpretations with them. This discussion prompted me, in beginning my first group at the Veteran's Administration Hospital that year, to let the four group members arrange themselves and communicate with each other as they saw fit, while I lay down on one of four couches. However, I became increasingly aware, as time went on, that my observations and procedures were influenced by the psychoanalytic concepts of my training.

I had been practicing group therapy for some time and was teaching psychiatry to general practitioners at the University of Texas Post Graduate School of Medicine. Instead of lecturing to them, I formed a group and let them initiate the activity. Dr. Grant Taylor, Dean of the school at the time, sat in at these classes. He wondered at my manner of acceptance—the ease with which the doctors followed their own needs and formulations and participated actively and creatively. In other words, their leadership abilities were able to emerge. Dr. Taylor is a dedicated teacher and an inspired leader in postgraduate education. His quiet support and affirmation made it possible for me to venture into new and larger group modes (Mendell 1964), despite the anxiety and opposition of important faculty members and agencies.

A good leader facilitates and brings out the leadership of others. He helps each member of a therapy group to reach the goal of facultative leadership. Each group member has qualities of competency and strength which must be brought out in full in order for him to function as a creative human being. Leadership is the inverse of pathology. It counteracts frustration and the blocking of growth and creativity.

Realizing that the group leader has to be aware of himself and the influences which shape his methods and decisions, I sought out Seymour Fisher, an expert on projective testing to work out my family theme. This is it: "Life is tough and supplies are scarce. It would be wise to find a protected place or role and to stay there, but that would constitute passivity, weakness, and surrender. So one must be adventurous, mobile, and assertive." The Scylla and Charybdis of overactivity and passivity is a continual challenge to me in practice (1).

I see the group leader initially as the decision maker. He determines the boundaries of the group and its subsystems. He structures the therapy to a desired module. The group leader decides what issues to focus upon and what issues to avoid. The importance of decisions at crucial points of therapy, and life in general, impressed me. I view much of the work in psychotherapy as preparation for a few essential decisions, such as taking over one's due leadership in his family.

This may relate to some of my own difficulties in making decisions. I hate questionnaires. When it comes to buying a new car, I have to study all makes and models for months. When eventually I buy one, I am satisfied and keep it for as long as ten years.

In previous papers (Mendell and Fisher, 1956; Fisher and Mendell, 1958), I have proposed that the patient coming for help to the therapist is the family representative who occupies a leadership role. It is he who signals his family group's inability to solve some basic problem common to all the family (Mendell and Fisher, 1956).

When the therapist accepts the patient and his family for therapy, he has joined the family group, not only as an individual, but also as a representative of his own formal and informal groups. And just as the qualities of leadership inherent in individual group members are shaped and influenced by family and other groupings, so are those of the group leader. His system of leadership, his procedures, and his decisions are all influenced by these larger systems. I hope here to probe more deeply into my own systems than I have previously done. This will hopefully give the reader a more realistic and complete appraisal of my approach.

An enlightening experience for me came when Richard Evans, well-known social psychologist, gave a party in his home attended by fellow faculty and myself. Evans proposed a game—"try to be non-authoritarian." Whoever had the floor was to avoid any authoritarian statement or attitude. Whoever caught him failing to do so would take over the floor. To remain unauthoritarian seemed an easy task to me. To my surprise, the floor was taken from me repeatedly, and also rather quickly. Upon consideration, I realized that these attitudes in me stemmed from my father—a very authoritarian figure. These qualities were transmitted though generations of my father's family and certainly could not be eliminated by a few years of psychoanalysis.

The group leader shares to a varying extent the forming and modifying of goals in the group. I, for example, may have a more authoritarian approach to the therapy group than would other group leaders. I add new members to the group without consulting the present members. I rationalize this in some way, making an analogy of the addition of a member to a therapy group to the arrival of a new member in a family. However, when the decision is made, whether slowly or quickly, I initiate activity. For example, while building up a mental hygiene unit in the service, I also organized the Mental Hygiene Society in Fresno County. On my return to Houston I initiated the organization of the Houston Psychiatric Society and then the Southwestern Group Psychotherapy Society. These are still strong today.

My desires and motives to lead therapy groups seem to come from a capacity and feeling for leadership, strongly interwoven with residual difficulties in being myself. These difficulties I share with the other group members. They are a vital link to closer understanding and empathy between myself and members of the group. It would follow, therefore, that a therapist, whether he realizes it or not, ultimately chooses the techniques or modifications that best fit his own makeup.

The therapy group, as described in this chapter, is congruent with the family group. The family is a system for survival and problem solving. Leadership qualities are developed and passed on from generation to generation. A group is a number of people with a common goal and mutually agreed upon leadership. A therapy group reconstitutes elements missing from the family of each group member. The participants are united with the leader to remedy this deficiency. Each group must have a primary goal in order to survive—a unifying pull which holds it together and urges it onward. This counteracts the inertia and resistance of each member and his family. The group leader helps the group achieve direction, adds to it and gives support; he is a mediator and he controls the tempo. He may pursue a topic when the patient or group is judged able to do so, even when one patient is anxious and hesitant about continuing. The group leader brings out the desires of the group, although these obviously are not always his and may be uncomfortably contradictory to his own. The leader must, therefore, be able to tolerate periods of isolation from the group. He must inter-react and be shaped by the group. As the sessions progress, he modifies and develops his ideas and desires in response to those of the group. He functions like a valve between group members and the inter-reacting systems of those members. He modulates the tone and pressure of the group, sometimes allowing the depth of feeling to escalate and sometimes attempting to reverse it. He will steer to de-escalate a buildup of neurotic conflict. The group leader maintains his self esteem among group members and remains objective, handling unfair behavior or attack without retaliation. The leader does not put down the downputter; he points to another way which creates appreciation and increased understanding.

As the group progresses and the previously inhibited qualities of facultative leadership among group members begin to emerge, the group leader's role will be modified. The individual members will then gradually take initiative and introduce changes. They will carry these qualities into their respective families and later to other groups outside the family.

For any group to be successful, optimal information input from its members is essential. In an environment where each member is free to be himself, he can supply that information which is unique to himself. That information may be crucial for the goals of the group and necessary for valid decisions to be reached. Therefore, the leadership given by a member at that point not only contributes meaningfully to the group but reinforces the unique qualities of leadership in that individual.

A very anxious, disturbed, young married woman was so self-conscious that she would run out of the group if she felt anyone was critical or angry with her. As her therapy progressed she became one of the mainstays of the group. Her outstanding qualities of empathic support touched the group deeply. She often quickly saw through dissembling and evasion, going sensitively and lovingly to the heart of the matter, even before the group leader or other members perceived it. Her hypersensitivity, which previously had been her Achilles heel, was now a trusted sensor for her and the group. Also, she could help her husband to work out his problem with his father and to go on to parenthood, from which both she and her husband had been holding back.

The therapy group searches to uncover and develop the members' uniqueness and leadership qualities, in order that they can be shared effectively, rather than be used for the manipulation of others. When facultative leadership is developed in an individual, there must necessarily follow increased communication and constructive relationship to others. Responsibility, initiative, self-esteem, creativity, perseverance, acceptance of one's own weaknesses, and empathy with others are qualities concomitant with the development of facultative leadership.

How does the group leader encourage these qualities in members of the group? His leadership is a manifestation of that which has been brought out by other environments, other systems than that in which he is now placed. He now must direct the group, but not dominate, while encouraging members to speak of their own experiences; he must make them aware not only of their conscious minds but also of the unconscious, the nonverbal, the consciousness of dreams. The leader must listen to and quietly accept the members' contributions, thus encouraging them to trust their own thoughts and feelings. This also raises the information level of free association and gives further material for meaningful interpretations. The leader represents a unity of decisions. He decides ultimately the rules for the group and monitors the rank-ordering of mutually accepted value orientations. Thus priorities are clarified.

Each group member, including the leader, represents a transaction between an overlapping of systems—those of the therapy group, of family, other organizations, and groupings of all kinds. Scrutiny of the interface of these systems will bring intense focus on a group member's conflicting allegiances. The group facilitates the sharing of information among numerous families, something that can happen under no other circumstance, even if the families are exposed to one another. The individual is confronted with conflicting values, such as doing versus being, the traditions of one culture versus those of another, and so on. The group, the leader, and individual group members help resolve these conflicts.

The younger daughter in a family, aged three, had violent tantrums and destructive rages. The mother was an only child whose own mother had insisted that any woman who had more than one child was a nymphomaniac. Despite her husband's objections, the wife dutifully heeded her mother's feelings. After some years the husband had his way. With the advent of the second daughter, the mother reacted with feelings of guilt to her mother's disapproval. The child's symptoms developed alongside the wife's helpless reaction to the conflicting pulls of her mother and her child. She had to clarify her priorities, decide who was to come first, and then act accordingly and consistently. This enabled her to assume leadership in her family and to become free of her mother's domination.

A young wife harassed by her mother-in-law may have to confront her husband to decide whether she or his mother is to come first with him. In our culture the wife has reason to expect to be first with her husband. The group leader must be aware of cultural differences and be prepared to deal with them.

The leader can demand a direct decision from the patient. For example, he may ask a female patient to decide, if she awoke to find her home in flames and could save either her mother or her child, which one she would choose. Such alternatives, and the conflict which the patient cannot avoid facing, point out the situation as it is, rather than as it should be. Thus, in the context of the therapy group the woman can get a fresh viewpoint within the ordering of a value system different from that of her own family.

People live in groups, are integral parts of groups. If the unresolved conflicts which prevent these groupings from functioning adequately can be resolved within the context of another group, the individuals may regain equilibrium. The therapy group is a system. It is more than the sum of its parts. The common goal allows each member to transcend his effort and capacity. By the same token, the group can help the therapist transcend his own limitations.

NOTE

1. This is a continuation of my thrust to share the systems of the therapist as well as the patients in dealing with the therapeutic interaction. See also my chapter on "Family Therapy: A Synergistic Systems Approach," in *Group Therapy*, Editors Wolberg and Schwartz (New York: Intercontinental Medical Book Corp., 1973).

REFERENCES

Fisher, S., and Mendell, D. "The Communication of Neurotic Patterns Over Two and Three Generations." *Psychiatry* 19 (1966):41-46.

Fisher, S., and Mendell, D. "The Spread of Psychotherapeutic Effects from the Patient to His Family Group." *Psychiatry* 21, 2 (May 1958):133-140.

Mendell, D. and Fisher, S. "An Approach to Neurotic Behavior in Terms of a Three Generation Family Model." *Journal of Nervous and Mental Disease* 123, 3 (February 1956):171-180.

Mendel, D. "Family Therapy: A Synergistic Systems Approach. *Group Therapy*, edited by Wolberg, L. and Schwartz, E. (New York: Intercontinental Medical Book Corp., 1973).

Mendell, D. "Creative Communication at Scientific Meetings and Lectures using 'Group Therapy' Modes." Presented at the First International Congress of Social Psychiatry, London, England, August 19, 1964.

29. The Leader in Group, Couples, and Family Therapy

HARRIET STRACHSTEIN

Leader concepts evolve out of varying personality traits as well as a therapist's background. These traits may have a certain psycho-therapeutic impact upon patients, depending upon the therapist's use of himself as a group leader, or they may prove to be an obstacle.

They may be an advantage (Grotjahn 1971) when the therapist proves that he is a master of communication, whether that communication is with himself or with the group members he tries to understand. It is this communication with himself, extending into his unconscious, which helps him say what he truly feels. How much he says, to whom and when, and—most important—how he says it, is a question of his style.

The therapist's personality traits may be an obstacle (Wolf and Schwartz, 1971) when he is predisposed by his own or his patient's disequilibrium to act out. It is at this point that he is faced with the danger of losing his reasonable, examining, discerning, and objective role—to which his training may have been structured.

While exploring several therapists' published descriptions of their concepts of themselves as leaders in group, couples, and family therapy, this writer found similarities as well as differences in their opinions with corresponding variations in methods.

GROUP THERAPISTS

Wolf's (1964) conception of leader qualifications for what he specifies as "psychoanalysis in groups" calls upon the therapist to interpret and work with fantasies, dreams, free associations, slips of the tongue, identification, transference, resistance, defensiveness, displacement, and

173

neurotic alliances. He views effective leadership (1950) as that which is combined with continuous attention to the emerging potentials in various group members so that a new family unit is created, where each participant realizes increasingly gratifying levels of adjustment.

For Grotjahn (1971) the use of his own personal spontaneity is an important technical device. He has learned to depend upon his hunches and to see himself as an orchestra conductor in the group. To balance the fact that patients often trust their peers more than they trust him, he has struggled to invite their faith in him by dealing with his own countertransferences and thereby working more effectively as a leader.

But the therapist, according to Bernstein, Wacks, and Christ (1969) is never really identified with the group. His value lies mainly in his personal flexibility. He may move into the group and out of it again. He may be included in the group process by partaking in both the conscious and the latent problem solving. Yet it is conceivable that his own problems, which he consciously or unconsciously brings into the group, will be dealt with in the same way as the patient's reactions are dealt with; that is, they are taken up by the group as a problem. Some neurotic traits which may hinder the effectiveness of certain leaders are the tendency to dominate patients, to want to be included as a group member, to be taken care of, or even to see patients as faithful pupils. Such therapists may unconsciously build monuments to themselves as group leaders in order to insure their immortality.

Yalom (1970) employs his leadership to develop the group into a cohesive unit with an atmosphere conducive to such curative factors as mutual acceptance, support, hope, the experience of universality, opportunities for altruistic behavior, interpersonal feedback, testing, and learning. An elusive distinction between patient and therapist has its roots not in what the therapist does or what he is in reality, but what he evokes in the fantasy of each patient. Many analytic therapists consider the clarification of the patient-therapist transference distortions as the paramount and even the sole mutative process in therapy.

A strong leader as envisaged by Kaplan and Sadock (1971) is one who makes decisions for the group, who decides which member should be discussed in any particular group session. These therapists maintain that spontaneity allows the withdrawn patients to avoid participating. "Structured interactional psychotherapy," as they call it, encourages change by forced participation. When certain patient areas require more intensive exploration, it is the therapist who allots the time and even provides the topic, with the goal of encouraging the patient under discussion to bring his feelings out into the open.

Variations of these leader concepts in the field of group therapy are utilized in couples and family treatment. More analytically bound therapists, however, express doubts about the value of working with related patients in the same setting. Wolf and Schwartz (1971) claim that group therapy ought to be limited to patients initially unknown to each other; that it may not be appropriate to make parents and children, or husbands and wives, aware of one another's unconscious processes. There may be too much potential for mutual destructiveness from such exposures. They concede, however, that it may be possible to treat married couples in groups when the leader plays some interpretative, supportive, guiding, and mediating role.

COUPLES GROUP THERAPISTS

Papanek (1971) defines her leader concept in couples group therapy as one which psychologically modifies the neurotic interaction between married partners. She strives for the improvement of their behavior so that they can move toward individual as well as mutual understanding and growth. At the same time, she does not avoid dealing with unconscious material, using dreams as one method to help couples free themselves from their distorted images of one another and from the neurotic binds that strangle their relationship.

By limiting the number of sessions in couples groups, Kadis and Markowitz (1968), as co-therapists, employed firm leadership roles. They dealt chiefly with a problem in analytic resistance: that patients, in their fantasy lives, expect an unlimited amount of time. A definitely time-structured experience became a kind of emotional weaning which elicited anxiety and pertinent defenses relating to the "unweaned state" of the individual. Both leaders also reacted to the transference distortions imposed upon them by confronting group members with their aim to split "the parents" into good and bad parts.

Grotjahn (1960) finds himself continuously challenged in his leadership of couples groups by the fact that each one of the embattled pair needs to be right. To deal with this impasse, he uses his role to increase communication and to establish what he calls "in-fighting." He helps each mate to understand and gain insight into the other's unconscious meanings. His most important tool is his own acknowledgment and discipline of his countertransferences, which then gives him the empathy to deal with his patients' difficulties.

A different concept of couples group leadership is offered by Everett (1968). He and his co-therapist appoint "lawyers" to represent the quarreling partners. Other members serve as "judges" and "marriage counselors." After the evidence is in, the appointees offer an analysis of the dispute and constructive advice to the couple. The co-therapists urge "judges" and "counselors" to be as objective and impartial as possible, whereas the "lawyers" are expected to be completely partisan. Since "lawyers" and "marriage counselors" are fellow patients, the therapists can preserve their unbiased image and so avoid their patients' hostile reactions.

Framo (1965) directly confronts his couples with their fear of exploring the marriage relationship in the group, and exposes the tactics they use to "cover up." "How long have you both felt that this marriage hasn't really existed?" he will inquire. Taken off guard by such a bold approach, some partners may admit that they have long ago abandoned honesty in their relationship. They may have tried early in the marriage to share real feelings with one another, but surrendered because neither mate would see the other's point of view. Each was using the language of his own background, where words of love, closeness, jealousy, intimacy, and aggression had different meanings. They finally wrote each other off and played roles by not letting the other know any true feelings. It is these roles which Framo confronts, challenges, and seeks to change.

Bowen (1966) finds that leadership concepts in couples groups have remained much the same over the years, with some changes in emphasis and modification of theories. In the past, the communication of feelings and the analysis of the unconscious through dreams were stressed. Now, a method of watching a step-by-step process of externalizing and separating the fantasy, a feeling and thinking system has evolved. With this, a process of knowing one's own self and the self of the other has been developed.

This author has used a directive approach as well as an analytic one in leading couples groups: Beginning with the very first session, the leader directs the partners to sit separately, in different parts of the room. This is used to prevent the mates from forming isolated islands of protection for one another. Such physical apartness allows each group member to speak without constantly searching for protection and/or permission from the other. The more passive partner finds the daring to speak and is encouraged by other possibly non-talkative patients who gain strength from his courage. When a mate panics under the accusing eye of his partner, he is usually cautioned not to be afraid: "Go on!" "You're doing great!" "We're right behind you." There is more interaction and a loosening of the tight neurotic binds which each couple brings ready-made into the group. Each patient gradually experiences a freedom, a permission to be alone, to be individuated. Occasionally, a panicky patient may look longingly across the room for assistance from a mate, but this is usually picked up and interpreted as a need for "mama."

Such a need for "mama" or "daddy" develops into a growing awareness of the distorted images which each mate has imposed upon the other and how each one manages to provoke the other into acting out a piece of history.

Dreams, fantasies, slips of the tongue are explored and interpreted. This brings into the open the patient's infantile hold upon the past which blocks his enjoyment of the present. There is, of course, ensuing shock and resistance while giving up these old "pleasures," but later, as communication opens, partners slowly realize relief at the recognition of their true selves. "I wish I could have known this about you years ago." "We were just fooling each other." "Maybe you really do care about me."

Couples groups are "chancey" but the results are often like turning on the lights in a dark room where each partner has been groping and stumbling against each other. Now he can see that the individual against whom he has been fighting for years is not his hated father, mother, or sibling, but a human being he could possibly love today.

FAMILY GROUP THERAPISTS

In this field, the usual technique is one of exploring and attempting to shift the balance of pathogenic relating among family members so that new forms of relating become possible. It presumes a notion that the family is a homeostatic system in which change in one part is likely to effect change in other parts (Jackson 1957).

Satir's concept (1967) is that the leader must be a resource person who can report impartially on what he sees and hears. He must check out meaning *given* with meaning *received*. When defending someone, he must clearly state that he is doing so. Satir searches out the covert roles which family members play and then focuses primarily on each mate as a partner in the marriage. Their marital pain is what the identified patient and the other children are attuned to and affected by. For the leader, the knotty question is how to be an expert without appearing to be all-powerful. In revealing himself without fear, he gives the group its first experience with really clear communication.

Haley (1963) agrees with the concept that the family therapist must set the framework for being the expert in charge. He then proceeds to encourage the family members to take over by gradually but constantly removing himself from responsibility. When he finds it necessary to ask the family to undergo a painful ordeal, such as a discussion of something they would rather not talk about, he will define this request as a positive goal for each member. By giving them the feeling that he is working for the benefit of the family as a whole, he prevents the formation of splinter groups which are a major means of resistance in this kind of treatment. His premise is to avoid dealing with the underlying hostility but rather to expose the difficulties in the relationships which are the root of the hostilities.

Minuchin's (1967) concept is that of a highly active participant leader. He performs like a play director, pressuring family members into seeking new methods of interacting and demanding that they fulfill his expectations. He also utilizes a traditional role, that of interpreting underlying dynamics and teaching the family a new experiential language. He challenges the family structure by modifying the direction of its transactional pathways, such as interrupting a wife by telling her to stop "taking over," or he initiates dialogue from father to son when another family member is monopolizing the relationship. He thus creates new experiences, new understandings, which the family learns to interpret and use as they shed their old ways of interacting.

When the leader asks for an interaction in an unfamiliar way, he is not attempting to break a habit by the simple means of creating another. He seeks for an awareness of covert motivations while providing a means for more beneficial ways of attacking a problem.

In his treatment of families in groups, Ackerman (1966) supported health and counteracted sickness by shifting his leader functions at various stages; he might create changes in family allegiances by exposing the complementarity of their needs; he might protect a weaker member against the attack of a stronger, he could as well selectively penetrate family defenses, patterns of complicity and disguises of deeper currents of conflicts and fears. While probing for the interpersonal, he sought to explore the intrapersonal levels. By counteracting scapegoating as a specific barrier against anxiety, he returned the underlying problem to its place of origin in the family.

Bell (1960) takes the initiative in family treatment by acting as an agent to start a chain reaction. He may slip out of the present into the past; he may have to fight against being driven into himself and out of touch, but with directness and freedom from ambiguity, he challenges the family to join him in action. Thereafter, his function comes to an end. The family takes over; they decide what parts they will perform. Bell claims that his intent as a group therapist is to lead the members to change, to reduce their isolation, to free communication, to deepen their trust, promote their fun and fulfillment and, finally, to help each member be a part of the most important group anyone can have: his family.

CASE STUDY

The following report by this writer deals with a leadership concept from a psychoanalytic point of view in the treatment of a family of four on a weekly basis for about eighteen months.

> Mark, the father, forty-three, was the only son of a domineering mother whose husband had died when the child was two. She went to work and, as soon as he could, Mark found odd jobs and became part of a gang of children who lived mostly on the streets. At ten, he was hit by a truck and suffered a broken leg. Because he was supposed to be "man enough" to take care of himself, his mother beat him while he was still lying in the gutter. Her visits to the hospital interfered with his mother's new-found interest in gambling.
>
> While in high school, Mark and an attractive girl, Sara, became engaged. They graduated at seventeen secured jobs and planned to marry, but her parents urged them to wait. Mark went to live with them while he studied accountancy, and Sara continued her job as secretary. They were married when they were nineteen, and four years later moved into their own apartment.
>
> Sara was the youngest of four daughters. She was born when her mother, at fifty, made a final attempt to bear a son. Viewed as a disappointment, Sarah responded with many childhood ills.

Since her oldest sister, Ida, took care of her, Sara had no experience of any real mothering. When Ida married a successful businessman and moved into a better neighborhood, Sara gloried in her achievement and envied her. Everyone felt the impact of Ida's determination to raise the family's living standards. Her father, however, refused to give up his tailorshop. No amount of her mother's whining could move him.

Under Ida's influence, Sara developed into a fashionable, blond young woman with heavy false eyelashes and seductive clothes which her sister handed down to her. Only one part of her life remained guarded: her relationship with Mark. He enjoyed her femininity, even her childishness. She made him feel protective, manly, needed. Mark provided the importance and appreciation she had not been given as a child. Mark respected his father-in-law's independence, his sense of worth. But when Sara began to connive with Ida and accepted money to furnish their apartment, Mark sensed danger. He was "man enough" to take care of his wife and himself. He fought to keep Ida out of their lives but Sara began whining: she was pregnant; she would have to give up her job; Mark ought to be grateful to Ida, whose husband offered Mark a job at a higher salary. This threat silenced Mark. He hated the hero worship everyone extended to his rich brother-in-law. He hoped that when the baby arrived, Sara would relax again. All her plans were for her son.

Since Ida had a son and a daughter, in that order, Sara reacted with disappointment when she gave birth to a girl, Beth. She returned to work almost immediately, handing over her baby's care to Mark. He took a night job and relived his early rejection by his mother in Sara's rejection of Beth.

Beth grew up in an atmosphere of bickering. She loved her father. He took her to basketball and baseball games. In an effort to identify with him, she dressed like a boy: shirts, pants, dark curly hair cut close to her head. When Beth was nine, her brother Josh was born.

This was a triumph Sara wanted Mark to share. Now he must take that better-paying job. Money was needed for private schools such as Ida's children attended. When Mark protested that a public school had been good enough for Beth and should be good enough for Josh, Sara ridiculed his shortsightedness. A boy had to become a "professional." Beth defended her father, but her weeping and complaining made her appear to be a carbon copy of her mother. Mark finally took the job with his brother-in-law. He allowed Sara to give their bedroom to Josh and shared a couch with his wife in the living room. Beth was relegated to an alcove off the kitchen. Only one part of Mark remained intact: his secret interest in gambling. This had been going on for months. Their savings were gone and he had begun to borrow. When Ida's husband revealed that he had signed a note for Mark, Sara turned on Mark in a rage. Mark experienced a strange satisfaction—somehow, he was getting back at his mother. He had also started a relationship with another woman and managed for Sara to discover that, too. The brawls in the kitchen off Beth's room increased. Beth joined the quarrels. She was tired of babysitting for Josh, sick of being exploited and ignored. At sixteen, when she graduated high school, she asked to be sent to an out-of-town college. There was no money. Screaming could not produce it. In a tantrum, Beth swallowed an overdose of her mother's sleeping pills. After her hospitalization, she was sent for psychotherapy. The entire family was then asked to come, including Josh, aged seven, a chubby, baby-faced boy.

Mark remained silent the first few weeks, although he never missed a session. Sara berated him and complained about the uselessness of treatment. She said that Beth's attitude had worsened; she would not help in the house; Mark came home only to watch television. When the therapist tried to elicit history from each group member, Mark resisted telling about his childhood. There was no problem getting such facts from Sara.

Beth blurted out her feeling of being divided between her loyalty to her father and her pity for her mother. She had been her mother's confidante when Mark was unfaithful and lost money gambling. Sara interrupted Beth and called her "Ida," her sister's name. Beth remarked that her mother often made this slip. Mark's derisive glance at his wife provoked her into revealing that Mark sometimes called her "Mom."

Mark came early to the next session. When his family arrived, he told a dream, the first one offered since the group began. Something in his rectum bothered him. He reached down and pulled out a snake. He kept pulling and pulling, but there was no end to the snake.

He had had the dream the night after the last meeting. He had awakened Sara to tell her, and she had reminded him that his mother had given him enemas. Maybe it meant that his mother was a snake and that he could not get rid of her, no matter how hard he tried. Mark looked dubious but thoughtful. Later in the session, Beth said that she had been thinking about her father's dream. The snake might be her mother whom Mark so often called "Mom." Mark mumbled that there was no end to his wife's complaints, they went on and on; that he and Sara had been so happy before Ida butted in and the children came. Sara pounced on Beth and Mark for being in league against her. She said that only Josh appreciated her. Josh complained that he and Beth fought whenever they were left alone, that she called him a spoiled brat, she never stopped picking on him. Mark suggested his children might be doing an imitation of him and his wife.

The problems were brought up again and again the first four months and were often repeated during the drive home. Only more communication was established; less recrimination, a little more insight and understanding emerged. During the time between sessions, the family developed a means of going over what had already been said but with attempts to reach out instead of withdrawing into silences or anger.

Mark had been right about Beth and her brother. They were reliving their parents' relationship. Sara had tried and failed to make a big sister out of Beth, whom she resented and envied for having Mark. Mark had once reveled in his exclusive relationship with Sara. When it was destroyed, he relived his boyhood pain.

Toward the end of the fifth month of therapy, Sara brought in a dream about going to the toilet, defecating, and getting herself soiled. This, she said, showed how much she was blamed for all her family's troubles. If she was so messed up, she must be very unattractive to Mark, Beth and even to Josh—the same disappointment to everyone, just as she had been to her mother. Here the therapist intervened, saying that it was possible that a good word from Mark and some help in the house from Beth might keep Sara from feeling so unappreciated. Sara worked at a job all day, cooked and cleaned at night. Maybe her complaints were valid. Sara wept; Mark reached out his hand to her. He muttered something about trying to make things easier, that he and Beth and Josh ought to pitch in and help. Beth watched and listened, somewhat uneasily.

Weeks later, Beth reported a relationship begun with a boy, Tom, whom she had met at City College. When she had told him about their family sessions, he asked if he could join. No one raised an objection. He was a tall, pale, shy young man of eighteen who had little contact with his parents and was quite dependent upon Beth. Whenever she could, she pushed him into the limelight. Now that her father no longer needed her, she found in the passive Tom someone who did.

By this time, Mark had dropped his gambling and his extramarital affair. He had located a well-paid job with an accountancy firm which got him off the hook with his brother-in-law. He had paid off his debts, managing to do this without financial help from Sarah. It was gratifying to watch him grow in the non-critical, approving group atmosphere. His independence strengthened Sara. She could now lean on him without surrendering her identity. The therapist had also supported her, believed in her. As the communication between Sara and Mark developed, it allowed the children room for their own growth. Even Josh landed a job, delivering newspapers in the neighborhood.

The transference changed as the family reacted to a tolerant "mother" who accepted and tried to understand them. One serious crisis developed when the therapist announced that she was taking a six-week vacation. The morning preceding her departure, Sara telephoned to say that Mark had been unable to sleep and had been weeping all night. She asked for an emergency session. Mark arrived and broke into heavy weeping. He told a dream. He had opened a coke bottle and it cracked in his mouth as he was drinking.

He shook agitatedly. When he was a little boy, he had loved cokes and always drank them from the bottle. It was the one indulgence he had received from his mother, but it was usually accompanied with a slap or a complaint. Nothing he ever received from her had come without pain. Now that he had begun to trust the therapist, she was deserting him, like his mother and Sara had done. Maybe she would never come back.

The therapist arranged a date and hour for their next session, which was to be soon after her return. This was confirmed with Sara, who was waiting for Mark. They left with the appointment card clutched in Mark's hand.

The whole family returned for two-hour sessions weekly in the fall (previously, the sessions had been ninety minutes). Everyone had a chance to do more talking. Subjects were repeated and discussed, such as Mark's constant hunger for attention which he provoked by losing his way on the drive home and thus forcing Sara into her backseat driving act; Sara's need to go into her martyr role whenever Beth neglected helping with the housework. This brought up the topic of Beth's moving into her own apartment with the money she earned as a part-time bookkeeper while still in college. Sara burst into a tirade about Beth's being a baby, and Mark was worried that she would not be able to protect herself properly.

Beth had changed. Now she was an attractive girl—long, curly hair, dresses she herself had made, skin and figure showing the attention and care she gave herself. In a private session, she confided to the therapist her doubts and fears about sex. No one had told her about contraceptives. She and Tom wanted to live together before marriage.

This new problem resulted in further upheavals in the sessions, of which Tom was still a member. Beth and Tom set a limit of one year to their living together without marriage. No one else in the family would have to be told, particularly Ida or the grandparents. Finally, Sara conceded that Beth might be doing a "smart thing." At least, she would let go of her parents sooner than Sara had done. Tom could learn to stand on his own feet. To this, Mark nodded approvingly. He appeared to understand the therapist's goal. With Beth gone, he said, he and Sara could have a life together without so many family problems. He encouraged Beth in her independence and Josh in his efforts to become "a small businessman."

In the last months of treatment, Josh had become more boy than "baby." Ida's influence had weakened as Sara recognized that what she had believed to be admiration for her sister had really been envy.

The family visits to the therapist tapered off to twice and then once a month. Then there were only occasional telephone calls from different members, but even these dwindled with time.

CONCLUSIONS

All the leaders in this report had these aims in common: To help each group participant achieve a more gratifying level of adjustment, to increase his ability to communicate, and to provide him with the feeling of being part of a cohesive unit.

The groups could be gatherings of patients previously unknown to one another, or couples groups where partners cling to deeply rooted neurotic binds, or family groups where scapegoating and habitual modes of hostile interaction act as powerful barriers against the therapist's efforts to reach the source of the real pain—the mates themselves.

How the therapists deal with such goals is reflected by their personal qualities, as well as in their training. Some use their flexibility to reach for more response from the group members. Patients are likely to reflect the therapist's ease, his willingness to take chances, his lack of discomfort in the face of the unexpected or angry interaction, or even an attack upon the leader himself. Another related trait, the leader's spontaneity, may supply him with the intuitiveness and imagination he needs to gain greater insight into his patient's unconscious and to attempt more innovative approaches.

When he also utilizes his countertransferences without making a patient of himself in the group, yet remains the leader who is still in touch with his patients' problems, he improves his qualifications as a therapist. He may discover that his groups are effective supervisors against his acting out.

More decidedly active are the leaders in couples and family therapy. Their directiveness helps break up old patterns of behavior that otherwise remain hardened against other means of approach. But the leader may also be quite nondirective when he purposefully guides the group members toward their own rhythm of growth as new insights develop and potentials for change appear.

A characteristic that enables some therapists to cope with resistances is their ability to confront transference distortions boldly and to set limits on irrational demands which may be blindly pursued by their patients. While these effects are desirable, leaders try to retain a nonjudgmental attitude, yet remain honest enough so that their group members can use them as models.

This nonjudgmental quality, paired with honesty, originates from the therapist's own humaneness in the face of suffering, his empathy for those who may be in the wrong, and his earnest desire to help his patients free themselves from their webs of neurotic misery.

Such a willingness may call upon the leader to abdicate his position of power as a leader at times and to bestow it upon the participants who, as peers, can supply a group member with the strength and courage to go on where the therapist as the authority figure might fail.

The group leader's chief quality is his dedication to the most optimal approach, to the goal where hope is the major resource. At no time can his sincerity and belief in his work be clouded by cynicism.

REFERENCES

Ackerman, N. W. "Family Psychotherapy—Theory and Practices." *Am. J. Psychother.* 20 (July 1966) 3:405-414.

Bell, J. E. "The Family Group Therapist: An Agent of Change." *Int. J. Group Psychother.* 14 (Jan. 1960):72-83.

Bernstein, S.; Wacks, J.; Christ, J. "The Effect of Group Psychotherapy on the Psychotherapist." *Am. J. Psychother.* 23 (April 1969), No. 2.

Boszormenji-Nagi, I. and Framo, J. L. *Intensive Family Therapy* (New York: Harper & Row, 1965).

Bowen, M. "The Use of Family Theory in Clinical Practice." *Comprehensive Psychiat.* 7 (1966):345-374.

Everett, H. C. "The Adversary System in Married Couples Group Therapy." *Int. J. Group Psychother.* 18, 1 (Jan. 1968):70-74.

Grotjahn, M. *Psychoanalytic and Family Neuroses* (New York: W. W. Norton, 1960).

———— "The Qualities of the Group Therapist." *Comprehensive Group Psychotherapy*, Kaplan, H. L., Sadock, B. J., eds. (Baltimore: Williams & Wilkins, 1971).

Haley, J. *Strategies of Psychotherapy* (New York: Grune & Stratton, 1963).

Jackson, D. D. "The Question of Family Homeostasis." *Psychiatr. Quart. Suppl.* 31 (1957):79-90.

Kadis, A. L. and Markowitz, M. "Short-term Analytic Treatment of Married Couples in a Group by a Therapist Couple." *New Directions in Mental Health* ed. by Reiss, B. F. (New York: Grune & Stratton, 1968).

Kaplan, H. I. and Sadock, B. J. "Structured Interaction: A New Technique in Group Psychotherapy." *Am. J. Psychother.* 25 (July 1971), No. 3.

Minuchin, S.; Montalvo, B.; Guerney, J.; Rosman, B. G.; Rosman, B. L.; Schumer, F. *Families of the Slums* (New York: Basic Books, 1967).

Papanek, H. "Group Therapy with Married Couples." *Comprehensive Group Psychotherapy* Kaplan, H. L., Sadock B. J., eds. (Baltimore: Williams & Wilkins, 1971).

Satir, V. *Conjoint Family Therapy* (Palo Alto, Calif.: Science and Behavior Books, 1967).

Wolf, A. "The Psychoanalysis of Groups." *Am. J. Psychother.* 4 (Jan. 1950). No. 1.

———— "Psychoanalytic Group Therapy." *Current Psychiatric Therapies* 4, Masserman, J., ed. (New York: Grune & Stratton, 1964).

———— and Schwartz, E. K. "Psychoanalysis in Groups." *Comprehensive Group Psychotherapy* Kaplan, H. I., Sadock, B. J., eds. (Baltimore: Williams & Wilkins, 1971).

Yalom, D.: *The Theory and Practice of Group Psychotherapy* (New York: Basic Books, 1970).

30. The Leader Using Audiovisual Methods

GERALD J. McCARTY

The evolution of psychoanalytic treatment from individual consultation into psychoanalysis in groups has required creative leaps in the concepts and conduct of the psychotherapeutic process. There have been many innovative approaches in psychotherapy, as there have been many in the teaching and learning process of psychotherapy. Freud's use of free association was innovative. Nonsense syllables have been used as an experimental approach to teach therapists to focus on feelings independent of intellectual content. The group is an attempt to go beyond the associative approach. The alternate session is a way of stimulating active patient participation in a therapeutic process so as to change it from a vertical relationship into a self-help process. In these expansions of the technical armamentarium of the therapist to help the patient develop a stronger and more reflective ego, the patient becomes increasingly more active and assumes more leadership in the treatment process.

The conceptual basis for the use of television techniques in group psychotherapy is the value of such methods for fostering an observing ego and self-help or leadership functions in the patient. The empirical rationale is a derivative of different personal experiences. Closed circuit video (CCV) techniques employ direct display of camera information to the monitors so that group members may watch ongoing behaviors. This is distinguished from the use of a videotape recorder (VTR) to store visual and auditory information for instant or delayed replay.

The impact and interaction of perceptual processes with personality and characterological factors was the focus of research reported in a book entitled *Perceptual Processes in Psychopathology* (McCarty

1961). The use of the conference phone and verbatim transcripts of the calls was the basis of a book exploring the teaching and learning process of group psychotherapy (Wolf et al., 1970). The telephone has also been the medium by which to continue psychoanalytic therapy with patients who have found it necessary to move from the locale of the therapist to remote areas, as well as for supervision of group therapists in a distant city (Saul 1951; Wolf et al., 1969; McCarty 1969). The use of audio tapes and written notes in the psychotherapeutic process is not uncommon. The presentation of lecture material on VTR, followed by telephone discussion and interaction with the presentor, is now being used in a training program of municipal court probation workers (McCarty 1973).

Berger (1970) presents a very thorough description of the use of VTR in the process of confrontation. In his thinking, the immediate or later replay of the exchanges in the group results in a confrontation between the patient's self-image and others' observations and perceptions. Such confrontations can be merely a gimmick and an interference or can be meaningful, depending upon the skill and timing of the therapist.

Rogers (1968) has used photographs and phonograph recordings effectively. Cornelison and Arnsenian (1960) have used photographs to help patients in redirecting libido outward. In a sense they use the photographs of the patients as transitional objects between narcissistic ego functions and object relations. Geertsma and Reivich (1965) found changes in self concept with the use of VTR playbacks.

The opportunity to observe my own interaction and dialogue with a colleague on prerecorded tapes of an educational television series gave direct impetus to the beginning conceptualization of the use of CCV and VTR in group psychotherapy.

The physical arrangement of our office space was developed specifically for the use of CCV and VTR. The office was prewired for the use of cameras, recorders, and monitors in any individual or group consultation room. The design includes remote control operation of the equipment from a fingertip operated console in the main television group room. Another control console is located in the storeroom where the VTR is routinely stationed.

Ordinary operation of the equipment uses information from five cameras. A fixed camera is located in each corner of the room approximately 18 inches below ceiling level. It is focused to pick up the opposite quadrant of the room. A camera mounted on a servomotor is located in the ceiling at the center of the room and rotates 360 degrees under the control of a matching servomotor on the console. The image of this camera can be electronically tilted so as to provide a close-up of either short or tall patients without requiring movement of the camera in a vertical direction. All wires are buried in the wall except for the short power cord and video information package running from any particular camera to the prewired outlet immediately behind the camera. Monitors for viewing are mounted on two walls of the main studio just above the heads of the patients to allow either CCV or VTR presentations. The microphone for audio information is located in the ceiling in the center of the room. Other monitor stations are located in the other group rooms, individual consultation rooms, and in the storage control center.

The display of information may be initiated by the therapist's decision or a patient's request. Visual information is displayed directly from a camera over a monitor without voice. A closed circuit simultaneous broadcast of audio and visual information from the VTR is displayed as an instant replay, or later broadcast, of previously recorded information for patients' associations and reactions. Presentations may be visual, audio and visual, slow motion, or reverse slow motion. This latter procedure can be particularly helpful in studying the components of gestures. We may replay an earlier part of the meeting with no predetermined purpose other than to discover new associations and understandings.

Any of these processes of confrontation is particularly useful in the beginning phases of new groups or with new patients in an existing group. They are helpful in teaching a patient how to be observant of nonverbal, tonal, and other communication processes. Atypical media or parameters for psychotherapeutic intervention are aimed at strengthening the patient's ego function to enable him to engage more actively in the therapeutic process as a participant-helper.

One may rely on environmental manipulation as a means to afford triangulation in instances of pathological tendencies for dyadic fusion. For example, a boy of seven years of age was unable to attend regular classrooms because he was functionally mute. His father had been killed in a plane crash, and the boy became silent, and the mother lonely. She was quite unaware of the way in which she was finding fulfillment of her romantic needs in her regressive emotional attachment to her son. He seemed to be trying to absorb her or be absorbed by her as a defense against the anxiety and insecurity caused by the sudden loss of his father. The resumption of normal psychic growth and development for the boy followed upon the therapist intruding between the boy and his mother. The therapist's influence was a limited version of the father's role as conceptually articulated by Forrest (1967) regarding the influence and role of the father in male character development.

Using video techniques, the therapist or patient focuses upon a silent member or another person's verbal or nonverbal interaction which affords both the person who is in focus and the others a confrontation with the triangularity of their involvements.

Just as I will encourage a patient to take certain psychological tests, including projective tests during initial phases of appraisal, I also encourage him to bring in art work, professional papers, poetry or prose. Particularly, if patients have difficulty with verbal articulation, I encourage them to take time to free associate on paper between sessions as a way of becoming observers of their own mental processes. A deaf and dumb man for whom therapy consisted of notes written back and forth across the desk is a special case of this type of approach. Notes are an intermediary of distance between the patient and his or her own thoughts as well as between the patient and the therapist. The interpersonal differentiation and distance permit intrapsychic differentiation. One patient to whom I recommended this method made tape recordings, and then transcribed the tape recordings for other patients in the group, and brought the tape recordings in for them to hear. The patient began to become more visible and verbal in the group and more active in her life away from the therapy group. Such a change in therapeutic productivity overcoming a stalemate is similar to the findings of Stern who reports that the use of audio playback of recorded analytic sessions does not interfere with the analytic process and is helpful in overcoming resistances. As he describes it:

> Relistening in a state of detachment allows the patients to objectify their behavior in greater independence from the analyst and to integrate more efficiently the insight gained in the analytic process (Stern 1970, p. 597).

The use of CCV or VTR presentations of patients' interactions, the use of conference phones, transcripts, and other intermediary procedures, stimulate the patient to take on a reflective posture in regard to his own inner life and his and others' interactive productions. It provides an opportunity for free-floating attention to his own associative flow and thus puts him in the position of being his own helper. Transference reactions and fantasy elaborations are stimulated. The relationships between patients take on a quality where the patients are able to "play with" various associations and ideas about themselves and each other. Group sessions become more spontaneous.

The CCV and VTR replays attenuate the vertical vector in the therapy. There is much anxiety and defensive maneuvering as a consequence of the stimulation of new visual cues. Patients become rapidly aware of projected feelings about others in the group. The procedure is helpful from the countertransferential point of view in that the therapist becomes confronted with his projections on the patients.

People are initially exhilarated and dismayed, entranced, anxious, frightened and delighted by seeing and hearing themselves. Through the continued use of these procedures, they seem to evolve realistic and consensually validated self-images. A therapist should certainly see himself on videotape recording if he is to utilize this equipment. It allows immediate empathy with the patients. Seeing oneself on the tapes allows an opportunity to observe oneself in action and certainly encourages openness in any supervisory experience.

With my students I engage in co-therapist experiences where we alternately operate the control console. This provides an opportunity for the trainee to observe my decision making, selection of input to the videotape recorder, as well as my timing of replay. When the trainee operates the console, it allows me to observe his selection or avoidance of material and permits an opportunity for viewing myself on his decision basis rather than on my own. The opportunity is there for reflective speculation about the nature of my own participation in the group. The VTR is a marvelous instrument for studying interaction patterns and resistances. Therapists who use a VTR in groups where they are not directly supervised have an opportunity to become their own supervisors.

Videotape recording serves as a teacher, as a source of example, as an exposure of oneself and as a reminder of one's faults, as a means to recall particular exchanges, and for repetitive review of complex interactions. Of course recordings can be useful as cross-sectional indices of growth. The various procedures which I have described can be means of circumventing some of the situational interferences with the learning process. In group therapy we must be able to show ourselves and not be afraid to be seen, just as it is important for the patient to allow himself to be visible without fear. Video techniques are extensions of this view of us by others, so that we are able to join the others in viewing ourselves.

Certain patients manifest anxiety in regard to attendance at the alternate session in group psychoanalysis. Many of these same patients are frightened by the use of video techniques. This is particularly evident in forms of boundary-line disturbance; a psychodynamic constellation involving anxiety about fusion with or separation from a real or symbolic mother. Confrontation with the self over VTR is very upsetting for these patients for whom object relationships are characterized by the investment of emotions in a person who is not fully or clearly differentiated from the self. This is similar to Fairbairn's concept of primary identification (Fairbairn 1954).

What appears to be an obsessional syndrome, or an hysterical syndrome, is rather the context in which a more basic ego disorder is expressed. The identity problem preempts later developmental issues but precipitates ego-adaptive mechanisms in the style of the particular developmental phase. The ego must be liberated to allow the normal forward thrust which has been blocked by whatever the situations have been which have fostered the attempt at regressive fusion at the later phase. The group analytic matrix, particularly including the use of alternate sessions and CCV or VTR presentations, is especially suited to accomplish this liberation of the ego. Patients whose personalities are dominated by narcissistic features are more easily confronted with their magical fantasies and omnipotent qualities when the therapy includes the use of CCV and VTR. These methods provide for a beginning of self-helping ego functions and the opportunity to use the time in therapy more effectively.

Obsessive patients are more easily confronted with their fantasies of dominance, power, and control which are often vested in transference to the therapist. Those whose personalities take on the wrappings of an hysterical characterology are exposed to their competitiveness, their strivings for adequacy, and their attempts to gain leadership posture as a means to achieve security and a sense of ego identity or self-esteem. As the psychotherapy group becomes an extension of the therapist's intervention with the particular patient, as the group provides an opportunity for self-help, CCV and VTR act as an extension of the therapist's and patient's interpretive processes and provide the opportunity for self-development.

In the beginning phases of psychotherapy, whether working in the dyadic context or in the group context, the single most important objective is to establish a strong, dependable, intellectually crystallized alliance between the helper and the person being helped. Various authors use different language to describe this collaboration. Greenson describes it as the

> working alliance [or] the relatively nonneurotic rational relationship between patient and analyst which makes it possible for the patient to work purposefully in the analytic situation (Greenson 1967, p. 46).

The use of such parameters as groups, alternate sessions, written notes, CCV and VTR deviates from classical techniques. I introduce such parameters early in the process of treatment to build the capacity for object relations and healthier ego functions and to help the patients identify with my attitudes and methods. In the middle phases the patient is able to utilize classical psychoanalytic interventions more efficiently. In the working through process confrontation, clarification and interpretation can be accomplished as much by the use of CCV or VTR as by verbal methods.

The self-analytic process which is the goal of all psychoanalytic psychotherapy requires a resilient ego. For this reason neurotic patients initially have more positive reactions to the use of CCV and VTR than do psychotic patients. For example, Marjorie reacted extremely unfavorably to the introduction of alternate sessions in the group, as was reported in a previous publication (Wolf, et al. 1970), and was equally frightened by the prospect of the use of CCV and VTR. When the alternate session was first introduced she was fearful of the group meeting without the therapist and referred to it as being "alone."

Analysis of this resistance led to further understanding of her transferential tendency to fuse with the therapist as she had historically lived in a relationship of fusion with her mother. The overwhelming fusion with her mother was exemplified shortly after the introduction of the alternate session.

One weekend the therapist was viewing a new house open to the public. Marjorie, accompanied by her mother who had never met the therapist, was in the group viewing the house. The mother tripped and fell and was assisted to her feet by the therapist who was still unidentified to her. The mother expressed thanks and the scene dissolved. At the next group meeting Marjorie had no recollection of having seen the therapist the previous day. She fully remembered the incident of her mother's fall and of a man assisting her mother, but did not have any awareness of the identity of the man. Analysis revealed that this information was repressed because her own ego was absorbed by her mother's when she was with her. Since the mother did not know the therapist, the patient did not know him.

At the first group session where we were to use the new video equipment, Marjorie unconsciously managed to move her chair out of range of all the cameras. She was frightened and revolted by the prospect of seeing herself on TV and by the prospect of intensified exposure to analysis. Her confrontation with her own body ego and independent existence would lead to the obsolescence of mother. When I replayed the section of the VTR material which showed Marjorie moving out of range of the cameras, she and the others had a new opportunity to work through her symbiotic problem. With the repeated use of CCV and VTR presentations Marjorie became able to view and differentiate herself.

I have observed such phenomena as unconscious identification with a significant relative in so striking a manner as to merit special comment here. A patient named Peter is a man with borderline ego function in a character structure with mixtures of narcissistic symptoms (alcoholism and gambling), obsessive symptoms (much scrupulousness and severe problems in managing bladder, bowel, money, time, etc.), and hysterical features (much sexual conflict, conscience-ridden behavior, role conflict). His father was considered worthless by his mother's family. After the father died, he and his mother lived with his maternal grandparents and an aunt, who was a nun. Then his mother died traumatically. When word came to the grandmother's house about the death of her daughter, she became hysterical and ran about the house literally tearing out her hair. Peter had no recollections of this incident during the initial phases of our therapy.

During a particularly moving group session Martha, a single woman (twice previously married and childless), was lamenting and mourning over recently relinquishing her illegitimate infant child for adoption. While she was grieving, group members were interacting with Martha. I had selected the camera which was focused on Peter and two other patients for input to the VTR. Martha did not happen to be seated in that same quadrant. The example portrays quite clearly how VTR can be useful as a means of triangulation as well as for a stepping-off point for associations and interpretive analysis.

All the members were focused on Martha, but the camera was focused on some others and gave us their bodily and facial reactions to the situation. I noted that Peter was pulling vigorously at his bushy eyebrows. I wondered what this behavior might be expressing. I interrupted the group process and asked the group to watch a segment of the tape with me. I invited their associations, feelings, thoughts, and reactions to this portion of tape without suggesting who or what in the picture they focus upon. Several patients commented on the sad appearance of Angela. Others noted the bored indifference as a defense on the part of Harry. Surprisingly, Peter immediately commented upon his behavior of pulling at his eyebrow and wondered about its meaning. He said the discussion of Martha's problem reminded him of the time when his mother died. He said how awful he felt about Martha relinquishing her child and how awful he felt about the sudden parental abandonment of himself to his grandparents. He remembered how grief-stricken his grandmother was at the news of his mother's death and how she had run about the house tearing out her hair. He associated his eyebrow pulling to her hysterical hair pulling and said "I guess I am feeling like grandmother did and like I felt at losing my mother. When Martha tells us about giving up her child and the grief at the loss, I am reminded of my grief." This eyebrow pulling gesture had been a frequent habit in anxious moments. Since this opportunity for interpretation of its meaning and other opportunities for working through his grief, it has completely dropped away. He and the group are now working on another facial habit he has of rolling his eyes up under the upper lids giving an Orphan Annie appearance.

The VTR or CCV also allows us to see ourselves as others in the group do. Angela, a woman of Italian heritage, customarily wears a sad face. She has become able to recognize how she uses her depressive mood to coerce the group into some new attempt at giving her solace. The VTR permitted her a profound awareness of her depressive tactics and of the pathological interactions and character style which has resulted in her self-defeating involvements with her husband, her family, and others.

The playbacks and occasional visual-without-auditory display of ongoing materials allow patients to see and hear their own over- and underreactions and inappropriate reactions. It confronts them with their systems of repression, denial, reaction formations, and the gamut of ego defenses. Viewings often precipitate break throughs. Patients see the multilevel messages in their serious words accompanied by a glib or cute manner, aggressive words but self-effacing manner, or attempts to gait or monitor other patients' responses. Harriet engages in frequent examples of this latter procedure. While interacting with others in the group, she vigorously shakes her head in the negative though consciously and verbally attempting to elicit an affirmative response.

Patients portray a variety of roles through words, accents, intonations, facial expressions and grimaces, posture, courting, mimicking, aggressive movements, pointing, first shaking, grasping, suppliant movements, supportive and nurturant movements, penitent postures, guilty avoidance of eye contact, Uriah Heep-like hand wringing and nail picking. The VTR magnifies these often microscopic or momentary allegorical or metaphorical messages and gives us additional opportunities to explore and wonder about their meanings.

The material from the VTR provides us all an experience as valuable in the therapeutic process as free associations, dream material, artistic or projective materials for discerning the multiple determinants of patient's behaviors. Insight is heightened as we see ourselves as others see us.

My clinical groups are all open-ended. Old patients leave and new patients enter. There is a rhythmic ebb and flow of patients. This factor tends to obscure the commonly described phases of group development, work, and demise evident in closed groups.

When beginning a new group using video techniques, one can assist the formation of a working alliance among the patients by such procedures as: asking for contrasts between anticipatory fantasies and actual observations of themselves in the group; eliciting recent dreams which reveal conflict and anxiety about the group; asking for expectations or explicit concerns about the group; going around on any of these matters or just going around in terms of reactions to and interactions with the others in the group or to instant replays or replays of early parts of the meeting.

As new patients enter an existing open-ended group the therapist employs these techniques with them. The experienced patients in the group will spontaneously assist the newcomer. Every time a new patient enters an existing group, members will handle the intrusion by their usual character defenses, and the new patient will mount his best defenses. The entrance of the new member then becomes diagnostic for all and gradually they integrate and work through a new self-awareness.

When Marlene, a nun whose community now dresses in ordinary street clothing, entered as a new member in an existing group, she introduced herself as Sister Marlene but very quickly corrected and said Marlene. Only one of the other six patients in the group and the therapist heard the "Sister" title. After the first moment of introduction Harriet, who was having a great deal of conflict about her marriage and who was engaged at that time in an extramarital affair, was guiltily discussing her clandestine involvement and attempting to elicit support and endorsement from the group for her conduct, while at the same time engaging in her routine of wagging her head "no." After some discussion of this situation, LaVerne, who was sitting next to Marlene and had heard her use the word Sister, quite charmingly and invitingly asked her if that indeed was what she had said. Others in the group felt that she had not introduced herself as Sister Marlene. A replay of the opening of the group session produced shocked awareness of some of the defensive processes of the members. Tim recalled that he had heard what she said but didn't believe it and passed it by, though he immediately began to relate to Marlene as if she were his own frigid mother. Peter said he hadn't heard it at all but on the replay began to associate to his need to ignore what was so clearly stated. He was able to realize immediately how anxious he was about having a nun in the group who reminded him of his aunt who was a nun and who criticized and manipulated his life for so many years. She also reminded him of his grandmother who was the dominating figure in his early life. George, who is routinely aloof and silent in the group, became curious, his face became more interested and mobile and he began to interact with Marlene and the others. His mother and father had divorced when he was a child, and his mother had sent George to a nursery from which he used to escape and wander through the neighborhood. His characteristic style is a detached presence. For the first time he warmed up in the group and began to break through his own silence. The impetus for this change seemed to have come from his reactions to Marlene who was strongly committed to being a religious woman but who, at the same time, sought a romantic—but sexless—tie with a man.

As patients nearing termination or interruption of psychotherapy are working through conflicts, anxieties, and defenses relative to separation and loss, the midphase patients and the new members have a foretaste of issues they must work through. While the member who is leaving works through relinquishing dependency ties and gratifications, the members who are staying work through loss of the other and anxieties about death.

For example, when Elinor was leaving the group and we replayed a segment of the tape from that session, other members of the group associated to her relaxed posture and her smooth features. They pointed out how, when she had first been in the group, she had assumed a guilty posture, had a severely furrowed brow and down-turned mouth, and would shield her eyes from the group and look down and away. Her own association to herself at the outset of her therapy was that she was the "poor little matchstick girl." Her early family life had been characterized by a situation where her brothers were more important, where masculinity was more important and where her own artistic interests were rejected and considered worthless. The family related to her brother as the most important person, and even Elinor herself would often think of him as the most important man in the United States Government. She depreciated her own artistic productions, though they were well accepted publicly. While she had made major changes in her therapy and had become more open and relaxed, it was the replay of a tape showing her new behavior which enabled Elinor and the group to appreciate her dramatically different approach to people.

I see my role as therapist as one of friend, observer, and reservoir of certain expert information. My task is to provide understanding, to explain mental and emotional functions and connections; to relate the immediate to the historical, the conscious to the unconscious, the rational to the nonrational, the remembered to the forgotten, the real to the imagined. To this end I use confrontation, observations, interpretations, humor, serious advice, communication of my own associations, feelings, fantasies, or countertransference reactions in timely or selectively determined circumstances. There is no basic change in my approach from the beginning to the end of the therapy, though I am more informative and supportive in the beginning and work toward a less directive and less supportive role during midphase. At the terminal phase I am more visible and share more of myself with patients.

In my association with the patient I try to use every facet of myself selectively and discriminately as the patient works through various phases of establishing basic trust and faith in himself and in me; as he establishes a sense of discipline and independence, a capacity for competitiveness, creativeness, and for emulating others whose way of life he appreciates. The final aim is to help the patient effect a healthy separation and interaction of intrapsychic processes and an independent but humane interaction with those in his life who count. To accomplish this requires that I make myself visible. Such a requirement is quite the contrary of the classical anonymity and abstinence of the analyst. I allow patients to see my interests and my activities, while focusing on the transferences evident in their projections upon me.

The group provides the patients the basis for facing themselves and for self-esteem. It provides structure, expectations, sanctions, discipline, and authority which enable the patient to work through a new inner discipline and an outer functional autonomy. It provides models for men and women to work through a sense of sexual and social roles.

In the group I encourage the patients to verbalize ideas, feelings, and fantasies about me and each other—positive and negative, fanciful or mundane—and to use me and the others as they use a dream or dream symbol as an associative stepping-off point.

For example, during another session Harriet was discussing her conflict between staying with her husband or running off with her lover. She became instantly angry at LaVerne for "laughing at me." A replay of this segment of tape afforded an opportunity for Harriet, LaVerne, and the others to associate to LaVerne's response to this incident. The tape showed an anxious smile. LaVerne's own association was that this kind of smiling reaction was her only defense at her most anxious moments. She was highly concerned about Harriet and in no manner considered the incident humorous. At the same time, Harriet had seen the therapist as angry and unaccepting of her. The different members of the group had different associations to that section of tape and, in fact, the variety of emotions that were perceived in the therapist made it patently evident that they were, for the most part, transference projections. Each became able to see his own response to Harriet more dimensionally by associating to her reaction to LaVerne, and the therapist, and their own differential responses to the replay of the tape. That video techniques provide such stepping-off points is frequently evident. It was the case with Peter and his eyebrow pulling, or Marjorie and her fear of seeing herself on TV.

I am generally affable in the group and use a joke, a story, an association, an allegory, or metaphor to crystallize an intrapsychic event or an interpersonal exchange. I then ask the patients or group members to associate to my intervention. There is a constant focus on the responsibility of the patients to explore, expose, wonder about, associate to their own and other's productions. Eventually patients learn to step back and observe their own inner life and interaction patterns. Group members become involved in the analytic task with respect to both themselves and others. They learn that they are both helped and helpers. They de-idealize me, and in the process de-idealize themselves and discover they are neither as helpless nor as omnipotent as they had felt and fancied themselves.

Of the many things therapists do which are destructive to mental and emotional maturity of patients, the reliance on mystiques about group dynamics is most prevalent. The idea that some transcendent group forces will automatically be reparative is seen in know-nothing approaches to group work. I would classify as mystiques all approaches which do not focus on the individuals in the group selectively and differentially.

It is important to avoid interventions which are designed to extricate information from resistant patients. It is most important to encourage all members to share expectations, anticipations, dreams, hopes, fears about the therapist, the others, the group and therapy in general. The approach must maintain the individuality of each patient while fostering horizontal peer exchange. The therapist must subtly discourage attempts on the part of patients to reestablish a vertical, dyadic, therapeutic involvement and analyze the underlying motivations for this. There may be unconscious collusion of other group members in this attempt to establish a vertical involvement. The patients may sponsor each other in taking turns with the therapist rather than interacting. They may collectively ostracize one or another member or the therapist.

Most patients are consciously, positively motivated. The therapist can use group members' associations to new members, or to resistive silent patients, which will reveal anxiety and defensive processes of both the verbal and the resistive patient. The group will tame the monopolizer, as will observation of his nonstop talking on CCV or VTR.

While I am careful for obvious reasons to exclude patients who are dangerously acting out, if a patient becomes boisterous or destructive, I will encourage him to try something different. Whenever a patient is behaving in a manner resistive to the contract, I encourage him to try something different.

For example, I encouraged Megan to try and be purposefully silent at specific times during departmental social occasions rather than always trying to talk, though feeling unable to do so. At the same time I urged her to approach others in the campus coffee shop and initiate discussions with a direct communication of her loneliness rather than to feel like an ugly duckling and sit by herself.

The fearful patient is encouraged to listen and is asked frequently by me and then more by others in the group for his ideas, feelings, and associations. Often the group members will offer some of their own fears as encouragement and support.

The central theoretical focus of this chapter is the use of atypical media to accomplish sufficient ego functions and reflective ego capacity so that a therapeutic alliance can develop, and we can work through basic characterological problems. The psychoanalytic approach in groups is more thoroughly and extensively explained by Wolf and Schwartz (1962). The use of CCV and VTR has been described in detail by several authors and probably most thoroughly by Berger (1970).

The primary advantage of CCV and VTR is in developing these reflective ego functions. It is accomplished through: observing body and facial nonverbal communications which add dimensionality to or contradict verbal communications; study of physical and verbal response characteristics of the patient; the opportunity for new associations to previous thoughts, affects, and interactions; a new opportunity to elaborate, editorialize on, and extend one's own interactions, both verbal and physical; an opportunity for all to associate to behavior and speech as one would to dream contents or associative materials.

There are certain limitations to this approach. Theoretically the use of CCV or VTR constitutes the introduction of parameters which interfere with traditional psychoanalysis. Any group poses the same limitation. More realistic limitations are physical and economic. It is expensive to design space properly, accomplish the wiring, buy the equipment, pay for the maintenance, and, most frustrating of all, to put up with repeated mechanical failures. It is important not to waste precious therapy time in unnecessary review of VTR material, and to maintain sensitivity to the approach and not permit it to become a gimmick which wears off.

As we look to the future we can expect improvements in audiovisual technology which will provide our patients with audiovisual interpretations and confrontations more easily and economically in the group.

Perhaps circumstances will allow for every group member to have a control panel to select material for CCV display or instant VTR replay. With the advent of the videophone even patients in remote areas, or patients who are temporarily ill or out of town, can participate in the group therapy session over videophone. Perhaps one of the most common, and delaying, resistances to therapeutic procedure can be preempted. That is the "obviously" excusable absence at a time when a breakthrough is imminent.

REFERENCES

Berger, M. *Videotape Techniques in Psychiatric Training and Treatment*. (New York: Brunner/Mazel, 1970).

Cornelison, F. S., and Arsenian, J. "A Study of the Responses of Psychotic Patients to Photographing Self-Image Experience." *Psychiat. Quart.* 34 (1960):1-8.

Fairbairn, W. *An Object Relations Theory of the Personality* (New York: Basic Books, 1954).

Forrest, Tess. "The Paternal Roots of Male Character Development." *Psychoanal. Rev.* 54 (1964), 2.

Geertsma, R. H., and Reivich, R. S. "Repetitive Self-Observation by Videotape Playback." *J. Nerv. Ment. Dis.* (1965) 141:29-41.

Greenson, R. R. *The Technique and Practice of Psychoanalysis* (New York: International Universities Press, 1967).

McCarty, G. J. "Small Group Interaction and Perceptual Changes in a Perceptual Conflict Situation." *Perceptual Changes in Psychopathology*, W. H. Ittelson and S. B. Kutash, eds. (New Brunswick, N. J.: Rutgers University Press, 1961).

McCarty, G. J. Training Program for Delauney Clinic, Portland, Oregon, 1969.

McCarty, G. J. Training Program for Seattle Municipal Court Probation Services, 1973.

Rogers, A. H. "Videotape Feedback in Group Psychotherapy." *Psychother. Theory, Res., Pract.* 5, 1 (1968):37-40.

Saul, L. J. "A Note on the Telephone as a Technical Aid." *Psychoan. Quart.* 20 (1951):287.

Stern, M. M. "Therapeutic Playback, Self-Objectification and the Analytic Process." *J. Am. Psychoan. Assoc.* 18, 3 (1970):562-597.

Wolf, A. "Psychoanalysis in Groups: The Alternate Session." *American Imago* 17 (1960):101.

Wolf, A., and Schwartz, E. K. *Psychoanalysis in Groups* (New York: Grune & Stratton, 1962).

Wolf, A.; Schwartz, E. K.; McCarty, G. J.; and Goldberg, I. A. *Beyond the Couch: Dialogues in Teaching and Learning Psychoanalysis in Groups* (New York: Jason Aronson, 1970).

Wolf, A.; Schwartz, E. K.; McCarty, G. J.; and Goldberg, I. A. "Training in Psychoanalysis in Groups Without Face-to-Face Contact." *Am. J. Psychother.* 23, 3 (July, 1969):488-494.

31. The Existential Leader

RUTH C. COHN

Human experiences, behavior and communication are ordered by interactional and intercosmic laws. They are not isolated events but interrelated with all past, present and future persons, events, and particles in time and space. As humans we are both conditioned and free to choose; we are bound by natural law and bonded by existential postulates. Our effectuality and our maturity grow with growing consciousness. This paper deals with existential postulates and auxiliary guide rules as part of the theme-centered interactional method.

The theme-centered interactional method promotes awareness of existential postulates and uses auxiliary guide rules in their behalf. These guide rules have been derived from psychoanalytic concepts and experiential and Gestalt methodologies. They are used in living-learning groups which may be educational, therapeutic or organizational. The theme-centered interactional method is based on (1) reverence for life as an axiomatic belief and (2) the working hypothesis that in living-learning groups three constituent factors are to be regarded as equally important: the individual person "I"; the group as a collective entity "We"; and the theme "It" around which the group gathers. It is stipulated that these three factors command an equal share of the available effort.

A group is a group when the members participate simultaneously in awareness of a common focus—be it a feeling tone, a task, a perception, a theory: the theme. The relationship among each participant, the group, and the theme can be visualized as a triangle in concentric transparent globes; the "I" (the self), the "We" (the cohesive group), and the "It" (the focused-upon theme) are centered in the environmental human and time-space milieu. The process of skillfully balancing these three equally important factors makes for functional versus fractured or ineffectual group interaction. Such balancing and making the implicit existential postulates explicit in groups belong to the group leader's functions.

At some appropriate moment, within the first ten or fifteen minutes of introducing a workshop series or interactional group meetings, I say something like:

> Be the chairperson of yourself. Speak or don't speak—as you want to. Try to get from this session and give to it as much as you want to get and give. Be your own chairperson—follow your own agenda with regard to our theme or whatever may be in your way so you cannot relate to it; I will do the same.

Slowly, as the workshop progresses, the concept of "Being the chairperson of myself" becomes more apparent. A good chairperson has a well thought-through, relevant agenda, and works with respect for his own recognition of the situation and for the multiple attitudes of the committee members, the organization or the community they represent. As the "chairperson of myself" I chair my "inside committee" and get in touch with the various strivings of my inner self: my body's needs; the flow of my emotions; the flashes of thoughts, fantasies, ideas, intuitions, judgments, values, intentions; plans. I accept being as I am, which includes wishes for change; I am aware of my feelings and check my shoulds and impulses against my physical capacity and my judgment of what my environmental reality is and demands.

"Being my own chairperson" in an interactional group means to perceive and respect others, their personal psychological and physical givens, their own chairmanship and our mutual task. It means to take myself, you, and our pursuits seriously.

"To be my own chairperson" means to recognize myself as a unique psychobiological, autonomous being, defined within the limits of my body-mind, time-space existence, including my need for survival and self-actualization in the living-learning process. It also means to acknowledge my bonding with humankind and matter as an interdependent part and partner of the universe. Growth means to become increasingly aware of realistic givens concerning this partnership.

"To be my own chairperson" then means to recognize my limitations in energy and time bondage as an earthly human being. I am not omnipotent, nor am I impotent; I have limited potency. "To be my own chairperson" means to focus awareness on the reality of my wants and the givens of partnerships in which I can fulfill my life in interaction with my surroundings.

Except by violence nobody ever really "chairs another person"; we can only influence someone else's thoughts, feelings, values. Even inside the womb, the child has his own growing power and fortitude; when the infant is born, the mother can offer food, but the child chooses to swallow or reject; a teacher can offer and share—he cannot implement knowledge into the student. A priest cannot convey God, he can only state his own faith. Leaders are not the creators of groups, they can only be their optimal selves, using skills to guide the group —skills which include their ability to promote self-awareness, interaction, and a sense of individual responsibility for the participants.

Not to be aware or to pretend that I am not my own chairperson means to walk the illusory pathway between dependency which claims to be helpless, clamoring for powerful parent-like caretakers and detached autism which creates a fantasy world of nonresponsive and irresponsible independence. "To be my own chairperson" means to be aware of and to use the interdependence of give-and-take and the autonomy of accepting my own ability and responsibility in making choices.

If as a group leader I state the directive of "Be your own chairperson," I appeal to the participants' responsiveness and responsibility to make themselves aware of what each of us is, wants, can do. I am neither blindly "doing my own thing" nor submissively following an irrational "should." I am a whole human being endowed with the abilities of my body and cursed with its frailty; a human being who can enjoy a large scale of intense and subtle emotions and must endure their pain as well as their blessings; a human being who can think—connect and understand—and who has the ability and the perspective which reaches beyond my present here and now to memories of my past and the image of my future; and whose vision can ever reach beyond awareness of myself to encompass and anticipate aspects of the human and material world—today, yesterday, tomorrow.

The meaningful emphasis on the here and now is often misunderstood. Here and now does not exclude the impact of past experiences, psychodynamic connections, environmental conditioning, memories, or goals and anticipations. Here and now is the vantage point of perceiving, thinking, and doing—a pinpoint in time and space, overlooking and containing past and future by memory, by language, by motivation, in imagery, and vision. The denial of the importance of the there and then is as unrealistic as denying the immediate as the point of experience and moment of choice. The here and now fantasy life of trips by whiskey, train, drugs, sex, or rockets has no valid philosophical foundation; here and now can be as much of an escape as the there and then daydreaming of the unfulfilled child or the hallucinations of the insane.

The basic directive of "Be your own chairperson" is supplemented with such words as:

> Disturbances and passionate involvements take precedence: if you are unable to be concerned with what goes on in the group; if you are angry, bored, upset, preoccupied, excited, and can't get yourself to be interested in what the group is all about—please say so. Stating yourself this way helps you to get with the group and does help the group to know where you are at.

Disturbances, indeed, take precedence, whether such directive and "permission" is stated or not. Severe pain or exhilaration stand in the way of accomplishing interactional tasks. Strong antagonism or preoccupations may occur in any group member's consciousness and sap away concentration on the group's purpose. This is true for all meetings—in business, classrooms, government, and agency staff meetings —but it is rarely acknowledged in the work process (although major decisions have been made by such "absentee" voters). People pretend to work at their desks, put presence but not purpose into staff meetings, or eat their worries into physical symptoms. The impersonal university, factory, or office find themselves confronted with either accepting, submissive and pained, or rebellious and revolutionary people, whose frustration of not living fully fails not only the individual but also undermines the institutions they can build and uphold or destroy.

Openly giving precedence to disturbances and passionate involvements means nothing more than accepting reality and opening the flow of interaction to reinclude the absentee-participant.

The individual, his abilities, sorrows, and pleasures are of primary importance for the philosophical credo of the theme-centered, interactional approach.

Group phenomena are seen as reflecting the influence of participants on each other within given circumstances and activities. Group silence, group activity, group hysteria, group climate, etc., are based on the building bricks of separate persons. *The "We" of the group arises from centering around a theme (a subject, purpose, common feeling, task, etc.)*—be it the given stated theme, a subtheme or a feeling, or a sidetracking group concern. It is on the basis of this credo that the theme-centered, interactional system takes cognizance of and makes room for the reality of personal and interpersonal interferences. Instead of pushing disturbances underground, they are accepted as part of each individual's inalienable right to own up to his psychophysical reality and to share his disturbances or passions with the group. Such sharing more often than not is a sufficiently gratifying cathartic and communicative experience to free the participant to return with full concentration to his commitment within the group structure.

However, there are individuals with "permanent" disturbances or involvements which cannot be resolved through brief interaction. If a person cannot concentrate on anything but his preoccupation, group participation could only be fruitful if the theme of the group would coincide with his interest (such as "Marital Conflicts and Cooperation" or "Finding Myself in a Group," etc.). In such cases the disturbance of the individual, the "I," can no longer take precedence, because dealing with his permanent disturbance would then become destructive to the group and its theme; the group disturbance takes precedence over this (here) untreatable individual concern. In emergency situations, where a group has to come to a very speedy decision, a similar restraint of not staying with an individual's disturbance is sometimes necessary. The axiom of "Reality Takes Precedence" may help to make such a decision.

The amazing effectuality of the method's directives is rooted in the fact that they are not simply guidelines or skill rules but verbalizations of existential phenomena. They are existential postulates rather than ground rules. Their formulation combines the pragmatism of psychoanalytic experience (resistance, expression of fixated anxiety must be diminished before work on content can be meaningful) and the existential position that each person has a unique place in this world. I *am* my own chairperson whether I state it or deny it. I *do* give to and try to get from situations what I want—whether I admit to this or not; and whatever disturbances or passionate involvements are stronger than my task orientation do take precedence. These "directives" are as binding as the law of gravity. And *as awareness of gravity helps to build bridges and airplanes, so does awareness of existential directives help to choose more effectively within the realistic givens.* They are, in fact, when elevated into awareness, as practical and useful as the knowledge of physical laws. Flying against the law of gravity does not work. *Educational and social communication are doomed to failure if they do not recognize the axiomatic postulate of man's autonomy and interdependence—the "chairperson" rule.* Recognition of this existential postulate throws off the notion of the fictional dependency-authority seesaw in which teacher, priest, organizer, group leader, etc., are endowed with fictitious power, and students and other common men burdened with equally fictitious powerlessness. Neglect of emphasis on each person's own chairpersonship promotes empty authoritarianism. It misleads the person on top into perverting leadership into the "thinging" of people—and the person at the bottom into the pretense of "being chaired." *Creative dealing with reality, being my own guide, avoids the stagnant choice of either "living for the other" or "putting someone down"—both unrealistic games.*

Guiding participants toward awareness of existential givens, stating them as postulates, and restating them again and again to oneself is the enzyme in the living-learning process of growth. Regardless of where we happen to be and what theme we are focusing upon, we always—except in ill or comatose states—sense, feel, perceive, value, think, and choose. Training awareness of what is going on within and around me and choosing accordingly and directly is what "Be your own chairperson" tries to encompass; it is what most people take away from W.I.L.L.[1] theme-centered interactional workshops and keep in awareness, regardless of what the immediate accomplishment within the specific theme and task may have been.

The existential postulates in the theme-centered method are supplemented by practical (auxiliary) ground rules which support and fortify the major directives. These can be varied and multiplied to fit each situation, but require tact in their use; indiscriminate insistence on any rule damages the very spirit it is meant to serve.

AUXILIARY RULES

1. State yourself—speak for yourself, per "I"
rather than per "we."

REASONS: The editorial "we" of the "we believe," "one does," "everybody thinks," "no one should" almost always are hiding places.

The speaker does not take full responsibility for what he states. He employs public opinion or a nonsubstantiated majority vote to convince himself and the listener. If my statement is rooted in my own substantiated convictions, it does not gain by numeric support by others; yet, if I wish to get confirmation I must check out whether such confirmation is actually forthcoming. In workshops statements like "the group thinks," "we are all bored," "everybody disagrees with you," "nobody wants a coffee break" are more often than not fictitious. The rule to speak per I, and per I only, helps to avoid projections or avoid hiding personal creativity or failures.

2. *If more than one person speaks or wants to speak at the*
   same time, converse with each other on what you
   want to speak about.

REASONS: All the would-be speakers' concerns are ventilated this way before full group interaction resumes. A brief communication relieves some of each person's need to share and get the group acquainted with things that want to be said.

Through this procedure various autonomous decisions, between the would-be speakers, about communications come to pass; the sequence of speaking may be determined by the strength of need which becomes very clear; by the stronger response of other group members to one or the other statement; by finding common denominators in what is being said.

In any case, the brief communications between the would-be speakers provide the whole group with a variety of threads that may be picked up immediately and/or much later, rather than leaving a person either stuck and distracted with what he had wanted to say and didn't get to, or having him forget something that was important to him. The alternative, if no such rule is set, usually supports customary roles of being shy or outgoing, dominant or submissive, and encourages the leader or leading participant to decide who should speak first. This, in turn, arouses authority problems of submission or rebellion, or leads to apathy of noninteraction.

3. *Side conversations take precedence; they usually contain*
   very important things for the whole group. Would you
   try to share what you wanted to say with all of us?

REASONS: If group members direct their conversation to their neighbors rather than the group, they are likely to be highly involved in what they say. A person may want to say something important but feels too shy to do so; he may feel hostile to something that is going on and need help to state himself to the group; he may be out of the whole process and try to find reentry on a private track rather than to the whole group.

4. One at a time, please.

REASONS: Nobody can listen to more than one statement at the same time. Concentration on each individual and what is being said requires alternate communications. Group cohesion results from each participant being concerned with the same subtheme simultaneously. This rule primarily pertains to verbal expressions although often non-verbal communications, gestures, pairing, etc., are just as distracting as verbal statements and may best be picked up and brought into the mainstream. There are, of course, exceptions where this rule would not apply, such as when the group is split up in small workgroups, or when special encounter techniques with different rules have been introduced.

5. State yourself by making statements. Ask questions for
information only. If you ask such questions, also make
statements about what the questions mean to you.

REASONS: Only questions which ask for information are authentic. All other questions are statements in disguise. Authentic questions ask for information which is essential to pursue a subject further or to understand what has been said. Such questions are substantiated by stating why this information has been requested. More often than not, group members ask authentic questions which don't express requests for information but avoid communication of their own experiences or get involved in some inquisitive power-game. The questioned person, more or less aware of this situation, usually reacts defensively. He takes the question more seriously than it has been asked, and gets away from the theme-focused communication into a scapegoat question-and-answer game, or he plays one-upmanship, giving false response or counterquestions. Such procedures lead into an unproductive, defensive climate.

If participants make statements about their experiences and thoughts before or instead of asking questions, they inspire the flow of inter-action. People tend to respond to statements with communication of their own experiences and ideas. Authentic communication is contagious; so are defensive maneuvers.

6. *Be aware of what you really want to say or do;*
   not what you ought to or what you feel like
   saying or doing.

The word "want" in the theme-centered approach expresses the person's voluntary act of decision and choice among various strivings within the self, in awareness of the pertinent reality.

REASONS: What I *ought* to say or do lacks my own evaluative agreement or support by the given reality; it is based on blind conformity—be it with the group norm or my internalized, parental "should." What I *feel like* similarly lacks considered judgment, here with my own system of values and/or the given circumstances and environment.

Examples: I *ought* to stay in this group. I really don't *want* to. I *want* to use my time at home with my family. I *feel like* running out of this group. I won't because I really *want* to learn how to fight back.

7. *Postpone interpretation of others as long as possible;*
   give your personal reactions instead.

REASONS: Interpretations may be timely and correct or untimely or incorrect; if they are correct and timely they cement what needs to be said; however, if they are correct but premature or if they are incorrect, they arouse defensiveness and interfere with the forward process. On the other hand, personal authentic reactions induce reactivity and promote spontaneous interaction.

8. *Postpone generalizations.*

REASONS: Like interpretations, they are apt to stop the group process. They are in place only if a subtheme has been thoroughly discussed, and a change of subject matter is desirable.

While existential postulates are universally valid and, therefore, benefit us by continuous awareness, rules are aids, not absolutes. If you deify them and use them to subdue spontaneous exchange, you nullify their purpose.

NOTE

1. W.I.L.L. (Workshop Institute for Living-Learning). A training institute for groupleading, specializing in the theme-centered interactional method.

32. The Leader Using Object-Relations Theory

JEROME W. KOSSEFF

There are a considerable number of patients who are put in therapy groups nowadays because the individual therapist or patient—or both —feel that something else is needed to further the treatment process. There is a kind of puzzlement as to "what next?" can be done to make any further change in the patient's psychic status. The therapist may be frustrated, or worn down, self-questioning or even counter-transferentially resentful—or even worse—despairing; the patient waiting stoically, wondering what's wrong with him or his therapist, may find himself retreating and withdrawing emotionally from the treatment encounter. What to do?

Like other therapists, I have been faced with this predicament; and, as a matter of course, went through the usual self-examination and review of the case material, discussed the impasse with colleagues, but got little further ahead with the patient (Wile 1972).

In these situations, I have gone on, empirically, experimentally, and intuitively, with firm and patient determination that, somehow, some-thing had to work, and with fierce faith in both the patient and myself, to try various expedients, generally by mutual agreement with the patient. I have terminated individual treatment and placed the patient in a group of my own; placed him in someone else's group while continuing individual treatment; placed him in two groups at once, with or without individual treatment; attempted another treatment modality (such as hypnosis for specific psychosomatic problems) while in a group with me; or even interrupted individual treatment at various points for varying lengths of time, while continuing the patient in the group. Each of these procedures has produced some beneficial results in some cases, and has particularly led me to begin to seek for a fuller understanding of the difficulties encountered with these patients and how they got resolved.

The patients being referred to here are not the total body of those who have presented problems in treatment for me, nor was referral to group the only resource employed for all. I am focusing on a substantial number of "difficult" patients in my practice who fall into the designation "character disorders" (Giovacchini 1973; Kernberg 1970a), whom I suspect are fairly representative of the difficult patients encountered by other therapists, and for whom group treatment seems to have been a markedly facilitating modality. What, or where, or who was the logjam in individual treatment? What changed, and what facilitated further growth in the group situation? Why the instinctive reliance on group in these stubbornly resistive cases?

A few of the answers to these questions have been emerging, while others are still in the works. Those which I have to offer at this time seem to fall into these categories:

1. the need for a more inclusive theory of analytic group phenomena;
2. the need for a fuller understanding of the difficult patients mentioned above;
3. the need for a more comprehensive statement of the group's effect on such patients.

ISSUES AND DEFINITIONS

I shall proceed to discuss these categories in detail as we go along. Just now I shall indicate that the first issue will take up the possible value of object-relations theory for the understanding of group phenomena. The term "object" is used here in the analytic sense of the "whole person." It has unfortunate connotations, suggesting an inanimate object or a person treated as inanimate (for example Buber's "I-It"; woman as "sexual object"). Further complication has come from using it to describe both the real or external person and also the introjected image, the imago, of such persons. But it will be retained here because of its familiarity as the title of the theory. In personal communication, Harry Guntrip indicated his preference for "personal-relations theory" as the properly denotative title, but acknowledged the confusions involved in changing its already established name in the literature.

The second point of inquiry is also related to object-relations theory which, in reformulating analytic ego psychology generally, points to the centrality of a schizoid base for all psychopathology (Fairbairn, 1952, pp. 28-58). Possibly schizoid elements in such patients play a much more determining role in their negative therapeutic reactions than I had realized. The term "schizoid" will be used throughout as equivalent to "borderline personality organization" (Kernberg 1967, 1968, 1970b), but in the same special sense Guntrip does (1971, p. 173). It will refer more to a psychopathological undercurrent rather than to just a particular nosological entity visible in greater or lesser degree in many apparently diverse diagnostic categories, such as obsession, paranoia, psychosomatic problems, phobia, hysteria, and sexual problems. It is a postulate of object-relations theory that the schizoid position is the ultimate base dynamic on *all* psychopathology, and must be reached and worked through in treatment if full reconstructive change in the psyche is to be effected.

The pursuit of the third point of inquiry will bring this far-flung search back to solid earth—to the functions of the analytic therapy group. I shall offer the hypothesis that the therapy group performs a special service in our therapeutic armamentarium, of particular significance in the treatment of the patients just cited and generally in our culture at large: In the terminology of object-relations theory, the therapy group performs the service of "transitional objects" (Winnicott 1971). Briefly, a "transitional object" is one which is chosen as a special possession of the child, usually something soft and cuddly, and which serves as a beginning step in the differentiation of himself from his objects. "It is not the object, of course, that is transitional. The object represents the infant's transition from a state of being merged with the mother to a state of being in relation to the mother as something outside and separate." The "transitional object" is thus a first *creative* act by the infant, in finding a representation of the mother to hang onto, in helping him master his anxiety in the process of differentiation and separation from her. It is also a first effort in symbol formation, the rudiment of thought; and a first step toward play, the basis of all cultural activity, according to Winnicott (1971). It also has an *illusory* quality, since it is *both* mother and not-mother, *both* separated child and not-so-separated child. It occupies an intermediate position between the baby's inability and his growing ability to recognize and accept reality, with room in between for fluctuations in the proportions of mother-with-child or child-without-mother illusion as is necessary. There is the "illusion" that the mother or her breast is within the control of the child to the extent that she presents herself at the moment that the baby requires her. This is his inner realiy, which *at the moment* corresponds to the outer reality. The transitional object partakes of this illusion and also partakes of the beginning process of disillusionment when she is the not-so-available mother (Winnicott 1958, pp. 223-224). It is to this intermediate area between merging and individuation that Winnicott points as the "natural root of grouping among human beings" (Winnicott 1971, pp. 1-14).

This paper, then, will be restricted to one aspect of object-relations theory: its usefulness in looking at the analytic therapy group from a somewhat new, possibly additionally stimulating vantage point, and, hopefully, a vantage point offering the group leader more creative notions for encompassing its multifarious data. While it may appear an unseemly analogy to liken a therapy group to a scrap of smelly, dirty blanket, we shall see I hope that it is not so far-fetched as it may now appear, and it is far from a devaluing concept. In viewing the analytic group as a "transitional object," I am not merely referring to the frequent use of the group as a sort of "graduating class," following on completion of individual therapy, and intended primarily for re-socialization of the patient. Rather, I am seeking to focus the rays of object-relations theory down to a particular spot of light: the manner in which the therapy group may serve *both* intrapsychic and interpersonal functions at the same time, and to observe the many aspects of the "transitional object" embedded in the operations of the therapy group and its influence for change within the individual member.

OBJECT-RELATIONS THEORY

In order to properly assess the value of object-relations theory to the purposes and problems of analytic group therapy, we shall first have to review the essential principles of object-relations theory; this much review seems necessary both because American-trained psychoanalysts seem relatively ignorant of object-relations constructs, and also because these constructs seem at first somewhat mystical, compared to more classical ego-psychological concepts. This review of object-relations theory will involve (1) its view of the ego and its development; (2) its focus on the phenomenon of "splitting" of *both* object and ego under conditions of deprivation; and (3) the concept of infantile dependence in the form of schizoid manifestations as the fundament of *all* psychopathological conditions (rather than the Oedipus complex).

Object-relations theory is a British import, the principal figures in its development being Klein, Sutherland, Balint, Bowlby, Fairbairn, Guntrip, Khan, and Winnicott. The evolution of this theory has been amply and lucidly described by Guntrip (1971) and Kernberg (1970b). Suffice it to say that both attribute its beginnings to Freud's "putting ego analysis in the center of the field of inquiry . . . from Freud's ego and superego, through Melanie Klein's internal objects, projection and introjection, to Fairbairn's splitting of both ego and objects in relationship, and finally Winnicott's tracing of the absolute origin of the ego in the maternal relationship, we have a highly important view of what happens to the individual psyche under the impact of personal relations in "real life" (Guntrip 1969, pp. 312, 389).

> What is object-relations theory? In essence, it is the psycho-analytic approach to the internalization of interpersonal relations, the study of how interpersonal relations determine intrapsychic structures, and how these intrapsychic structures preserve, modify, and reactivate past internalized relations with others in the context of present interpersonal relations. Object-relations theory deals with the interactions between the internal world of objects (the internalized relations with others) and the actual interpersonal relations of the individual (Kernberg 1970b, p. 1).

More specifically, it is a way of understanding human behavior in terms of what the subject

> gives to, and takes from, the human relationship in any situation . . . from the most primitive "object" relations of infancy to the more interdependent relations of adulthood; . . . the ego constructs a body of experience relating to that balance of giving and taking, of satisfaction and control, which has proved to be viable in the person's relationship with others (Laing et al., 1966, p. 40).

The Ego, Its Development and Vicissitudes

Object-relations theory starts with the premise that the

> ultimate goal of the libido is the object; . . . the baby sucking his thumb seeks not only to provide for himself what he cannot obtain from the object, but to provide for himself an object which he cannot obtain. . . . It is a technique which originates in

an oral context, and which always retains the impress of its oral origin. It is thus intimately associated with incorporation of the object—which is, after all, only another aspect of the process whereby the individual attempts to deal with frustration in oral relationships. In view of this ultimate association it will be seen at the very outset that thumbsucking, as an autoerotic (and erotic) activity, acquires the significance of a relationship with an internalized object. It is no exaggeration to say that *the whole course of libidinal development depends on the extent to which objects are incorporated and the nature of the techniques which are employed to deal with incorporated objects* (Fairbairn 1952, pp. 31-34, 126).

To Fairbairn, erogenous zones are the channels by which the libido of the subject flows to the object, serving as energic means to the goal of object-relationships. Libidinal development, therefore, is no longer seen as biologically derived from instinctual sources, but rather based on the libidinal attitudes of the ego to its objects, that is the quality of its dependence—whether infantile, ambivalent or mature— on its objects. Consequently, the libido is defined by Fairbairn and Balint as the striving of the ego for good object-relationships; "not a thing-in-itself, but as the object-seeking drive of the primary natural ego or psychic self." Impulses are not psychic energies, but reactions of the ego to objects. Fairbairn viewed the ego as "a pristine dynamic ego," a giver. "The libidinal quest for objects is the source of the capacity to love, and the maintenance of loving relationships is the major self-expressive behavior of the total self." Thus, the aim of all human striving is "to be able to love in peace" (Balint 1968, pp. 65, 67; Guntrip 1961, pp. 288-290; 1969, p. 91). This view of the ego does not deny or minimize the biological bases of human behavior; rather it seeks to avoid the dichotomous biological-psychological difficulties that have beset classical psychoanalytic theory. It seeks to establish a unitary *psychological* theory of human behavior from the earliest moments of birth onward. "The key biological formula is the adaptation of the organism to the environment. The key psychological formula is the relationship of the person to the human environment" (Guntrip 1969, p. 18).

Object-relations theory begins with the notion of an infant beginning life with a basic unitary ego, whose functions are *adaptive* in enabling the child to seek satisfactions in and with objects according to the conditions of the environment, *integrative* in organizing the perceptions of its reality and in coordinating its behavioral responses, and *discriminative* between inner and outer reality. This ego is thus the primary organizing agent for human behavior, involved in making, maintaining and developing relationships with others. The ego develops not merely by *reacting to* and *adapting to* its objects, but also by *incorporating* aspects of its objects. "The basic drive to object-relations is at the same time the drive to self-development and self-fulfillment as a person. The importance of object-relations lies in the fact that without them the ego cannot develop" (Guntrip 1969, p. 91).

The first social relationship, of course, is that of the child with his mother, with the mother's breast as his initial libidinal part object and his mouth the beginning of a partial body ego. The energy for this first object-relationship is the need to receive and give love. Each of the two parties is both subject and object, and each enters into the other's personality by reactions, by introjections, and by projections (Guntrip 1961, p. 32). Grinker (1957, p. 382) amplifies this process of identification and beginning self-differentiation:

> . . . the infant internalizes the mother's image *and her concept of him as a recipient of care* [italics ours]. . . . There is not only an image of the object but also a mirror image of the object's attitude. Thus, personality structure is primarily organized from internalizations of social objects. . . . What is internalized is always a reciprocal interaction pattern of matched or complementary expectations. . . . This constitutes internalization of the parent-mother in her role as the source of care, and identification of that aspect of her with the self that has stood in a meaningful relationship. . . . Thus, introjection, as a psychological analogue of the biological prototype of incorporation, leads to internalization of subject-object transactions. . . .

This is the origin of "ego relatedness," the basis for ego-strength, and the capacity to tolerate separation from objects. If there is "good-enough" mothering, the infant internalizes the good object as the basis of a positive, confident self-concept, a "good me" and is gradually able to give up the experiencing of omnipotent control and adopt more mature sharing behavior with a "not-me" mother and others. This is the "true self," which collects together the details of the "experience of aliveness," out of which comes a sense of things being real, and the spontaneous gesture and the original idea—uniqueness of the individual. The "true self" develops as soon as there is any mental organization at all, develops complexity rapidly and relates to external reality by natural growth processes. The infant can then react to a stimulus without trauma because *"the stimulus has a counterpart in the individual's inner, psychic reality"* (italics ours).

Object-relations theory also attempts to discriminate *real* relationships in the outside world—the ego relatedness of the subject and the *actual* uses to which the object is put—from the internalized ego-object relations, the latter always consisting of only immature relationship patterns. Additionally it recognizes the difficulties inherent in being bound to such immature behavioral sequences on the unconscious level, while at the same time trying to cope with mature relationships consciously in the outside world (Guntrip, 1961, pp. 359, 360; 1969, p. 388). There is a constant interchange

> between the introjection of external objects and the projection of internalized objects. . . . The "inner world" is a psychodynamic legacy, compound of all the unsolved problems of disturbed ego development in infancy and childhood; it is a purely psychic world that the individual lives in, largely if not wholly unconsciously, where his lack of internal unity as a self is manifested in dreams, fantasies and symptoms, as experiences of highly emotionally charged relationships of parts or aspects of himself with internalized good and bad objects. In this "inner world," which is both withdrawn and repressed though it breaks into consciousness as pathological disturbance, a needy deprived infantile ego clamors for good objects, and an angry, sadistic infantile ego hates its bad objects, and the whole is shot through with fears of internal bad objects destroying internal good objects in fantasy, leading to depression and despair. This whole pathologically dynamic "inner world" is the active unconscious, and it masks the more secret phenomenon of the regressed, withdrawn, or even as yet barely evoked true or natural self, a potential self, awaiting a chance to be reborn into an environment in which it is possible to live and grow (Guntrip 1969, pp. 222, 409; Winnicott 1971, p. 88; 1965, p. 149).

Splitting

If, in the process of maturation, there are continuing deficiencies in mothering, the originally internalized "preambivalent," total-mother image is split into a "good-mother" image and a "bad-mother" image, "good" and "bad" here signifying degrees of satisfaction associated with each. The issue is not, however, merely one of lack of gratification from the "bad" mother. The insistent view of the object-relations theory is here most evident: it is rather that essential *ego experience* has been lost at a crucial developmental point, and it may be that very psychic deficit which later becomes the basis for feelings that "the world is a frightening emptiness when it does not respond and meet the infant's needs and a frightening persecutor when it actively and hurtfully impinges" (Guntrip 1969, p. 68). It is along in here that the fate of the ego is determined (Guntrip 1969, pp. 418, 421).

The first object, the total-mother image, is incorporated by the mutual interaction of mother and child, which involves also mutual identification. This incorporation of the total-mother image by the child becomes, therefore, by both introjection and identification processes part and parcel of the initial development of the child's ego (Kernberg 1966, p. 239; Mahler 1968, pp. 43-47). This being so, any splitting of this object, the mother image, automatically involves a parallel fragmentation and dissociation in the child's primary unitary ego connected with it, that piece of ego associated with the "good" (or idealized) mother splitting off in conjunction, and similarly with the 'bad-mother" image. Further splitting of ego and object parts takes place as maturation progresses, with "layering" and "fusion" of internal objects and their respective ego components into complex composite structures (Fairbairn 1952, pp. 123, 175), having much to do with psychosexual development and maldevelopment (Winnicott 1965a, p. 117). Each split object has attached to it a related split-ego segment. The unsatisfying aspect of mother is matched by a perpetually hungry part of the ego, the satisfying aspect of mother by an idealizing "central ego." The child is struggling to coerce his frustrating aspect of mother into a more satisfying response by internalizing her "bad" image—the real mother not being manageable—and dealing with it in his internal world of omnipotent control. His struggle has in it aggression, rage, and the intensity of his need of the mother. So we now have a split-object, a split-ego fragment, and the affect associated with this splitting process, all three associated as a unit.

These "units" (Kernberg 1970b, p. 16) of ego-object-affect are repressed, in order not to create further conflict in the outside world with the depended-upon, actual external object. A "central ego," manifesting compliant behavior with a neutralized object, may then be the observable external relationship, a "false self" united with a wishy-washy idealized image of the mother. At the same time, in the secret life of the inner world, these units of ego-object-affect are still clamoring for resolution of the frustrations which internalization did not truly accomplish. There is unfulfillment within each unit and conflicting demands between units; there is the continuing pressure from the central ego system to maintain the repression of these deeply internalized split systems. They are the "nonmetabolized" internal object-relations (Kernberg 1968, p. 604), which the psyche has not been able to "digest." To the extent that the aggression, which makes the object feel real and external to the self, does not get integrated with the libidinal (affectational, erotic, and intimacy-seeking) goals toward the object, there may be several malignant consequences: (1) the energy which is used for keeping these units in a "split" condition is available only limitedly for ego growth; (2) a situation of "ego weakness," manifested by feelings of inadequacy in handling life situations develops; and (3) various forms of sexual problems arise, depending on the proportions of conflicting aggressive and erotic drives toward the object.

Given the proper external situations currently evoking them, these archaic, internal, dissociated object-relations may erupt, be projected into the outside world once again, and be imposed on the human relationships existing there, the extent depending on the "closeness of fit" of the two worlds.

> Objects are only internalized later in life . . . by fusion with already existing internal-object structures. In adult life, situations in outer reality are interpreted in the light of these situations persisting in unconscious, inner, and purely psychic reality. We live in the outer world with the emotions generated in the inner one (Guntrip 1969, p. 23).

If sufficiently extreme, such eruptions may seriously affect the identity of self and the realistic recognition of others, these dissociated fantasy relationships leading to disruption of real dyadic and triadic relationships. Additionally, there is the apperceptive consequence that the outer world gets "to derive its meaning too exclusively from the inner world" (Fairbairn 1952, p. 18).

In treatment, such issues involving "not-good-enough" mothering are manifested by an unusual degree of primary identification, diffuse and primitive jealousies and projections, magical expectations and fears, and some impairment of object relationships (Greenacre 1971, p. 330). Evidence of splitting of the ego can also be observed when a person makes a simultaneous denial and acknowledgment of the same attitude, or displays abrupt shifts in his feelings in a seemingly contradictory way (Kernberg 1967, p. 667; Katan 1964, p. 241).

> An inner psychic world has been set up, duplicating an original frustrating situation, an unhappy world in which one is tied to bad objects . . . who will therafter dwell in the unconscious as an abiding fifth column of secret persecutors, at once exciting desire and denying satisfaction; and feeling therefore always frustrated, hungry, angry and guilty, and profoundly anxious, with constant temptations to seek transient inner relief by projecting it back into the external world (Guntrip 1969, pp. 22, 45).

The Concept of Dependence

Object-relations theory also suggests a more economic concept than the "repetition compulsion" to explain the tendency to cling to painful experiences; it is rather out of the relationship with bad, though nevertheless desired, objects:

> Patients cling tenaciously to their *external* bad objects because they represent *internal* bad objects whom they feel incapable of leaving. . . . The infantile ego cannot just give them up, for in that internal world it feels like being left with nobody at all. . . . Bad parents are better than none. . . . To part with internalized bad parent figures sets up two kinds of fear-reaction: it plays on repressed death wishes about the bad parent in childhood; arouses the unconscious feeling of having now destroyed this bad parent in the inner world, leading to guilt and punishment; it also creates the unconscious feeling of being now, for the first time in life, left utterly alone, bringing with it the fear of ego loss, of depersonalization, of dying, unless and until they are replaced by someone better" (Guntrip 1969, pp. 342ff).

It will have been evident also to the reader that Fairbairn has postulated as a basic dynamic of his object-relations, ego psychology: "the whole vast theme of the individual traveling from dependence to independence." He views this process as having three stages, the first being *infantile dependence*, which involves sucking, taking, or rejecting behavior towards the mother's breast in the early phase, or sucking or biting in the later stage. The early phase of infantile dependence is preambivalent, with total love. The later phase is characterized by ambivalence, the love-hate object being the mother with breasts, but not yet sufficiently differentiated as separate. The *transitional stage* is the second of the three major stages, in which active and persistent efforts at individuation are made. The final stage is that of *mature dependence* (where whole genital objects are related (Fairbairn 1952, pp. 38-39) (1). "Dependence vs. independence is the basic neurotic conflict. The person one turns to is the person one must get away from" (Guntrip 1971, p, 116). During this progression toward independence, integration of the ego takes place as the "unreal abstractions of separate good and bad objects are once more unified as different aspects of one real person, and then real people become real, and neither have to be ideal lovers nor sinister persecutors" (Guntrip 1969, p. 417).

The overall contributions of object-relations theory are already impressive. It has been of crucial importance in the understanding and treatment of severe forms of psychopathology in the diagnosis and treatment of severe marital crises; in sorting out observer influence on projective tests; in firming up the metapsychology of ego and super-ego formation; in providing particular criteria for (1) depth and stability of internal relations with others, (2) tolerance of ambivalence and temporary aggression toward loved objects, (3) capacity for tolerating guilt and separation and working through of depressive crises, (4) the extent of integration of the self-concept and its behavioral manifestations.

The possible contributions of object-relations theory to analytic group therapy are these:

1. Object-relations theory meets Anthony's (1970) criterion as a theory at once "developmental, dynamic, and inclusive of psychopathology."
2. It also meets Parloff's (1968) criteria as (a) based on the individual's uniqueness, yet (b) focusing also on the relationship of the individual with others, at least to the extent of the manner in which others are incorporated in the self. Admittedly, there is still a gap in a full theoretical statement of "I-Thou"-type relationships (Laing 1969, p. 7; Guntrip 1969, p. 389).
3. Object-relations theory is a "here-and-now" conceptualization; uses an energy concept, the libidinal goal of object-relationships; employs the notion of a central ego which is dynamically related to both "inside" and "outside" worlds, with a series of subsidiary, split-off, closed-off ego- and

object-segments, each in strong repressed relationship to the others. These aspects of object-relations theory meet the criteria set forth by systems theory.

4. Object-relations theory also meets G. Klein's (1969-70) requirements of a proper ego psychology: that it offer as constructs adaptational types of controls, rather than the more delimited defense-type controls, and that it shift from the narrower sexual and aggressive motives to a broader motivational base of human relationships generally.

5. Object-relations theory encompasses Bion's observations on the "basic assumptions group," on the fantasied dangers of incorporation-expulsion, the self-same dangers feared by the schizoid person in his personal relations, and thereby offers an emotion-bridge between the phenomena of the internal world of the individual and his functioning in the outside, group world. It offers a bridge, therefore, to span with the same constructs the multifarious data of individual development and dynamics and the dynamics of interpersonal life.

THE ISSUE OF THE SCHIZOID POSITION

Having come some way through this steamy jungle in the dark interior of the object-relations psyche, it is now time to move to the point of inquiry of this inner paper—the effort to better understand the dynamics of the patients with schizoid elements.

It has been a commonly accepted fact that in our time we are increasingly breeding a population of alienated personalities. "The plight of people in contemporary society as expressed in the experience of alienation, loneliness and lack of identity is presented clearly by patients in the group" (Ruitenbeek 1969, p. 342; Guntrip 1969, pp. 46-47, 62-63; 355; Scheidlinger 1964, p. 303). What we have to deal with in the patients I am discussing is a considerable range of behavior of varying degrees of severity of symptom and varying degrees of therapeutic readiness. In all of these cases we are considering the possibility of an underlying schizoid base (Winnicott 1965a, p. 59; 1971, p. 66), defined here as "the withdrawal of the libidinal ego from *external* objects, and the libidinal cathexis of *internal* objects" (Fairbairn 1952, pp. 50-52). Such a base consists

structurally in an early splitting of the ego, *aetiologically* in a reaction of intense oral sadistic libidinal need in the face of deprivation of mother-love, *dynamically* and *emotionally* in a refusal to risk libidinal object-relations in the outer world because of the terrifying dangers felt to be involved in loving and seeking love, and hence a radical introversion to the inner world. . . . "I can't make moderate demands of anyone, so I don't make any at all" (Guntrip 1961, p. 282).

We might interpret this last statement as meaning:

I don't expect to find anyone who can stand me" (Winnicott 1965, p. 218).

Schizoid dynamics have their origin in the child's experience of his parents not loving him in his own right, and/or in feeling that his love for them is not accepted. This conception of "nonloving" might come about either by deprivation of the child's needs or by overwhelming of the as yet weak ego by too soon or too great "impingement" on him. If, therefore, love doesn't work, he is left with the only two other basic emotions to relate with—fear and aggression—in seeking object-relations. "Yet the schizoid fear is not so much on behalf of the object as on behalf of the ego and the consequences to it of losing the object" (Guntrip 1969). The "tragedy" of the schizoid is, first, that he feels his love is destructive of those he loves. For example, when the mother cannot tolerate the infant's demandingness, his ego interprets her rejecting attitude and internalizes in the personalized mode: "My love is unacceptable because it is ruthless, greedy and destructive!" Or, he develops a compulsive reaction-formation to rejection and settles for an object-relation of hating and being hated, while all along he has the deep desire to love and be loved (Fairbairn 1952, p. 26). So he comes to feel driven to build defenses, not only against his love for others, but also against their love for him. He has some stake therefore in regression, in "not being found" and in not having to respond to the other or to be responded to. Yet, while he must remain hidden, it is disaster if he is not "found" or at least in some degree recognized.

The "false self," based on compliance, then becomes the vehicle which can handle these simultaneous needs to be part of, yet apart from. Winnicott (1958) calls the false self *"one of the most successful defense organizations* designed for the protection of the true self's core." The false self also involves a feeling of unreality and futility and "badness," even when sensually or realistically rewarding; while the products of the true self generally seem real and good, even if aggressive. This regression to the false self also has a positive side; it is *"a freezing of the failure situation"* at the point where environmental deprivation took place, making possible a return to it when conditions such as in the therapeutic relationship are ripe for reworking this unfinished bit of developmental business. "The mother holds a situation in time."

What happens as the child grows up into the adult more-or-less schizoid patient?

There are those oedipal-level patients who can "take in"; they can internalize the analyst and the tensions of the working-through process. There are others who cannot, but rather "spit out"; they resort to externalization as a defense, using such devices as splitting, acting-out, projection and projective identification, primitive idealization, self-idealization, confusion, denial, and depersonalization. These and another group of patients who *seemingly* "take in" anything and everything in the therapeutic process while somehow "their innermost self remains largely uninfluenced by it, are . . . among the many patients who are described as 'deeply disturbed,' 'profoundly split,' 'seriously schizoid,' 'having a much too weak or immature ego,' 'highly narcissistic,' or suffering from 'a deep narcissistic wound,' and so on" (Balint 1968, p. 12).

Kernberg (1968, 1970b) prefers the term "borderline personality organization" to denote their remarkably stable pathology which, while located between neurosis and psychosis, does not fluctuate between the two.

Patients described in these terms are the ones Balint refers to as suffering primarily from pre-genital fixations, which he prefers to call "the basic fault." "Basic" refers to the two-person psychology involved in their dynamics, compared to the more complex three-person psychology of the oedipal-level patient. "Fault" differentiates their psychic dilemma from that of a conflict and signifies that the patient himself feels something is wrong inside him that has to be put to rights, and the fault is there because "somebody has either failed the patient or *defaulted* on him." In treatment, this emerges as a great anxiety that the therapist *must* "find him and reach him, that is, not fail him," since he cannot himself open himself to view. This fixation in and preoccupation with inner reality is the hallmark of the schizoid personality, however much there may be masking of the essential isolation and detachment by a "false self"; indeed, there are many disguises behind which the schizoid aspect is concealed; inner reality may be substituted for outer reality, identified with it or super-imposed on it (Fairbairn 1952, p. 76; Balint 1965, p. 21; Guntrip 1969, pp. 105-106, 1971, p. 185). An additional complication is that in this two-person relationship, only the subject matters; the object is felt as most powerful, but is recognized only to the extent that he does not fulfill his needs, the patient responds by feelings of emptiness is an intense oral aggressive aspect in his functioning. If the analyst does not fulfill his needs, the patient responds by feelings of emptiness and futility. He may discount good things as chance occurrences, but frustrations are invariably interpreted as maliciously inspired. At the same time, he "is capable of differentiating the self from external per-ception, and reality testing is also preserved to a major extent. This capacity is lost, however, during transference regression" (Kernberg 1968, pp. 606-607). The comparatively good differentiation of self from object which obtains sufficiently under ordinary circumstances becomes subject to projective identification and refusion with idealized objects, with resultant anxiety and withdrawal from close interpersonal involvement. While deficient in feelings of guilt and concern over objects, these patients are liable to erupt with various forms of ex-pression of primitive and impotent rage reactions and feelings of defeat, but this is "love made hungry," the schizoid position with its essential emptiness and futility, rather than "love made angry," the depressive position with its guilt, ambivalence and rage (Kernberg 1967, pp. 664-673; Guntrip 1969, p. 24). At the same time, internalized bad object images of a sadistic kind are intolerably punitive, and have to be reprojected as external bad objects, especially in their demanding and prohibitive aspects. This tendency to devalue objects then inter-feres with acceptance of realistic demands from actual parental images, and with internalization of the parents as valid superego images.

These patients tend to be exploitative, unreasonably demanding, tactlessly manipulative and inconsiderate. Their sexual behavior, since it has intermixed pregenital and prematurely genital features, has al-ways an aggressive coloration. Their self-preoccupation and narcissism represents a "primitive fusion of idealized self and object images, used against the 'bad' self- and object-images, and the 'bad' external objects." This results in a lack of stable object relationships in relation to the self, Erikson's "identity diffusion" (Kernberg 1967, pp. 676-677). With other real people, the tendencies to identify with the love object and also with the object of aggression lead to constant oscillation of roles. It is equally as frightening to be like the other one as to be different, because likeness threatens to destroy the self, and difference the object (Jacobson 1964, p. 69).

The Dilemma of the Schizoid Patient and His Therapist

This brings us to the issue of therapy. Many writers have particularly focused on these sticky issues of the treatment of borderline patients. Their work has been well summarized by Kernberg (1968, 1970). I shall therefore attempt to concentrate our attention on those difficulties in treating schizoid patients that specifically suggest referral for group and shall try to begin framing these difficulties in object-relation terms.

Most of the difficulties in treating the schizoid or schizoidlike patient may be best described as originating in the dynamic bipolarity of their personality structure, in the constant oscillation between "keeping in touch" and withdrawing from real objects, this oscillation reflecting the same struggle going on within. This bipolar behavior is simply *the fear of, and wish for, both merging and emerging,* in relational terms. Let us keep this particular bipolarity of "merging-emerging" in mind, as we summarize the problems of treatment.

In treatment, the first issue we encourage with such a patient arises out of his desperate struggle to preserve his ego. We have seen that his ego regression began when he felt the failure of his parents to love him for himself, as a separate person. This was the failure of his environment to be sufficiently "facilitating" and provide the proper conditions, in the form of human relationships, for his psychic maturation. Since he is in no position to flee physically from this cold and unloving world into which he has been born and on which his growth depends, he resorts to the only avenue open to him: he retreats in fear into the inner psychic world where he may once more hope for a better growth situation, or at least a lessening of the deprivation.

But he is there confronted with an insufficiency again. He is trying to build anew a sense of self-regard, *but he has only the old building-blocks—the ego aspects already internalized from his deprived environment—with which to work.* He has "burned his bridges" behind him by premature repudiation of dependence and withdrawal out of fear, and he is now faced with the threat of personal dissolution, the loss of himself as a self, unless he can somehow control the internalized situation. He hates himself to the extent he goes on seeking love from others, since this makes him feel weak; so he attacks himself, tries to smother his desire to go on seeking love, setting up a sado-masochistic struggle inside himself. The paradoxical situation he then has to deal with is the denial of his own natural desire for intimate, loving relationships with a sort of sour-grapes false pride: "Who needs people, anyway?" This, then, is the vicious cycle into which his efforts to protect and help himself in the face of emotional adversity bring him. Neither the real people of his life, nor his internalized people are satisfying his craving for affectional exchange; he cannot get the love he requires either in the real world or in his incorporated world, since there are the very same depriving, frustrating people in both. He has turned away from them in the real world, hoping to find better inside; but to his dismay, finds himself once more faced with them just as he has always known them. While restrained by fear of further loss of love if he vents his rage in real life, he now can let loose the primitive, intense rage and hate on them as internalized images. But these internalized images are him also, the beginnings of his own ego structure, his self. So he is now taking out on himself what he had wanted to do to the real deniers of love in the outside world, but dared not do openly. It is the self caring for the self as a good mother, and the self punishing the self for exposure to the threat of additional humiliation and destruction by any further reaching out for love. In this way, the substantial residue of infantile dependence which has never been satisfied is repressed, but remains as an early false foundation on which the later aspects of the psyche build.

This "weakness" of his structure is largely denied by the schizoid person, who prefers to see himself as "bad" rather than "weak." To be "bad" implies strength to him, since "bad" has by now assumed more of an aura of false independence and self-sufficiency. To be "good" means to be weak, dependent on others for love, and this has by now acquired a repugnant quality of self-abasement. Similarly, he seeks out situations where he can test out his capacity for anxiety and temporary relief when it is felt, since pain proves to him that he is still real and has boundaries as an individual, and that he has not disintegrated. In object-relations terms,

> We see in our patient a "central ego" (the false self), delibidinized and dealing with outer reality, and a "regressed ego," the secretly preserved libidinal core of the self, and the intermediate internal world of bad objects he clings to as a compromise between the other two aspects of the self; this compromise solution prevents

the total loss of his objects and the world of reality on the one hand, in psychosis, or the loss of himself by depersonalization, on the other (Guntrip, 1962).

The first issue in treatment is then the provision of a real and good object in the person of the therapist, if the patient immersed in the struggle to preserve his ego is to have a lever by which to pry himself loose from his internal quagmire. The therapist has been approached initially as one who holds the promise of knowledgeable intervention in the patient's predicament. But, while the patient has sufficient appraisal of reality to engage the therapist, there may be either magical expectations of the therapist initially, or unconscious transferential reasons for choosing this particular therapist, or later evocation of negative transferential reactions to the therapist of sufficient potency to get in the way of straightforward use of the therapist. There may, of course, also be ways in which the therapist collaborates with the patient in this.

Resistance and Dependence

Individual treatment bogs down for such a patient because he cannot readily use the analytic situation for true uncovering and instead resorts to a kind of clinging behavior, but with fear of the dangerous closeness involved. Or, he might, equally obsessionally, avoid further transference regression and withdraw emotionally from the analyst. At the same time, simple supportive treatment is likely to fail with him, too, because of the investment such a patient has in avoiding a working alliance (Balint 1968, p. 72). Transference resistance becomes massive because of the patient's fear of reactivation of his profound dependency needs and also because of the fear he had that the analyst would function independently of him should he allow his dependency needs full expression. "It is as if the patient's life depended on keeping the analyst under control" (Kernberg 1968, pp. 601, 605). This happens when the therapeutic regression leads back to the more primitive identification and introjection mechanisms that interfere with the observing ego. The patient therefore is certain that his "absolute badness" will show, that his rage and envy will erupt and destroy the very one he counts on so heavily. His feeling of inequality with the analyst in the one-to-one situation results in immobilizing hate as a result of his dependent formulation of the relationship. He fears "being taken over" by the analyst, with the resultant dangers of being exploited, mistreated, frustrated, and humiliated (Bergmann 1966, p. 25; Kernberg 1968, p. 605). In object-relations terms

> rapidly alternating projections of self-images and object-images representing early pathological object relationships, produce a confusion of what is "inside" and "outside" in the patient's experience of his interactions with the therapist. This is a frightening experience which reflects a breakdown of ego boundaries (Kernberg 1968, p. 607).

The patient is seeing the fantasy images of his bad parents once again arising to haunt him in the person of the analyst; but paradoxically at the same time he is fearful that the analyst will rob him of these bad parents, the only ones he truly has (Guntrip 1969, p. 344). Or it may be put another way:

> the danger area that is arrived at sooner or later in all psychiatric treatments, the patient having felt secure and viable because of the analyst's reliability, adaptation to need, and willingness to become involved, and now feeling a need to shake free and to achieve autonomy; . . . the patient cannot become autonomous except in conjunction with the therapist's readiness to let go, and yet any move on the part of the therapist away from a state of being merged in with the patient is under dire suspicion, so that disaster threatens (Winnicott 1971, p. 107).

> Bad self cannot understand a good not-self until stronger boundaries are reconstituted (Grinker 1957, p. 386).

Also, to the extent these patients are narcissistic, they need to defeat the analyst, not being able to acknowledge having received help—something good from someone—because of intolerable guilt over their own aggression that would be evoked if they did acknowledge the help (Kernberg 1970a, p. 67).

THE GROUP AS TRANSITIONAL OBJECT

For a substantial group of patients, referral to analytic group therapy seems to bring about movement in their treatment and improvement in their functioning, both of which had been lacking for a considerable time in their prior individual treatment. The notion of the "group as a transitional object" (3) was advanced as an economical and provocative explanation for these changes. Let us see, now, how our previous understanding of object-relations theory and of the schizoid position can provide further understanding of what has happened *to* and *in* these patients prior to and after referral to group and what it really means then to describe the group as a "transitional object."

We have seen that the patients we are discussing have been somewhat more than the rest of us stuck in that intermediate stage of personal evolution Fairbairn called the transitional stage (Guntrip 1961, p. 291), the second of his three-stage description of the individual's growth toward "mature dependence." Characteristic of this stage is that the self has not as yet become "separated out" from its objects. We conclude from this that usual individual therapeutic efforts have stalled at the very same point in the transference as the original childhood situation, where the enormous fantasy fears of the patient destroying the object while seeking to emancipate himself from it are so compelling that he is forced to retreat in confusion into himself, becoming unclear as to who is subject and who is object. Were he able to trust in his self and his therapist enough, he would chance the awful catastrophes of his inner fantasy world whereby he could destroy the therapist by his omnipotence and in the process lose himself. Could he allow this fantasy free reign, of course, he would learn that his therapist and his own self would survive what was only a fantasy; he would learn that they were separate individuals, both real and true ego- and object-relatedness could begin for him (Winnicott 1971, pp. 86-94).

But it is precisely because he is frozen with fear of the awful consequences of his inner fury, precisely because he cannot risk the freeing of this "anti-libidinal ego" on the therapist, who is still viewed as part of him, that he remains immobilized.

> If the Regressed Ego can be saved from fear and helped back to secure relations with the outer world, the intermediate "closed system" of the inner world loses importance and fades. It is outflanked. The need in psychotherapy is to safeguard the Central Ego against breakdown while the Regressed Ego is being reached and its rebirth to active life fostered. . . . The two major obstacles to psychotherapy are the patient's antilibidinal fear and hate of his Regressed Ego, and therefore of the therapist who offers help to it, and his fear that his Regressed Ego, if allowed the security of a relationship to a Good-Object, will betray him into abject infantile dependence (Guntrip 1962, p. 187).

This is where the group can become the opportune agent of change for the adult patient, much as the scrap of blanket serves the infant. Patient and child are both engaged in the strenuous business of beginning moves toward separation and autonomy. There are many analogies in the two situations; the child's transitional object is generally his first self-chosen *non-me* possession, and "serves as a bridge between what is comfortably familiar and whatever is disturbingly unfamiliar. It facilitates the acceptance of the latter" (Greenacre 1971, p. 316). Similarly, the group becomes the transitional object for the patient, who is seeking to emancipate himself from his symbiotic tie to the therapist. The similarities can be detailed as follows:

1. The group is a tangible representation of a relationship between the patient and the therapist; it, like the child's blanket, has attributes of and connections with both of them, yet is neither one solely nor just the two of them alone. It thus has the security value for the patient of a part of himself that has already experienced a modicum of trust in the therapist and a glimmering awareness of the possibility of a new kind of self relatedness. Whatever beginning evocation of the hidden true self (the "repressed ego") the patient has already experienced in individual treatment with the therapist carries over into the group. Also, the patient is able, at least to some degree, to retain the illusory security prop of feeling the therapist still under his control in some degree.

2. The group carries the notion of some degree of separation from the therapist and may well represent to the patient the beginning of that combination of support and freedom which he did not or could not experience in previous dyadic relationships, with resultant arrest in personal growth. The act of being placed in the group by the therapist conveys to the patient that he is not necessarily so bound to his early objects; he also feels that the therapist has confidence in his ability to function in the "outside world" of the group. Group placement represents to the patient a hopeful sign, "a tangible symbol of a relationship undergoing change" (Greenacre 1971, p. 352), just as the blanket represents, in part, emancipatory possibilities.

3. The group is a bulwark against too great feelings of frustration, perhaps interpreted by the patient as punishment for his efforts at autonomous functioning in the individual analytic situation and offers the support of other members as an alternative. This is analogous to the child's transitional object as a source of comfort when the mother

is absent, or defaults in some way in her role, or attempts to rebind the child to her.

4. The group provides a"space between" the therapist and patient and makes an area of freedom for the patient to fill creatively (Winnicott 1971, p. 108). He may use the group as he chooses, playing roles with other members with a spontaneity and variety he may not have experienced in individual treatment. The plasticity of the group situation enables the patient to move back and forth between security and experimentation with himself, resting where he is or moving on as he is ready to do so. In contrast to the frozen rigidities of his individual relationship with the therapist, the patient is able to relax or tighten up his relationship with the therapist in the group, splitting his transferential identifications as he needs to.

5. The group may serve as a "convoy" in a patient's efforts to deal with his internalized bad objects via a new approach to the therapist in the group situation. This is again like the child venturing with his transitional object into the world of "me-without-mother," and returning with added independence to revise his relationship with mother.

6. The group as a "good-enough facilitating environment" provides a cushion against the enormous shock to the patient as he begins to give up the omnipotent fantasy that underlies his tie to the therapist. The group then substitutes for, and also denies the possibility of controlling the therapist. The patient who had all along clung to omnipotent fantasies as a defense against profound fears of helplessness has now the possibility of group encouragement and support in discovering that his fears are unwarranted. The child does the same thing when he takes his transitional object with him and leaves mother behind.

7. As the patient gives up his omnipotent fantasy with the therapist, with the help of the group, he becomes more able to differentiate reality from unreality, his own actual capacities from fantasied ones. Boundaries between group leader and patient become firmer and more real.

8. The group as a transitional object "absorbs neglect and even abuse as well as the most loving closeness; responds sensitively to the impulses and needs of its infant owner; and so in general makes strangeness and solitude more acceptable. . . . It is both the recipient and the donor of tender feelings . . . which is a step in object relatedness" (Greenacre 1971, pp. 316, 333, 336). The group promotes the

emergence of a "larval self" from the boundness to the therapist, and facilities the sense of mastery of self as the patient experiments with objects in a new way. Giving and receiving empathy, reassurance, understanding and self assertion in the group leads to freeing of impulses and capacity for greater closeness. The paralyzing rigidity of schizoid, outwardly compliant, inwardly resistant behavior in the individual treatment situation gradually gives way in the group to greater ego- and object-relatedness.

These analogies between child and patient demonstrate how it is possible to regard the group as a transitional object. Perhaps the way in which object-relations theory meets the need for a group therapy theory that would deal with both individual and group dynamics is best seen by a comparison of concepts. Wolf (1969, p. 70) says of the group patient:

> As he gradually becomes able to dispose of compulsive investments and discerns group members in fact, they become the *social bridge* [italics ours] to the establishment of normal communal relations.

By comparison, in similar terminology, Greenacre (1971, pp. 344-345) says of the child's transitional object:

> By its very plasticity the transitional object allows associative relatedness to many external objects . . . *a multidirectional bridge to external objects* (italics ours) which may provide further appropriate stimulations . . . which may then be represented in apparently random playful activity. . . . Play, which then gains the value of primitive experiment and reality testing, leading to knowledge . . . seems to precede each new maturational achievement. . . .

We can see here that both quotations are descriptions of a process of change in the individual, but that the former is a view of him from outside, while the latter is a view from within, not only of what happens *to* the person, but what happens *in* the person. Object-relations theory, represented here by its specific concept of the transitional object, delineates the way in which interpersonal relations get translated into intrapsychic structures, which in turn affect the interpersonal relations through the introjective-projective mechanisms.

The key concept in viewing the group as a transitional object is that of *identification.* We are speaking of patients for whom there has been no sufficiently reliable mother-figure to relate to and identify with, at a time in their development when this deficit led to a corresponding damage to ego growth and strength. The mother was incorporated as an ambivalent figure, at best, with emphasis on the destructive aspects of her behavior with the child. The child's identification was split, and the feared mother was taken in in two ways: "the child-as-unworthy-of-mother's-love," the weak image of self, and compensatorily, "the child-as-mother-who-can-do," the strong image of self. But this latter part of the split reacts then to the depriving mother with rage. The fear of destruction of the mother is fused with fear of the destruction of the self by the mother. It is the mother's destructive potential squared. The whole relationship is then so colored by its destructive potential that the child comes to view himself as mostly destructive and dangerous. The extent to which the mother is supportive and facilitating is submerged by the intolerable guilt over rage at her. The capacity for concern for others which arises from feeling cared for by the mother in a continuing way is hidden from the observing ego beneath the weight of the negative views of self. In the individual treatment of the schizoid patient, the fear of his destructive potential toward the therapist again becomes uppermost and becomes a formidable block to further exploration when the transference progresses far enough. This is especially true when the individual analyst fails to recognize the overwhelming fear the patient has of his own destructiveness and fails to help the patient by focusing first on the constructive and positive feelings the patient has towards him. Only then would the patient be able to face consciously and explore fully this destructive set of feelings. Sometimes too even the most careful efforts by the analyst to emphasize the real positive sides of the patient are insufficient to overcome the patient's enormous fears, since the person from whom this positive view of self is coming is also not to be trusted (Winnicott 1965, pp. 73-82).

In the group, this "single-parent anxiety" (Wolf 1969, p. 95), the fear of destroying the individual analyst, is mitigated. The continuity of the group, the possibilities of multiple and partial identifications with other group members, the exposure of others' similar attitudes, the feeling of therapeutic relationships with more equality in them, the acceptance of both positive tender feelings and of destructive ones also make it different for the schizoid patient. It is no longer "an environment empty of support" (Guntrip 1969, p. 106), which he had to view the individual treatment situation as being, whether or not it was so.

The group's value as a transitional object lies, then, in its facilitation of healthy identification processes. It can help the schizoid patient (1) shift from a set of internalized split-images of self to a more unitary representation of self by identification with other group members; (2) shift from the part-object seen as if it were the whole object (the therapist seen solely as destroyer) to the whole object seen as whole (the therapist as caring, neutral, and facilitating) (Grinker, p. 384); (3) shift from fears of being engulfed by the therapist to gradual recognition through other group members that this cannot happen because the group leader is not so powerful, and because they, by sharing him with the patient, interfere with the patient's longing for fusion. The group helps the patient let go of primitive idealizations of the therapist and his omnipotence by pointing out both the reality and the shortcomings of the therapist. As the patient is able to face these less positive attitudes toward the therapist, he is able "to change places" with him and see himself in a more worthwhile light. Where the patient in individual treatment would tend to overlook differences between his view of the therapist and the reality of the therapist, the other group members jar the patient's efforts at continuing pathological identification with the therapist or themselves and force him to acknowledge, and ultimately accept, his differences from others. Where the therapist's relative silence in individual treatment may tend to foster such pathological identification, visible group behavior and interaction force objective recognition of differences. What had been a sealed-off, dead-end identification with the therapist, a giving up of the real object and a substitution of an internalized, possibly idealized object, along with a giving up of the real potentialities of the self in favor of a false compliant self, now gives way to a recognition of the self as good and different from others. As the danger of fusion and immolation with the therapist subsides, the patient develops the hope and possibility of separation and true individuation. The possibility of coming unstuck, of renewing the process of growth, and of assimilating whatever aspects of identity from the therapist and other group members that can be real for the patient becomes once more possible.

Also, the splitting process might have been reactivated as a defense against closeness and being swallowed up in the individual treatment situation. In the group, it is halted by the fact that there are already multiple aspects of the self visible in the transferences to other group members, and the diffusion of self is guaranteed for a while. It is possible now for the patient to "integrate his disparate fragments" (Guntrip 1969, p. 311).

We may summarize this identification aspect of the group as a transitional object by saying that, when "one person functions as a group of persons" (Guntrip 1961, p. 138), accepting all of them as one person may not occur until there can first be a group of people to be one person, and only then can one person function more truly as one person. Oftentimes after the group has served a transitional purpose for the patient, the patient will return for more intensive individual treatment, functioning now on a more oedipal level.

NOTES

1. See also Mahler 1968, pp. 45-46; Greenacre 1971, pp. 329-333; Kernberg 1970, p. 23; Winnicott 1965, p. 88, for a rough chronology of the "normal" developmental sequences in psychic change and internal structure formation.
2. Yet it should be kept in mind that out of even this limited two-person psychology, given "good-enough" mothering, the "capacity for concern" for others eventually develops (Winnicott 1965, pp. 73-82).
3. This title has no mystical meanings. It is simply a succinct description of how the therapeutic group may be seen as serving the total needs, intrapsychic and interpersonal, of its individual members.

REFERENCES

Balint, M. *Primary Love and Psychoanalytic Technique* (New York: Liveright, 1965).

Balint, M. *The Basic Fault: Therapeutic Aspects of Regression* (London: Tavistock Publications, 1968).

Bergmann, M. S. "Processes of Internalization." Paper presented at the Postgraduate Center for Mental Health, New York, 1966.

Bergmann, M. S. "Psychoanalytic Observations on the Capacity to Love." *Separation-Individuation* (New York: International Universities Press, 1973).

Bowlby, J. *Attachment and Loss, I: Attachment* (New York: Basic Books, 1969).

Boyer, L., and Giovacchini, P. L. *Psychoanalytic Treatment of Schizophrenic and Characterological Disorders* (New York: Jason Aronson, 1967).

Cary, G. L. "The Borderline Condition: A Structural-Dynamic Viewpoint." *Psychoanalytic Review* 59, 1 (1972): 33-54.

De Mare, P. B. *Perspectives in Group Therapy* (London: Allen & Unwin, 1972).

Durkin, H. *The Group in Depth* (New York: International Universities Press, 1964).

Durkin, H. "Analytic Group Therapy and General Systems Theory," in Sager, C. J., and Kaplan, H. S., eds., *Progress in Group and Family Therapy* (New York: Brunner/Mazel, 1972), pp. 9-17.

Ezriel, H. "Notes on Psychoanalytic Group Therapy: Interpretation and Research." *Psychiatry* 15 (1952):119-126.

Fairbairn, W. R. D. *An Object-Relations Theory of the Personality* (New York: Basic Books, 1952).

Fried, E. "The Effect of Combined Therapy on the Productivity of Patients." *International Journal of Group Psychotherapy* 4, 1 (1954):42-55.

Fried, E. "Some Aspects of Group Dynamics and the Analysis of Transference and Defenses." *International Journal of Group Psychotherapy* 15, 1 (1965): 44-56.

Fried, E. "Basic Concepts in Group Psychotherapy," in Kaplan, H. I., and Sadock, B. J., eds., *Comprehensive Group Psychotherapy* (Baltimore: Williams & Wilkins, 1971), pp. 47-71.

Fried, E. "Individuation Through Group Psychotherapy," in Sager, C. J., and Kaplan, H. S., eds., *Progress in Group and Family Therapy* (New York: Brunner/Mazel, 1972), pp. 66-82.

Ganzarain, R. "Object-Relations Psychoanalytic Theory Applied to Group Therapy: On Intrapsychic Changes." Paper presented at the 29th American Group Psychotherapy Association Conference, New York, 1972.

Glatzer, H. "Working Through in Group Psychotherapy." *International Journal of Group Psychotherapy* 19 (1969):292-306.

Giovacchini, P. L. "Character Disorders: with Special Reference to the Borderline State." *International Journal of Psychoanalytic Psychotherapy*, 2 (1973): 7-36.

Goldman, G. "Some Applications of Harry Stack Sullivan's Theories of Group Therapy." In Ruitenbeek, H. M., ed., *Group Therapy Today* (New York: Aldine-Atherton, 1969), pp. 58-66.

Greenacre, P. *Emotional Growth, I* (New York: International Universities Press, 1971).

Grotjahn, M. "The Qualities of the Group Therapist," in Kaplan, H. I., and Sadock, B. J., eds., *Comprehenhive Group Psychotherapy* (Baltimore: Williams & Wilkins, 1971), pp. 757-773.

Grotjahn, M. "Learning from Dropout Patients: A Clinical View of Patients Who Discontinued Group Psychotherapy." *International Journal of Group Psychotherapy* 22 (1972):306-319.

Guntrip, H. *Personality Structure and Human Interaction* (New York: International Universities Press, 1961).

Guntrip, H. "Object-Relations Theory and Ego-Theory," in Salzman, L., and Masserman, J., eds., *Modern Concepts of Psychoanalysis* (New York: Citadel Press, 1962).

Guntrip, H. *Schizoid Phenomena, Object-Relations and the Self* (New York: International Universities Press, 1969).

Guntrip, H. *Psychoanalytic Theory, Therapy and the Self* (New York: Basic Books, 1971).

Guntrip, H. "Orthodoxy and Revolution in Psychology." *Bulletin of British Psychological Society* 25 (1972):275-280.

Haley, J. *Strategies of Psychotherapy* (New York: Grune & Stratton, 1963).

Harris, T. G. "1976—Things to Come and Then Some." *Intellectual Digest* 3, 5 (1973):84-87.

Jackson, D. D., ed. *Therapy, Communication and Change: Human Communication, Vol. II* (Palo Alto: Science and Behavior Books, 1968).

Jacobson, E. *The Self and the Object World* (New York: International Universities Press, 1964).

Josephson, E. and M. *Man Alone: Alienation in Modern Society* (New York: Dell, 1962).

Kafka, J. S. "The Body and Transitional Object: A Psychoanalytic Study of a

Self-Mutilating Patient." *British Journal of Medical Psychology* 42 (1969): 207-212.

Katan, M. "Fetishism, Splitting of the Ego, and Denial." *International Journal of Psychoanalysis* 45 (1964): parts 2-3, 237-245.

Kernberg, O. "Structural Derivatives of Object Relationships." *International Journal of Psychoanalysis* 47 (1966):237-253.

Kernberg, O. "Borderline Personality Organization." *Journal of American Psychoanalytic Association* 15 (1967):641-685.

Kernberg, O. "The Treatment of Patients with Borderline Personality Organization." *International Journal of Psychoanalysis* 49 (1968): part 4, 600-619.

Kernberg, O. "A Contribution to the Ego-Psychological Critique of the Kleinian School." *International Journal of Psychoanalysis* 50 (1969): part 3, 317-333.

Kernberg, O. "Factors in the Psychoanalytic Treatment of Narcissistic Personalities." *Journal of American Psychoanalytic Association* 18 (1970a):51-85.

Kernberg, O. "New Developments in Psychoanalytic Object-Relations Theory." (Topeka, Kansas: The Menninger Foundation, 1970b).

Klein, G. "The Ego in Psychoanalysis—A Concept in Search of Identity." *Psychoanalytic Review* 56, 4 (1969-70):510-525.

Klein, M., Heimann, P., and Money-Kyrle, R. *New Directions in Psychoanalysis* (New York: Basic Books, 1955).

Kohut, H. "Forms and Transformations of Narcissism." *Journal of American Psychoanalytic Association* 45 (1966):243-272.

Kohut, H. *The Analysis of the Self* (New York: International Universities Press, 1971).

Kubie, L. S. "The Distortion of the Symbolic Process in Neurosis and Psychosis." *Journal of American Psychoanalytic Association* 1 (1953): 59-86.

Laing, R. D. *The Divided Self* (New York: Pantheon Books, 1960).

Laing, R. D.; Phillipson, H.; and Lee, A. R. *Interpersonal Perception* (London: Tavistock Publications, 1966).

Lichtenstien, H. "Identity and Sexuality." *Journal of American Psychoanalytic Association* 9 (1961).

Mahler, M. S. *On Human Symbiosis and the Vicissitudes of Individuation. 1: Infantile Psychosis* (New York: International Universities Press, 1968).

Mahler, M. "Rapprochement Subphase of the Separation-Individuation Process." *Psychoanalytic Quarterly* 41, 4 (1972):487-506.

Mitscherlich, A. *Society Without the Father* (New York: Harcourt, Brace and World, 1963).

Neumann, E. *The Origins and History of Consciousness* (Princeton: Princeton University Press, 1954).

Parloff, M. B. "Analytic Group Psychotherapy" in Marmor, J., ed., *Modern Psychoanalysis* (New York: Basic Books, 1968).

Rice, A. K. *The Enterprise and Its Environment* (London: Tavistock Publications, 1963).

Rice, A. K. *Learning for Leadership* (London: Tavistock Publications, 1965).

Rice, A. K. "Individual, Group and Intergroup Processes." *Human Relations* 22 (1969):565-584.

Rioch, M. J. "The Work of Wilfred Bion on Groups." *Psychiatry* 33 (1970): 56-66.

Roiphe, H., and Galenson, E. "Object Loss and Early Sexual Development." *Psychoanalytic Quarterly* 42, 1 (1973):60-72.

Roland, A. "Contributions and Controversies in the Areas of Identity, Identification and Self-Image." *Psychoanalytic Monographs* 1:25-39 (National Psychological Association for Psychoanalysis, 1973).

Ruitenbeek, H. M., ed. *Group Therapy Today* (New York: Atherton Press, 1969).

Schafer, R. *Aspects of Internalization* (New York: International Universities Press, 1968).

Schafer, R. "Concepts of Self and Identity and the Experience of Separation-Individuation in Adolescence." *Psychoanalytic Quarterly* 42, 1 (1973):42-59.

Scheidlinger, S. "The Concept of Identification in Group Psychotherapy." *American Journal of Psychotherapy* 9, 4 (1955):661-672.

Scheidlinger, S. "Identification, the Sense of Belonging and of Identity in Small Groups." *International Journal of Group Psychotherapy* 14, 3 (1964): 291-306.

Scheidlinger, S. "The Concept of Regression in Group Psychotherapy." *International Journal of Group Psychotherapy* 18 (1968):3-20.

Schindler, W. "The Role of the Mother in Group Psychotherapy." *International Journal of Group Psychotherapy* 16 (1966): 198-202.

Schutz, W. C. *The Interpersonal Underworld* (Palo Alto: Science and Behavior Books, 1966).

Schwartz, E. K. "Group Psychotherapy: The Individual and the Group" in Reiss, B. F., ed., *New Directions in Mental Health* (New York: Grune & Stratton, 1969), II, pp. 9-15.

Schwartz, E. K. "Leadership and the Psychotherapist," in Reiss, B. F., ed., *New Directions in Mental Hetlth* (New York: Grune & Stratton, 1969), II, pp. 1-8.

Searles, H. H. *Collected Papers on Schizophrenia and Related Subjects* (New York: International Universities Press, 1965).

Sokol, R. J. "A Short-Term Technique of Psychotherapy for Psychotic Depressive Reactions." *International Journal of Psychoanalytic Psychotherapy* 2, 1 (February 1973).

Sutherland, J. D. "Object-Relations Theory and the Conceptual Model of Psychoanalysis." *British Journal of Medical Psychology* 36: 1963.

Watzlawick, P.; Beavin, J. H.; and Jackson, D. D. *Pragmatics of Human Communication* (New York: W. W. Norton, 1967).

Wile, D. B. "Negative Countertransference, Therapist Discouragement." *International Journal of Psychoanalytic Psychotherapy* 1, 3 (1972):36-67.

Winnicott, D. W. *The Child and the Family* (London: Tavistock Publications, 1957).

Winnicott, D. W. *Collected Papers: Through Paediatrics to Psychoanalysis* (London: Tavistock Publications, 1958).

Winnicott D. W. *The Maturational Processes and the Facilitating Environment* (New York: International Universities Press, 1965).

Winnicott, D. W. *The Family and Individual Development* (London: Tavistock Publications, 1965).

Winnicott, D. W. *Playing and Reality* (New York: Basic Books, 1971).

Wittkower. E. D., and Dubreuil, G. "Reflections on the Interface between Psychiatry and Anthropology," in Galdston, I., ed., *The Interface Between Psychiatry and Anthropology* (New York: Brunner/Mazel, 1971), pp. 19-20.

Wolf, A. "The Psychoanalysis of Groups," in Ruitenbeek, H. M., ed., *Group Therapy Today* (New York: Aldine-Atherton, 1969), pp. 67-96.

Wolf, A., and Schwartz, E. K. "Psychoanalysis in Groups," in Kaplan, H. I., and Sadock, B. J., eds., *Comprehensive Group Psychotherapy* (Baltimore: Williams & Wilkins, 1971), pp. 241-291.

Wolf, A.; Schwartz, E. K.,; McCarty, G. J.; and Goldberg, I. A. "Psychoanalysis in Groups: Contrasts with Other Group Therapies," in Sager, C. J., and Kaplan, H. S., eds., *Progress in Group and Family Therapy* (New York: Brunner/Mazel, 1971), pp. 47-53.

Zetzel, E. R. *The Capacity for Emotional Growth* (New York: International Universities Press, 1970).

Part IV

THE GROUP LEADER: OUTSIDE THE PSYCHOANALYTIC GROUP

Introduction

ZANVEL A. LIFF

In addition to their traditional group practice and their innovative modifications, group analytic leaders are making contributions beyond their immediate treatment activities.

Wolberg contrasts the paradox between democratic goals of the small group leader with the aggressive-repressive power needs of governmental and corporate structures. She states that it is incumbent upon the group leader to be aware of how malignant socio-political-economic pressures affect the individual patient. She also advocates activist behavior for group psychotherapists.

Observing the fragmentation in the group psychotherapy field, Leopold presses for a more comprehensive, integrated approach which brings together group therapy, training and education, and preventive methods. In addition, he promotes linking the work in small groups with larger community groups, and stresses the need for multiple techniques consistent with the different needs of different client populations.

Concerned with group methods both as art and science, Fidler explores training problems for professionals and paraprofessionals. He differentiates group leaders who are remote blank screens from the intimate, culturally sharing, and sometimes problem sharing leaders (e.g., former alcoholics and drug addicts). He states that such leaders are often better prepared to empathize than the extensively trained professional specialist and distinguishes between leaders who treat the individual and those who help humanity.

Rosenbaum makes a plea for skillful group psychotherapy based on sound theoretical rationale. He states that the boundaries of scientific psychotherapy have been opened to the religious revivalists of the larger cultural group movement with its emphasis on short-lived euphoria and an unreal sense of relatedness. It is recognized by him

245

that the pervasive group subculture in the United States is geared to overcome the emotional isolation of the participants as well as the leaders. In addition, he focuses on how leaders are attracted to the group medium because it provides an opportunity for gratification of power and control needs.

The problems and accomplishments of the group analyst in working with a community service are outlined by Lebovici. He describes his leadership functions in interrelating to the different needs of different agency departments and services, especially when being caught between intergroup conflicts. While not necessarily utilizing interpretation, he feels his power lies in his analytic understanding of crisscrossing, ambivalent transferences. He emphasizes the necessity of group leaders working within the community being able to identify with different client needs as well as cultural attitudes, and indicates that in community group leadership, responses are made more to what you are than to what you say.

33. The Leader and Society

ARLENE .R. WOLBERG

There is a basic paradox between the goals of the leader of the small, psychoanalytically-oriented group and the leadership objectives of so many of our governmental and corporate structures. In the small therapy group, the leader hopefully attempts to reduce his power and authority and distribute it democratically. Alexander Wolf represents the epitome of this approach in his use of peer interaction to break toxic parental bonds which are transferred onto the group leader (1962). The functioning of society in general, however, is based on a power structure whose goal is to broaden itself even at the expense of individual citizens.

The origin of authoritarian organization in our society is found in the primary group—the family. Children are socialized into approved modes of behavior by identification with parents who insure acceptance of their prescriptions by the exercise of superior power. The ultimate control of the parent may be actualized in a physically aggressive manner or, more subtly, through the use of psychological sanctions and rewards for appropriate behavior. In both cases, the parents use power aggressively and the child identifies with the aggressor out of fear.

The frustrations that this submission elicits stimulate, in turn, aggressive authoritarian needs in the child. Since aggression in the family is a consequence of repressive measures and disregard for the rights and needs of individuals, the authoritarian parent who persists in using such measures serves to perpetuate a cycle, developing children with a disproportionate fear and respect for authority, and a concomitant desire to wield repressive powers themselves. Thus, individuals characterized as authoritarian will be overly submissive in one context, and unduly repressive in the other.

The cultural pressures that the psychoanalytic group therapy leader is faced with are delineated in Stanley Milgram's work on *Obedience to Authority* (1973). The experimenter ordered naive subjects to administer allegedly painful electric shocks to subjects as part of a "learning" experiment. The results indicated that a majority of people are willing to induce pain in others if they are ordered to do so. Indeed, the machinery of government, the military-industrial complex, and corporate business operates on the expectation of obedience to these kinds of demands. While lip service is given to the ideals of participatory democracy, the power structure aims to broaden its base and is threatened by true independence of thought or action by individuals. Additionally, most people further undermine their own power by actually seeking to distribute authority outside of themselves. The search for an ideal, heroic figure or powerful institution in which to centralize authority is essentially a masochistic quest for a benevolent duplication of parental power and a continuation of the sado-masochistic power struggle of the family. A large portion of society is willing to subjugate its own power to the authority of the person or institution that it has tacitly agreed upon as the nucleus of control. Moreover, if that authoritative base is threatened, society responds with indignation along with the aggressor.

The prevalence of widespread identification with the aggressor is most evident in those cases where some persons do break out of the mold sufficiently to protest against the use of aggression by holders of power. The activists against the war in Vietnam and those working for the civil rights of minorities had as much to fear from middle America in the way of aggressive retaliation as they did from official agents of government. More recently, Watergate and the publication of the Pentagon Papers provide striking examples of this phenomenon. The threat to absolute power posed by the release of the Pentagon Papers precipitated a paranoiac, belligerent response which resulted in the installment of a massive network of wiretapping and political subterfuge, and provoked the determination to attempt to control the judicial proceedings that stemmed from these activities, all in the guise of national security and executive (or parental) privilege. It is no accident or even lack of perception that allowed Mr. Nixon to refer to the American people as his children in one of his speeches. In a government that purports to be a constitutional democracy of representative power, the executive branch has grown to dominate governmental processes and to regard challenges to this authoritarian control as treasonable. The "get them before they get you" attitude of the Nixon administration is a frightening demonstration of what happens when the previously undisputed control of the power elite appears to be in a precarious position.

While in the past society has generally accepted the centralization of power in the masochistic subordination to authority and denial of individual strength that is the imitation of the accustomed parent-child power distribution, the "rebels" in the Watergate situation (the House Judiciary Committee, the Senate Watergate Committee, and the newspapers) are powerful enough to have usurped, to a degree, executive control and to have generally won society over to their side. In this case, the aggressors with whom society identifies are those who are, at least in the eyes of the White House, the insubordinates. Thus, the shock, hurt, and confusion of the American public at the change of allegiances catalyzed by Watergate. Loyalties have switched from a once-revered and omnipotent President to a formerly suspect, "radical" press and moderate Congress.

Identification with the aggressor as a defense against harsh reality has caused millions of people to condone and encourage international and national aggression when they themselves are direct or indirect victims of it. Within the matrix of events of the Watergate scandal, however, American society is gradually beginning, through identification with what might be considered a more democratic aggressor, to recognize its own power.

The role of the psychoanalytic group leader is to change autocracy to democracy within the small group and to attempt to effect a similar change in society at large. The psychoanalytic group leader has special knowledge of forces leading to sado-masochistic patterns of dominance and submission, and it behooves him to direct this knowledge toward society as a whole. As Milgram states in *Obedience to Authority*, "We have a special obligation to place in a position of authority those most likely to be humane and wise. But man is a long range source of hope, too." The task of the therapeutic group leader is to inform the public and, in seeking to overcome submission to authority, work for a more democratic society. If the government is to serve the people rather than the other way around, the people have to be made aware of how their needs are manipulated to serve the needs of the holders of power.

The group leader must be constantly aware of the contradiction between the democratic goals of the microcosm and the autocratic goals of the macrocosm, and should strive to foster this awareness in others. He must become an activist on social and political levels as well as on personal levels, informing the public as to the ways in which its democratic preference are sacrificed to the perpetuation of the aggressive power of larger societal structures. Only with an active attempt to alter masochistic patterns of submission can the therapist contribute to changes in existing power concentration that ultimately undermines the movement towards autonomy made by therapeutic group members, and, more gradually, by American society itself as expressed in its reaction to the Watergate case.

REFERENCES

Milgrim, Stanley. *Obedience to Authority* (New York: Harper & Row, 1973).
Wolf, Alexander. *Psychoanalysis in Groups* (New York: Grune & Stratton, 1962).

34. The Leader with Psychotic Patients

HAROLD S. LEOPOLD

This discussion concerns itself with changes in the field of group psychotherapy, which have taken place during the last thirty years. The beginning of the period to be covered could coincide with the publication of Alexander Wolf's pioneering work "The Psychoanalysis of Groups" (1949). The present author, being a grateful, reverent, and admiring student of Al's, feels like a heretic whenever he deviates from the analytic framework or even suggests—as in this paper—modification of therapeutic approach. With a sense of humility and reservation he bows to Shopenhauer's statement,

> Every thirty years a new race comes into the world and after summarily devouring in all haste the results of human knowledge as they have been accumulated for thousands of years, aspires to be thought cleverer than the whole of the past.

The thousand years are in a sense equivalent to the time period embracing the history of group psychotherapy. In perspective it certainly looks like an eternity, considering the expansion of its domain and concentration of effort invested in it. By flashback we can observe the fast pace of development and the sequential phases of change in concepts of methodology and technique, leadership role, therapeutic objective and group composition. It would be difficult to enumerate the variety of group modalities, especially if one included groups which lie on the periphery or outside our traditional notion of group psychotherapy. But even within the narrow confines of "old fashioned," conventional practices, discrepancies and controversies are very much alive, and ideologies are worlds apart.

Various schools of thought in psychoanalysis and psychotherapy have provided a well-established frame of reference for their specific

251

adherents. None of the many ideological structures, however, could possibly have been able to provide a single therapeutic formula, a panacea to all the different patient types with their specific pathologies and symptoms. One of the greatest challenges to our field has been to find a treatment approach that would be in line with theories of modern psychiatry as well as those of learning and communication. However, theories are abstract structures which follow laws of logical thought. Translating theories into practice may meet with obstacles, especially when dealing with the intricacies, vicissitudes, and psychic complexities of human existence—complexities apparently determined by the multiplicity of forces that influence man, the inner ones as well as the cultural, socioeconomic, and social ones. It would indeed be indiscriminate to assume that the causality of illness is a result of an even distribution of all these etiological factors. However, one ought to consider the possibility that any of these factors can have a contributing and determining effect on the tenuous balance of the emotional scale. The effect of such causal possibilities and potentialities on the outcome of psychiatric illness ought to influence the therapist's treatment approach to individual or group. He would require flexibility in his therapeutic attitude since he no longer could be tied down by a scholastic orientation, which obstructs his view. He needs freedom of distance and perspective in order to see the total picture of the multi-faceted background to which his patient was exposed. In addition to such information, he must have compassion, which is of essence in any therapeutic relationship. As we know, the results of psychotherapy are determined not only by the training of the analyst and his choice of treatment approach but also by a more subtle and undefinable element—the artful application of human sensitivity. The quality of the human contact, which on some level transcends the sphere of awareness, often may be the most critical aspects of the therapeutic transaction.

The task of the therapist is indeed not an easy one. In hardly any other field is a professional's activity so continuously faced with the adversities, drama, and inequities of the patient's existence. The therapeutic function of interrupting the chain of the patient's repetitive, unwarranted, intrapsychic and social events requires favorable conditions for new interpersonal experiences. The question to be answered is: Which setting lends itself optimally to the therapeutic purpose? If it is the treatment goal to enhance the patient's self-esteem by ultimately providing a model for peer relationships, then the one-to-one relationship proves to be illusory when it is characterized by a vertical design in the therapeutic transaction. In addition to the symbolic manifestations (transference), there are frequently realistic disparities which relate to such important social aspects as cultural background, economic status, or education.

It may be one of the great advantages of group therapy that it provides not only symbolic representation but also the realities of the "here and now." It enables the participant to share and identify with other members in the problems of living and to protest against code, authority, or any social structure to which he fell victim. Needless to say, the group therapist under these circumstances often becomes the target of the patient's accusations. In the face of such challenges, he ought not to hide behind rhetoric and meaningless justifications that only widen the gap between him and his patients.

The group therapist's open communications, whether positive or negative, are possibly the best opportunities he can utilize for the patient's corrective experience. The following encounter may be illustrative:

> A patient conveyed his hostile feeling and disdain for the thera-
> pist by his silence, posture, and facial expression. When asked by
> the therapist, "I wonder how you feel toward me?" he replied,
> "Let's turn the table, how do you feel toward me?" Therapist:
> "At present, very unfriendly." Patient enraged, responded with a
> barrage of accusations in which he compared the therapist's be-
> havior and feelings with that of his noncaring father. At the end
> of the patient's angry outburst, the therapist remarked to him,
> "You never asked me why I feel unfriendly toward you. I have
> these feelings because for a number of sessions you have been
> inaccessible to me. The patient did not respond anymore. How-
> ever, he opened the next group session by remarking that his
> attitude toward the therapist had completely changed, that he
> admired his frankness which was in contrast to his father's self-
> righteous and untrustworthy behavior.

This example testifies to our experience that the admission of counter-transference reactions is indicated if they are therapeutic to the patient.

The relevance of a positive relationship opens up leading questions for the group therapist such as: How can he utilize this essential therapeutic tool in the face of the multiplicity of transactions taking place in the group? Does a group compensate for the loss of a dyadic therapeutic relationship? One could answer these questions summarily by stating that specific psychological laws are applicable to the group and its therapeutic potential. There may be differences though in handling the individual needs in the group, which depend on the group's therapeutic mission. In general, one can state that the small group displays a great deal of affect (positive and negative) and that the negative feelings—if therapeutically worked through—actually turn into empathy, understanding, warmth, and intimacy. The tool by which this will be accomplished depends on the leader's basic orientation.

Methodologies, process, and therapeutic potential have been established and successfully tested for the small group, which should not exceed the size of fifteen participants. But what about the larger group? What is the structure of such a group? What is the role of its leader? Probably these questions are interrelated. To cite some extremes, under authoritarian leadership the larger group will become an undifferentiated mass (complete individual ego diffusion) and under permissive leadership will be concerned with fragmentation and inter-group issues (group differentiation). The potential of the large group is probably very much related to the faculty and orientation of the leader.

In a profound research of encounter groups, Lieberman and Yalom (1971) have been able to relate the participants' experience to the leaders' role, type, and the groups they lead: "The experience differs with particular kinds of encounter groups, not only in how much change takes place, but also in the patterning of change and the areas of functioning affected." The authors differentiate seven types of leaders and focus in their comparative evaluation on two types: the "Energizers" and the "Providers." Most interesting is that the "Energizers," as the most charismatic of the leaders, produce the highest casualty rate. The "Energizers" have been described as being authoritarians, who often structured the events in the group and "thus asserted firm control and took over for the participants." It seems that responsible judgmental leadership is needed to steer such groups in directions which would avoid the unwelcome by-products of impulse-ridden acting out and unreasonable behavior. These primitive excesses, which are probably responsible for casualties in encounter groups, are reminiscent of Freud's mass psychological concepts where "affect becomes extraordinarily intensive while intellectual ability is markedly reduced."

The gradual transition from dyadic (one-to-one), to horizontal (small group), and finally to circular communication (large group) illustrates the historical development of group therapy. It also reflects the psychiatric concepts of and guidelines to the problems of mental health. The impact of such trends on group approaches has been very strongly felt insofar as the large group has gained in prominence and often has included the total social network, whether in family therapy, hospital psychiatry (therapeutic community meetings), or the community at large. In the face of such developments, it seems most crucial to discriminate among the multiple groups in operation and critically evaluate the merits of each modality and the competence of its leaders.

The many variables which are responsible for the known as well as the esoteric concepts of group methods, have led to the fragmentation of the field of group therapy. The plethora of group methods and techniques and the steady increase of new methods have led us to the crossroads. At this junction it is our professional responsibility to indicate the trend of direction. Schisms in our field have been created by obstacles to linguistic communication between various ideologies which have prevented unity in group approach. In order to streamline the practice of group therapy, one would have to raise some questions such as: Is it possible to bring divergent group methodologies which are rooted in the same basic principle under one umbrella? Furthermore, are the lines of demarcation between therapy and education groups clear enough to regard them as separate entities? I assume that the answers to these questions are in the affirmative.

There has been much thought given to these problems in recent research and publications. Ambitious efforts to establish a unified approach to training and study groups have been made by Klein and Astrachan (1971). "In order to learn about groups a theoretical model needs to be developed which combines elements of both T- and study-group theory. . . . In our work, we have tended to see the two theoretical positions as complementary. The study group, with its stress on covert feelings and behavior, provides a map of the primitive processes going on in the group. T-group theory is much more concerned with directly observable, modifiable behavior. In developing our group training conferences, we have seen the experiences as logically sequential."

The tendency to introduce current general systems theories as a structural framework applicable to group therapies has been discussed by Durkin (1972). She raises the question of "conceptual compatibility with analytic therapy concept." She arrives at the conclusion "that two conceptual systems are harmonious in principle and that their differences will eventually prove to be complementary rather than contradictory." The trend of fusion of related approaches seems to be a move in the right direction in order to reduce the fragmentation which has brought confusion to our field.

It is a difficult task, however, to merge related ideologies and to translate them into a meaningful, applicable frame of reference. To accomplish this objective we will have to change our professional attitude and demonstrate greater tolerance for deviance from our own frame of operation. It may be worthwhile to familiarize ourselves with other group methods and techniques. The broadening of leadership qualities would indeed enhance our therapeutic potential by providing flexibility in approach for the sake of a particular group or patient.

It is absolutely conceivable, for example, that multiple techniques ought to be available for the group treatment of the psychotic patient. Our observation of many hospital groups under different leaderships with different techniques did not provide a satisfactory answer as to the preferential choice of method. This author concludes that there is no one particular approach which can be successfully applied to the various types of psychotic pathology. Just as there are many types of schizophrenias, there are apparently specific therapies needed to deal with this complex diagnostic entity. For our purpose, it may be useful to separate the many types which all have been subsumed under one diagnostic entity. A discriminating selection of groups would enable us to form various group constellations and to test different therapies. One could compose, for example, homogeneous groups along such criteria as diagnostic category, symptom formation, and age. Also, attempts could be made to conduct various small groups with the composition of not more than five members of the same sex. These and various other therapeutic possibilities would have to be evaluated in order to secure guidelines for this large patient population which has not benefitted proportionately from the advances which group treatment, in general, has offered. Limited in our choice, we have been inclined to apply to groups of psychotics a treatment approach which originally was designed for neurotic groups. The tendency has been to regard similar phenomena occurring in both settings as if they were identically significant and sprang from the same pathological matrix. The interplay between psychological and social phenomena deserves special attention in group treatment with psychotic patients.

We see psychotherapy as an interpersonal process which is designed to bring about changes in an individual who has been suffering from intrapsychic emotional-mental disturbance and has experienced difficulties in his social fields. The small group provides a social field from which a patient can draw strength for the acquisition of interpersonal skills and gratifications from a corrective emotional experience.

The wide spectrum of divergent methods that all sail under the heading—or misnomer—of group therapy, requires the establishment of a methodical structure to clarify the various combinations of specific approaches, goals, techniques, and criteria of selection. Only the application of such a structure will make it possible to establish clearcut lines of distinction and the relative merits of respective group modalities.

It is my opinion that the existing variations of group methods can be subsumed under three categories: (1) therapy, (2) training and education, and (3) preventive measures in mental health. Such demarcation lines ought to be established even if a blurring of boundaries is occasionally unavoidable, as, for example, in training groups of "normals" where therapeutic gains may occur, but only as by-products of the experience.

The increasing specialization in psychiatry will present our field with challenging tasks in related fields of interest, such as social and community psychiatry. If social psychiatry focuses on the significance of the group to the individual and communications between groups, then group therapy attains a commanding position in the community. Therefore, it will be our responsibility to devise and provide sound training for those group leaders for whom a broad perspective and familiarity with the goals of the community become relevant. Such training would necessitate flexibility and commitment to multi-methods of treatment, whether in counseling family and other small groups, or large community groups. In addition to the leader's therapeutic responsibility would be his important function as consultant to agencies or community organizations.

The development of group psychotherapy is inseparable from the general trend of psychiatric thought, which reflects the impact of social currents of our time as well as that of the more permanent socio-cultural environment to which we are exposed. All these forces contribute to some degree to the shaping of the human personality and to emotional and mental growth.

Although group psychotherapy has established its own methodologies and theories, it is no longer a separate and airtight system; information and techniques filter in from neighboring areas such as family and community therapy. This "contamination" with other methods is not always desirable, since well-tested, constructive approaches should be preserved in their "pure" form. We refer here to the small analytic group which will survive as the treatment modality of choice for neurotic and character disorders. Its shortcoming lies only in its restricted applicability to a relatively small segment of the population.

The relevance and recognition of environmental forces is an important consideration in our attempt to reach that large sector of people who live under stressful conditions. Instability in the family and society and unfavorable sociocultural conditions are the breeding ground which nourishes the seeds of pathology. The impact of a "social" etiology must be considered in treatment. It requires of the group therapist that he become familiar with the background, value systems, geographical community and all other factors which may have affected his patient's development. Without this information, he will not know the inner reality of his patients but see only the projections of his theories and fantasies about them. The therapist's profound knowledge of intra- as well as extrapsychic influences on the development of man is essential as a prerequisite for successful therapy, as Alexander Wolf noted in 1949. "It enables the therapist who possesses an adequate understanding of the social character of man to unite this awareness with his methods of treatment of individuals who have been immobilized by the conflicts of our culture."

REFERENCES

Durkin, H. E. "General Systems Theory and Group Therapy: An Introduction." *International Journal of Group Psychotherapy* 22 (1972):159-166.
Fidler, J. W. "A Niche for Group Psychotherapy." *International Journal of Group Psychotherapy* 22 (1972):287-305.
Freud, S. *Group Psychology and the Analysis of the Ego* (New York: Bantam Books, 1960).
de Huszar. *The Intellectuals* (Chicago: The Free Press of Glencoe, 1962).

Kiev, A. *Social Psychiatry* (New York: Jason Aronson, 1969).

Klein, E. B., and Astrachan, B. "Learning in Groups: A Comparison of Study Groups and T-Groups." *Journal of Applied Behavioral Science* 7 (1971): 659-683.

Leopold, H. S. "Selection of Patients for Group Psychotherapy." *American Journal of Psychotherapy* 11 (1957):634-637.

Leopold, H. S. "The Problem of Working Through in Group Psychotherapy." *International Journal of Group Psychotherapy* 9 (1959):287-292.

Leopold, H. S. "Beyond the Traditional Therapy Group." Wolberg and Schwartz, eds., *Group Therapy 1973—An Overview* (New York: Intercontinental Medical Books Corp., 1973).

Leopold, H. S. "Training Groups for the Psychiatric Residents. A Comparison to Groups." Unpublished.

Wolf, A. "The Psychoanalysis of Groups." *American Journal of Psychotherapy* 3 (1949):525-558.

Wolf, A. and Schwartz, E. K. *Psychoanalysis in Groups* (New York: Grune & Stratton, 1962).

Wolberg, L. R. *The Technique of Psychotherapy* (New York: Grune & Stratton, 1954).

Yalom, I. and Lieberman, M. "A Study of Encounter Group Casualties." *Archives of General Psychiatry* 25, 1 (1971):16-30.

35. The Leader in the Community

JAY W. FIDLER

By now it is a platitude that the practice of a healing or helping profession is both a science and an art. This is true of medicine in general and perhaps especially of psychiatry. There is a temptation to feel that individual practitioners mix these two features in varying proportions. The "scientific" practitioner is more objective, puts greater emphasis on indirect data gleaned from laboratories and analyzes the problems in terms that seem more quantifiable. The "artful" practitioner is more subjective, puts greater emphasis on direct and intuitive data, and analyzes the problems in a style characteristic of the novel.

Treatment by these two polar representatives reflects the distant and relatively impersonal stance on the one hand and the proximal and more personal stance on the other. Commonly we observe that more of the former personality types choose surgery as a specialty and more of the latter choose psychiatry. But this is an oversimplification. Clearly there is a range within each profession, and there are nuances of practice and attitude which allow for a paradoxical effect in which the patient may perceive a reverse interpersonal situation. For example, we can easily imagine a surgeon utilizing other personnel to work with a patient—an intern, a nurse, an attendant, an anesthesiologist and a physiotherapist. In the total process, he may see the patient less than any one of these individuals and establish very little rapport. Asked five years later about the events of the surgical week, the surgeon will probably recall the pathology but not the name of the patient, but the patient will recall the name and personality of the surgeon and be much less clear about the other personnel.

The psychiatrist on some occasions also may delegate responsibilities, including psychotherapy, to other personnel, both professional and nonprofessional. On those few occasions when patients have been asked years after the hospital stay how to assess these personnel, we

260

find a different balance. Attendants and nurses are recalled as people and judged to be vital to the help gained while in the hospital. Psychiatrists are not ignored in these retrospectives, but they are relatively less the center of meaningful recall.

Despite the emphasized need for a strong empathic rapport between therapist and patient, there has been an intuitive awareness that the therapist may not be as empathic as he assumes. Presumably, individual psychotherapy cannot take place without the therapist just as surgery will not happen without the surgeon. Yet there have been many jokes about the therapist or the patient starting the session without the other, but I have never seen a cartoon or heard a joke about surgery that suggested treatment to be independent of the treater. Humor often derives from the less obvious or covert truth. There must be at least a reasonable doubt about whether the expert knowledge and training of the psychotherapist need be present and involved in the psychotherapeutic experience. The artistic component of this helping relationship, we might then conclude, is of large importance in psychotherapy and can be achieved, acquired, or inherited by people who have not had the scientific component in their training.

Our tendency to regard science and art as relatively independent entities has contributed to several manifestations of the split between the two. It may be seen for instance, in the social organization of the profession for at least the last fifty years. This would include the current increasing debate as to whether psychiatry should be a medical science or whether it should even operate in the field of mental health.

Science has tended to organize into professional societies and to function in universities. Accumulations of knowledge are shared and individuals are unlikely to be the subject of controversy except in the few instances when they make a major reorganization in the meaning of the discovered facts, as in the case of Darwin.

Art has tended to take the social form of schools in which one or a very few individuals are identified as the leaders. The ties in these schools are loose, and practitioners are likely to work alone. Individuals are frequently the subject of controversy and the relation of one man's art to that of another is the basis for a continuous game. The artist himself tends to minimize the derived nature of his work. The fellow artist or critic expends as much effort looking for just such derivations and relationships as he does trying to give meaning to any development in art.

On the scientific side of psychiatry, there have been relatively stable professional societies playing a role in the accumulation of data and minimizing controversy over individuals. The artful side of psychiatry has tended to develop schools with specific individuals as their leaders. The schools are more often seen as being in competition rather than as sharing in a common enterprise. These schools of psychoanalysis and their contemporary derivatives have taken a step of considerable practical importance as a reflection of their emphasis on art. By agreeing at an early stage to train nonmedical psychoanalysts and to acknowledge and support them as private practitioners, they started a tradition in which some of us now advocate, support, and even employ our own ex-patients as therapists for new patients. At the extreme pole the art of therapeutic intervention preempts the entire field and leaves little if anything to the science. What remains is a series of individual "schools" where any given practitioner may evolve his own art style, teach it to a few trainees or patients, encourage them to carry on the traditions, and thereby become a "school."

Just as psychiatry seems to magnify all the issues of the relationship between art and science, so group psychotherapy dramatizes our ambivalences in this field even further. In the literature and at the conferences, we were clear in stating that group psychotherapy is a subspecialty of psychotherapy. This would mean that the leader of the therapy group would have to first quality as a psychotherapist, and then with additional training and experience he could be the legitimate leader of a treatment group.

PARAPROFESSIONAL ASPECT

Almost from the beginning, however, the practice in the institutions and agencies was frequently in contrast to these assumptions. Groups of patients have been assembled under the leadership of ward attendants and many other staff categories. Despite the fact that we would not claim these group leaders were qualified as psychotherapists, we were often inclined to consider this activity group therapy.

Patients would frequently consider group therapy a lesser form of treatment, and the practices of the institutions supported this conclusion despite the sincere effort to substantiate our conviction that the group psychotherapist must be a psychotherapist with extra training rather than a person without basic training. The practice then reflected the art of psychotherapy rather than emphasizing the science.

We turn to science in an effort to help us be accountable for our practices and to evaluate our programs. Statistical reports and rating scales are applied after a group psychotherapy procedure. In the most effective studies, the measures and scales are used before and after the treatment procedures. This is an important phenomenon to stress. The scientific approach is applied before and after the transaction. The transaction itself is seen to be the art component and, as such, is less amenable to the measures and strictures of the scientific method. The artistic concepts cannot be linked in measurable ways to the body of knowledge about psychodynamics and personality change.

We find ourselves then in a position like the students of ESP. Since we do not have a body of data on neurophysiologic response to electromagnetic or other radiation, we cannot study the ESP process. Instead, we conduct observations before and after various procedures and attribute the results to ESP. We are then left with the "scientific" response of disbelief because the process cannot be rationalized. The "intuitive" response of other people, however, is that the demonstrations have proven the existence of ESP. The kind of research we do on psychotherapy leaves us in a similar vulnerable position. The "scientific" public is still convinced that within that black box called group psychotherapy there is no additional demonstrable measurable event, and that the group psychotherapist emperor is nude rather than bedecked in professional finery.

Yet another manifestation of the ambiguous concept of group psychotherapy is the development of group leaders from the population to be served. Part of the art of the group psychotherapeutic leader is to achieve an empathic rapport to be experienced by the patient as a relevant "real life" experience rather than as an asylum in a strange conceptual realm having no bearing on the familiar, everyday world. Experience shows that often the member or ex-member (the native member) of the patient group can achieve this rapport better than the (foreign) professional. The indigenous worker, the paraprofessional, and the mental health aide are identified as people able to help distressed people more efficiently. This is most especially true when the population to be served is farthest from the "intellectual, middle class" which is presumably the native population of the therapist. Intimacy in the therapeutic relationship in this framework is the kind of intimacy resulting from shared culture.

Culture is an organized group of learned responses characteristic of a particular society. If this is accepted as a definition of the broad social groupings usually referred to in sociological and anthropological literature, we may still find it acceptable in defining the subcultures of concern in the current community psychiatry movement, or it may apply to the individual psychotherapy group. Therapy then may take place in the framework of this empathic bond based on the organized group of learned responses. The question remains whether this intimacy constitutes a sufficient matrix for therapy, or whether it is only the art in need of a science to make it therapy.

From the perspective of the individual patient, this group empathic bond may very well constitute the outside help needed to make change possible. Before a person can effect change in his own social relations, fearful responses, distorted self-evaluation, or antisocial value systems, he needs to feel he has an essential core which isn't warped and that his aspirations are not those of a madman. To do this he must find others who feel as he does, who see what he sees, who identify with the same disharmony in life that he experiences. There must also be among them those who say what they see. For this we need a group that does indeed share a perspective, a group culture which encourages honest statements and a group leader wise enough to clarify the perceptions which are only partly identified or inaccurately stated.

Patients who are able to help themselves after this kind of reassurance and intimacy do not require and may find less helpful a leader who is personally proficient, but who has fewer shared "learned responses." For many years we have been aware that the alcohol experience creates a limited set of such learned responses. Treatment of alcoholics has been more effective in those group settings shared by and led by people who are also alcoholics or ex-alcoholics. Subjectively, the alcoholic patient feels greater understanding or empathy. Professionally, we suggest that one alcoholic can more readily see through the defenses of another.

This same basic concept plays an important role in more recent developments such as Synanon for drug addicts, gamblers groups, obesity groups, Neurotics Anonymous, and Recovery, Inc. This wide variety of identity groups for self-help does not achieve equal success in all categories. Less success should be expected if the unifying symptom allows for a greater variety of personal experience, with less chance of there being a similar acculturation experience. There is, of course, the alternate possibility that the pathology is actually more severe.

As the leadership of the specialized group approaches greater identity with the patient, there is an increasing danger of problems like the proverbial issue in analysis—countertransference is hard to control. The intimacy achieved by virtue of shared experience, expectations, nonverbal communication styles, and personal value systems can also enhance the intimacy of tenderness, sexuality, and hostility. At least on the surface, it would appear that as groups have undertaken the task of helping more serious problems, they have also manifested more overt signs of individual tenderness, sexuality, and hostility. Perhaps this is an inevitable part of any group which develops its own subculture, but it is just as likely that group leadership is compromised by being so closely identified with the members.

LEADERSHIP FUNCTION

The group for therapy has a task. A leadership function is the establishment of boundaries which both emphasize the functions which help with the task and minimize or eliminate those functions which are noncontributory or detrimental. Explicitly, many groups have been started with a semihumorous statement that physical violence is prohibited. This has the virtue of being completely acceptable to almost one hundred percent of patients seeking help. It also establishes the expectation that the group therapist has the function of setting boundaries. This is then followed by more subtle limit setting by the therapist showing interest in some statements and activities while ignoring others. It is in the realm of these more subtle boundary functions that the intimate identity between leader and member is likely to introduce distortions.

As group psychotherapists we undertake the professional responsibility of defining and transmitting the principles and practices of group leadership. The search has taken us into observation and participation in groups which meet success where we have failed. As a result we have changed our practices to build in what we have observed. A review of recent literature shows great variety in what we have observed. For some of us the essential change-inducing element in this intimacy is confrontation, for others it is extravagant emotional expression, still others see sexual revelation including nudity as vital. The range from screaming, to eye-balling, to muscular contortion, and beyond is contributing to a current group leadership subculture of its own. There is little apparent cohesiveness in this subculture, however, since agreement involves intensity of experience within the group and much disagreement persists about which aspect of experience needs to be intensified.

This problem of reconciling professional objectivity with the full impact of a subjective relationship is not unique to psychiatry. Clergymen face the same basic issues. In missionary work it is more blatant, but it is also present in the confines of the mother country. As in group therapy leadership there are professional missionaries and there are indigenous missionaries.

One of the characteristics of the professional is that he requires full financial support from his profession. The minister will get it from his church, while the group psychotherapist will get it from the patients or the institution. In contrast, the indigenous minister or therapist will earn his living by unrelated activities. The Pentecostal churches rely upon indigenous support more than other churches. A result is that their ministers are not considered professional despite their success in relating to people and in expanding religious practices. As with group psychotherapists, the ministry has developed a style of operation as well as a body of knowledge which marks the professional. We can look back with amusement at the tropical missions where missionaries built a rectory with a fireplace in which they presumably taught people how to argue about God. Perhaps it is less easy to be amused at our own strictures on physical movement and conversational content.

DILEMMA OF PURPOSE

The church is also confronted with a dilemma of purpose comparable to the dilemma of the community mental health center. Is their purpose to teach the gospel or to help humanity? Is our purpose to help individuals reach full emotional maturity or to help humanity? To take the broad objective of helping humanity invites the intimate relatedness of the indigenous worker and the flexible professional. To accept the limited goal of professional expertise invites the refinement of a standardized procedure and objectives with more precise goals and limited flexibility. Within these more limited bounds, it is possible to become expert and hence professional. When we expand the bounds without limit, we dilute professionalism to the point of extinction.

It is quite clear that the needs for professional integrity are strained by the expressed needs of the society. In medicine there is a popular argument that doctors should have fewer years of training and be more responsive to a larger proportion of the population. In the ministry there is ample evidence that people don't want to hear the preaching. They want to be shown a Christian way of life. From this need has grown the self-help church group called the "Jesus freaks." They have formed groups outside the church just as our self-help groups have often formed without professional sponsorship. The problem is whether to take these groups into the church and whether to include the self-help groups within the mental health center.

The question of intimacy then is both a challenge to our professionalism and the promise of greater effectiveness. But leadership style in group psychotherapy includes practices which might well be characterized as more remote. Certainly a stated objective of Freud was to approximate a blank screen as much as possible. The goal of reducing the impact of the personal response, the here and now relationship, or any other aspect of current reality, was to bring into focus all the fantasies and memories that would intrude into the patient's consciousness. In group psychotherapy there are some leaders who seem to approximate this blank screen impact as far as possible, despite the active interaction that occurs and, indeed, is encouraged between group members.

It is not a great conceptual distance from this picture of a relatively inactive, remote group leader to the assumption that the group can do a great deal, if not most, of the treatment itself. Twenty years ago, Dr. Alexander Wolf began working with groups by absenting himself from alternate meetings. At that point in time, his practice was very remote indeed. Since then there have been other variations on the theme. Some therapists have removed themselves from the patient circle and intervene only in an emergency or when there is an opportunity to be especially helpful. The most remote step has been in the form of the tape recorded leader. By programming a series of instructions, including when to turn the tape on and off, it has been possible to get the self-initiated groups to "operate" to the benefit of the members. One study of group therapy suggests that these groups have benefitted more than some of the standard groups led by competent professionals.

The process leading to beneficial change in these instances is not a product of intense empathy or of shared cultural responses, at least not with the leader. The leadership function is restricted to the process of defining a style of action and interaction as well as setting boundaries for themes and content to be discussed. If leadership is needed to perform that function, the therapy group must clearly have a different set of boundaries from the normal cultural ones and from any boundaries that would likely be established spontaneously by a group of patients who "accidentally" assemble for mutual support. The rules of the game must be unique in some manner, and the role of leadership must be, at a minimum, to establish and maintain those rules, however vague and flexible they may be.

The most remote as well as the most intimate group therapy leaders can both be said to have lost distance. The usual cultural expectation of group leadership includes face to face participation and a special status conferred by external credentials or by group consensus. The fact that a therapy group can reach its goal when the therapist is absent on the one hand or totally immersed in the group on the other hand, suggests that factors other than leadership style are of preeminent importance.

THE GROUP AS MINICULTURE

Conceiving of the therapy group as a cultural process in miniature will help to fit some of the observations together. As was pointed out earlier, there is important mental health support in the realization that one's perspective on the world is shared by an important person in one's life. The double bind proposition to explain the genesis of psychiatric disorders and the distortions of "reflected appraisal" frequently cited as a cause of disorder both indicate that lack of this consensus is detrimental to mental health.

Consensus is not ordinarily achieved by our patients because the conventions of public discourse and the social taboos necessitate the important part of the message or of the perception be unstated. Treatment then is partially a process of expanding the subject matter of discourse and violating the social taboos. We have all witnessed the relief expressed when one patient reveals his "private" perception and finds that others share his view, although none of them has spoken about it. Each feared his perception was unique and distorted. This consensual validation supports the self-respect necessary to reduce anxiety and to solve problems of living. It also establishes cohesiveness, which has been shown to correlate well with therapeutic benefit.

When the patient describes himself in a way that coincides with the description by the therapist, he is said to have insight. This consensual agreement is also considered important in treatment. Consensual validation then can be achieved in individual psychotherapy as well as in group whether the therapist is remote or intimate. When this cohesive phenomenon occurs, it often generates anger at the "other" people and other groups with whom this mutual understanding does not occur. Some of the cohesive force in any group is to be found in the competition or hostility generated against other groups. From the street gang to the nation, there is a tendency for the group to discover and emphasize its differences if there is no external antagonist to mobilize against. Some therapy group leaders will encourage anger at the "establishment" which did not "understand" the patients. This has the effect of enhancing the cohesion of the group.

Mental health concepts and practices have been defining the relationship between psychopathology and human systems such as families, neighborhoods, and industries. The demonstration of improvement in psychopathology may follow when a therapist works at change in what is currently called the "identified patient." Similar demonstrations now are shown to follow therapeutic work in changing the social context in which the patient is embedded. The therapist can be seen either as remote from the patient or as intimately involved in the social life of the patient. At times this broad social view of professional responsibility brings us in conflict with political, economic or religious establishments. It is hard to justify individual or even group treatment of twelve junior executives with ulcer symptoms, when we could cure them by treating one senior executive with paranoid symptoms.

The broad view of the task of the mental health professions generates concern that we must use all available tools to reduce anxieties, tensions, hostilities, violence, cruelty and destruction. The tools available include evaluations of the personality traits in decision-making leaders. We can also collect data on large numbers of followers with the aid of electronic memories. Such steps collide with our current political and ethical considerations. Despite the fact that the consequences of psychopathological leadership or hysterical mass mobilization can now have magnified consequences, including even nuclear destruction, there are many among us who feel that the use of such tools is immoral. The individual leader seems to have the "natural" right to make errors without regard to the magnitude of consequences. The follower we feel should be protected from the dehumanizing impact of computer records and the resultant impersonal accounts. Our enthusiasm for this latter protection diminishes when an individual impinges on our liberty, and we find he is a person "who should have been known to the police" because he was previously imprisoned or hospitalized.

Perhaps we as group psychotherapists will take the lead in studying our own personalities and related leadership styles. When these are correlated with the outcome of our group work, we will have a basis for approaching broader cultural leadership issues. We may find some facts which contradict the intuitive or common sense expectation about leaders. For instance, the encounter group movement makes much of the intimacy achieved and its importance in the helping process. By now it is a common experience to find a group member recall the experience with the line "I'll never forget what's his name." The mask of intimacy in the group is apparently ephemeral.

In a follow-up of groups handled by therapists with different leadership styles, it has been found that the charismatic leader who makes the greater personal impact on the patient will generate enthusiasm for his treatment, despite a lack of evidence that the patient has been helped. The more pedestrian leader generates less enthusiasm and apparently delivers more help. Studies to validate or alter these conclusions would not only be of help in defining the characteristics of an effective group psychotherapist, but would also give us a start at being able to live up to the expectations of the community psychiatry concept.

The remote and impersonal leadership style has come to exemplify the Establishment, which is currently so evocative of hostility and distrust. This emotional evaluation must be replaced by research findings to know whether this current intuitive reaction is valid or misleading. The intimate leadership style can also create problems based on irrelevant judgments. Each time the group leadership is assumed by someone with no training, or very little training which could be called professional, there is an additional challenge to our professional identity and practice. The rise of paraprofessionalism in numbers and in status is frequently applauded. Our enthusiasm diminishes, however, when the paraprofessional promises to replace the professional rather than work with him.

Group psychotherapy, at its present level of exploration into all variations of leadership styles—from the most remote and objective to the most intimate and subjective—is in a position to play a large role in helping the dream of community psychiatry come true.

36. The Leader and Cultural Change

MAX ROSENBAUM

When Alexander Wolf became interested in the concept of group psychotherapy some thirty-five years ago, he may have had some idea of the geometric expansion of the field. Indeed, he may have fantasied about the number of therapists who would become involved with the concepts of group therapy. But I wonder if he contemplated the Pandora's box that would be opened as all types of people set themselves up as "group psychotherapists," especially as they became aware of the enormous power that one can wield as "leader" of a group.

The field of group psychotherapy in the U.S.A. is a jumble of techniques and maneuvers, most of them very weak on theory, and many of them with an almost religious quality of cultism. Under the large theme of group psychotherapy, one organization held a conference this past year and included the following techniques: rolfing, body massage, group games, fantasy imagery, Alexander techniques, movement in depth, theater of encounter, psychosynthesis, transactional analysis, interactional analysis, consciousness raising, family therapy, bioenergetics, gestalt therapy, sensitivity training, and encounter. A practicing group psychotherapist from South America, after surveying just part of the field, commented to this writer, "It's like a large Hollywood production, but what happens to the patient?"

In our current culture there is an enormous need for people to have some type of relationship, especially with the breakdown of the neighborhood and the disenchantment with organized religion. Even the concept of the family as a nuclear unit is under attack. There is a quality of loneliness on the American scene. Job mobility is on the increase, new communities are built, it would seem, almost overnight, and what used to be considered permanent friendships become quite impermanent as people move about rather frequently from one locale to another. The concept of the group format has

271

become a substitute for religion, the political club, or the volunteer fire department. Many people who enter groups are looking for friendships and companionship. And many of the people who lead groups are quite lonely themselves. All too often, under the label of marathon groups, we will observe leaders who are looking for a solution to their own sense of loneliness. What better way than to organize a group which meets for a weekend or seventy-two hours? The group leader feels self-sacrificing and enormously dedicated professionally. The members of the group feel very involved. After all, isn't the leader giving up a weekend or seventy-two hours of his life? Like the parable, no one bothers to ask why the emperor isn't wearing clothes or phrased differently, "What would we do, where would we go, if we didn't have the new subculture of the group?"

What has occurred is the movement in our culture from a therapy technique to a surface philosophy of life. Tragically, the larger social question of what forces in our society lead to the alienation of the individual is ignored as "leaders" form groups to take care of any and all problems of the individual. It is a kind of "sop," and individuals often become "group bums" like "ski bums," following some new type of subculture. A unique problem then ensues: the leader has established a positive transference largely based on the loneliness of the group member. Because of the group member's sense of isolation, he will continue to reinforce the leader's sense of importance. Classic techniques of reinforcement are at work. I am speaking here of vast numbers of groups that are not psychoanalytic, and where the group leader has no awareness of the transference phenomenon at work, and even less desire to resolve the transferential processes.

Wolf, Rosenbaum and others have discussed and written about the neurotic needs of the group leader who, for example, may form a group so that he may sit and bask in the "admiration" of the group members. The various neurotic mechanisms that lead people to form groups have been covered in some detail, as have the neurotic fears that lead some professionals to avoid work with groups. But, to my knowledge, very few writers have been concerned about the deeper implications of the sense of isolation in our society that leads people to Esalen-type experiences, where they can experience a short-lived euphoria and have an "unreal" sense of relatedness.

The more I observed the short-lived type of "encounter" or "marathon" experience, the more I wondered about whether there could be a fundamental rule at work. A rereading of Freud's book, *Group*

Psychology and the Analysis of the Ego (1955), led to some insight. Freud stated:

> Let us keep before our eyes the nature of the emotional relations which hold between men in general. According to Schopenhauer's famous simile of the freezing porcupines, no one can tolerate a too intimate approach to his neighbor.

And Freud goes on to describe the Schopenhauer parable:

> A company of porcupines crowded themselves very close together one cold winter's day so as to profit by one another's warmth and to save themselves from being frozen to death. But soon they felt one another's quills, which induced them to separate again. And now, when the need for warmth brought them together again, the second evil arose once more. So that they were driven backwards and forwards from one trouble to another until they had discovered a mean distance at which they could most tolerably exist. (Paerega und Paralipomena, Pt. II, 31, "Glerchinisee und Parablen.")

There is a humorous quality to Freud's use of the term "mean distance" as he describes the porcupines, for another sense of the word "mean" refers to anger, and this is the area that is really not worked through. This seemed to be the fundamental rule that I had been searching for. How to relieve the isolation of many unhappy people and yet find the "mean distance" that Freud wrote about. The problem of negative transference, character traits, has been faced by the "newer" group therapies by establishing the "mean distance"—in this case, brief therapies that would meet no longer than a weekend and preferably in resort-type settings which would serve to dissipate any intense analysis of the unconscious, resistance, or transference.

In previous writings (Rosenbaum 1970, 1971, 1972) I have discussed the climate of anti-intellectualism that currently exists in education as well as in the field of psychotherapy, which is a type of education. The touch-feel experiences are all predicated upon the denial of the intellect, which is seen as intrusive to the "real inner self." Briefly summarized, I feel that the climate of anti-intellectualism eventually supports the concept of the powerful leader, which in turn leads to Fascism. This is the theme that Erich Fromm noted many years ago when he observed the strong needs of people to find a leader who would make major decisions for them. But the thrust of my comments at this time concerns the leader who misleads—who offers the *panacea of therapy* while, in truth, he is helping the group member find a technique which appears to be treatment but which simply mollifies the unconscious.

In this fashion, even the group leader's unconscious is not tampered with. One of the major results of this maneuver is that both group member and group leader have "conned" themselves into one of the greatest swindles. They have entered into a pact to avoid hostility. The agreement is that only loving and benign feelings are the important feelings. If people agree to sway together, roll together, gather together and urge someone to fall back with his eyes closed in order to stimulate trust—"Don't worry, we'll catch you,"—the pact is that therapy is at work. What is at work is the therapeutic version of Christianity—"love thy neighbor."

Freud was more "hard-nosed," and he knew that his concepts would be intolerable in the U.S.A. He noted that Adler's more superficial treatment of life-styles would be more palatable. He appears to have been accurate in his assessment of the American scene. Any technique that does not face the fundamental rage in people but encourages them to acquire new techniques of "relating" is acceptable. How else to account for the fact that Carl Rogers, formerly a theology student and one of the strongest supporters of the encounter movement, is someone who stresses the phrase "unconditional regard"? With reference to groups, Rogers calls the process and the dynamics "the immediate personal interaction" (Rogers 1968). But rather than describe these offshoots as stemming from humanistic psychology, as some observers see the trend, I would prefer to call these "here and now" techniques a palatable version of Christianity in therapeutic dress. One of the problems, as I perceive it, is how to reconcile Christianity and the individual's unresolved guilt about leaving a structured religion for a group that lacks structure.

Rogers has described the group experience as follows:

Milling around: which Rogers calls cocktail party talk.

Resistance to personal expression or exploration: When a member reveals some personal attitudes, other members are ambivalent in an effort to cut off the exchange of personal feelings.

Description of past feelings: Members describe past experiences and feelings come to the surface.

Expression of negative feelings: Rogers observes that the first feeling relative to other group members tends to be negative and he describes this as the test of trustworthiness. He explains that the expression of deeply positive feelings is much more inhibition-bound than the expression of negative feeling.

While Rogers' observations may or may not be accurate, Christianity stresses "love thy neighbor" and the murderous rage of the individual is never acceptable. Biblical theology in the New Testament stresses that hostility is sinful. There is a theory that the violence to be found in the Old Testament had to be counterbalanced by the preachings to be found in the New Testament. Perhaps this applies to the findings of Freud, especially his observations about Thanatos and Eros. While it is easy to describe his observations as those of a sick old man dying of cancer, they cannot be denied in a decade which has witnessed Bangladesh, India-Pakistan, Biafra and other atrocities which seem to confirm Freud's observations about man's destructiveness. (It is this writer's opinion that what Rogers describes as "expression of negative feelings" is part of the "swindle" where group member and group leader agree to get beyond negative material as quickly as possible so that "love" emerges.)

Rogers then describes:

Expression and exploration of personally meaningful material: based on Rogers' hypothesis that when negative feelings have been expressed and accepted, a climate of trust ensues which permits more open discussion of topics. (This writer believes that what Rogers calls a climate of trust is essentially part of the contract where two people agree that "you are not going to hit me too hard" and vice versa.)

Expression of immediate interpersonal feelings in the group: Here-and-now feelings that members experience toward one another are brought out into the open.

Development of a healing capacity in the group: The group members are supportive, making helpful suggestions and giving what Rogers calls "empathic acceptance."

Self-acceptance is the beginning of change: The group members begin to change as members accept their patterns of behavior.

This writer has not listed other stages which Rogers describes, but these are the major ones. Rogers also describes feedback where the group member begins to learn how he appears to others. If one reads carefully it has all the elements of a religious revival. The intrapsychic is carefully veered away from and the emphasis is upon acceptance. Rogers himself is benign in his manner and the nonverbal message is that "love" is the commodity that is being worked with. Freud was a much greater realist, since he was willing and eager to work with the repressed material of the unconscious.

Those exponents of the encounter method who want to work with hostility can use the techniques of Schutz (1967). Since he believes that hostility is inhibited at a very early age, he uses techniques such as pounding on pillows or on a couch. After this physical release, a person is supposedly able to express hostility verbally and with less anxiety. This is simply a series of conditioning exercises where anger expressed in pillow pounding inhibits the anxiety previously experienced by the individual if he were to express his hostile feelings. The group members enthusiastically support this type of ventilation of hostile feelings and they, in turn, serve as reinforcement for this conditioning. The nonverbal pact continues: "Hit the pillow—don't hit me." Occasionally the unconscious breaks through and there follow the reports of physical injury in encounter groups. In short, conditioning techniques have not worked.

There is no intent on the part of this writer to turn to theology, but one cannot help but notice that the leading sages of Judaism did not preach "love thy neighbor" but, instead, espoused the philosophy "do unto others as you would have them do unto you." Thus, Freud continued to be a realist in his efforts to ascertain an individual's potential—for both loving and murderous feelings.

What we see at work in the current scene is palatable Christianity applied to psychotherapy. It is quite similar to the feeling of well-being that is experienced by people who attend church on Sunday morning. The majority of encounter group leaders who were surveyed viewed the major function of the group as simply providing an intense emotional experience. This was found by Rogers himself in a survey (1967). Most of the participants reported satisfaction with their group experience. They were frequently described by others as showing an improvement in interpersonal skills. The group experience *does* provide an intense emotional experience. There is little evidence that significant personality changes or attitude changes result.

Much of what I have noted up to this point becomes relevant as one attempts to ascertain what group participants are looking for and what the leader intends to supply. It would appear that the situation is not unlike what religious leaders express when Billy Graham, the evangelist, "comes to town." There is a tremendous upswell of feeling for Christ, but the basic concepts of Christianity are ignored as participants in a Graham revival express enormous affect. The question is what is at work and how does it apply to the field of psychotherapy.

Since fundamental Christianity embodies the concept of "original guilt," it would seem likely that the individual will avoid a depth therapy which at the outset would conceivably reinforce guilt. This might happen since the individual becomes introspective as he considers intrapsychic forces at work. The person, busy searching, is led to consider a leader whose technique minimizes the intrapsychic and introspective and instead encourages a new behavior repertoire. It is the question of how to go to church, obtain salvation, and yet not be too upset by some of the fundamental questions that will be brought to the surface. Why not contribute to the Sunday collection plate and "screw your customer" Monday morning? Why not pound a pillow and avoid the fundamental rage that led you to become proprietor of a business that sells guns?

The current "scene" in psychotherapy emphasizes a surface handling of deepseated problems and the untrained group leader joins in the deception. This is all under the guise of American pragmatism. If it works, it is good. It's much easier to go to church and resolve your problems temporarily than consider the deeper implications of man's relation with his fellow man. It's much easier to gain the temporary euphoria than work toward larger goals.

What we currently have at work is a new *paradigm.* Historically, paradigms attract followers away from other methods of scientific inquiry. Also, new paradigms are open-ended so that they leave a grab bag of problems for new practitioners to solve. While Rogers and B. F. Skinner ostensibly would appear to be worlds apart, they are actually quite similar. Skinner believes in the concept of reductionism, and believes in the laboratory. Rogers stresses the concept of reductionism, but his reliance on the here-and-now experience is as laboratory oriented as Skinner's position. Recall that Skinner is concerned with manipulation and control (1971). Essentially, in his latest work, *Beyond Freedom and Dignity*, he is discussing social control.

Skinner has been a great influence, if not *the* influence, on students of "behavior modification." Their concern currently is with shaping, programmed learning, and token economies. In the "newer" therapies, despite the professed humanism of the group leader, the intent is behavior modification. Consider that Skinner postulates a "black box" view of man. He is concerned with studying the relationships that exist between the inputs and outputs from the "black box" and constructing a science based on these observations. Therefore, he has decided to research the observable relationships rather than "waste" time with concerns about changing the "unreadable" inside of man. The emphasis is on the externals of man and the externals can be manipulated. This is similar to the "new" approaches to group therapy which, while they profess a humanistic base, are basically concerned with devising a new behavioral repertoire. Skinner promotes the use of social control by people who are supposed to be concerned with the ultimate welfare of man. Since social control will be exercised by someone, Skinner has decided who the *someone* shall be. But the college students who study Skinner frequently ask, "Who will control the controllers?" Beyond this there is a fundamental problem which leaders of the "new" group therapies often ignore—either because they want to or because they really don't see the basic issue. To have the technical knowledge of manipulating people vests the leader with enormous power. Fascists and Communists know this very well. So we have a strange situation where humanists who use the new encounter techniques are busy shaping man and the future. They are essentially undermining the very freedom and dignity to which they pay lip service.

When people learn *techniques* of relating as a primary thrust, the very autonomy of man is undermined. The existential humanists speak of the "inside" of man, yet the "here and now" experience is worshipped. Every technique that the leader of the "here and now" experience promotes obfuscates fundamental values, since the group members are viewed as objects. This is in the same dimension as sex researchers who analyze physiological responses and deny the romance quality of the human experience.

When one surveys the field of operant conditioning, it is interesting that the first thing is to note the hunger of the subjects in the experiment. Pigeons who are hungry will take the pellets they are conditioned with. Human beings who are emotionally hungry and lonely will take the pellets of "trust exercises." How else to account for the fact that people will respond to advertisements, come to hotels in major cities of the U.S.A. dressed in casual clothing and ready to embark upon sensory awakening, sensory awareness, encounter experiences and meditation?

Gestalt therapy emphasizes awareness of the moment. The group participant is encouraged to enact his dreams and fantasies before the group. This is pure conditioning. The price of acceptance to the group is the leader's right to *demand* that fantasies be enacted before the group. When Perls, the leader of the Gestalt therapy movement was alive, he would consistently ridicule one psychotherapist who would attend his training centers. This unfortunate woman was locked into a positive transference where Perls served as her father figure, albeit the rejecting father. He was consistently hostile to the psychotherapist, and she kept returning to the rejection experience. There was never any discussion of transference or the unconscious forces that led the woman to return for her abuse.

In the sensory awakening and sensory awareness experience, the focus is on developing appreciation of taste, smell, hearing, sight, touch, and feel. A psychology of play is at work. In the encounter experience, historical material is denied since this is seen as resistance to the examination of current interactions. Again, like the pigeon, the idea is to work with what is happening "right now." The humanism of many of the leaders of the "newer group therapies" is not humanism. It is manipulation. They have developed a "hardware" to enable people to "fly" aircraft more safely. In this case the aircraft consists of emotions. The questions of whether the skies are overcrowded and there is pollution from the aircraft—these questions are not considered or are ignored. The person who does not want to "fly" is seen as unable to engage in "authentic relationships." The "mechanics" of living have supplanted the long term goal of the thoughtful, loving human being. The individual learns "how to adjust" at the expense of inner maturation. The robot-like quality of much human behavior is reinforced through techniques which teach behavioral repertoire. In a sense, the individual learns how to "act." Recall the familiar expression in our culture, "I'll act as if I care; I'll act as if I am pleased." This is in contrast to "I'll be pleased; I'll care."

It seems to me that this current state of affairs justifies Freud's anxiety about what would happen to depth therapy once it was introduced to the U.S.A. He felt that it would be vitiated and that the essential philosophical core would be ignored. In short, the technique would be stressed at the expense of the philosophy. Many psychoanalytically trained psychotherapists have been "technique" trained to the exclusion of the deeper implications of what they are engaged in. They have ended up in the same arena as the "mechanics" of sensitivity training. The very term sensitivity training implies how to train to become sensitive. The overemphasis on standardization of the psychoanalytic therapist's training has led to the total neglect of the philosophical basis of the work he is engaged in. The overpreoccupation with the clinical and the clinical distortions have led to emphasis on "relief." Because of a fundamental weakness in the philosophical training of psychoanalytic group therapists, they have either been unaware of or fearful of confronting directly the dangers of the "newer" therapies. Perhaps there is the fear of revealing one's ignorance. It is difficult to debate an adversary when you are not too sure of your own values. The reader is urged to study the training programs of the psychoanalytic institutes. He will find no statement of philosophical orientation. A lot of things are taken for granted about the background of candidates for training in depth therapy.

My plea here is *not* that we subscribe to old traditions for the sake of tradition, but rather that we understand our major responsibility to train people who are skilled enough to read behind charisma. The encounter movement and sensitivity technique use scientific language to elevate a process which consists of rapid excitement. It is like shadow boxing with an elusive opponent who does not abide by any standards and attacks any use of intellect. There is no specified goal, and the leader is thus able to encourage acting out. He is a willing witness to the tragedy of a group of people brought together for mutual exploitation primarily because of the social hunger that mobility in the U.S.A. has created. Europe has been able, to date, to fight off sensitivity movements because there is less social mobility and less leisure time activity where individuals feel guilty and uncomfortable and need to justify their spare-time activity. Also, Europeans don't get caught up in the concept of "basic goodness" of man where the "inner core" is considered good if only the disabling layers are stripped away. Last, Europeans are able to leave organized religion and go to new religions of the political far right and far left.

I believe the encounter movement to be basically encouraging of manipulative and destructive maneuvers. It is a dangerous technique in the hands of disturbed leaders. I believe that it has "crested out" and reached its zenith and will slowly decline. Therapists who are trained in depth should have been less reluctant until now to have confronted a questionable technique masquerading under the guise of science. There is always anxiety at work when psychoanalysts have to confront in the public arena group therapy leaders who are in truth leaders of cults. This was a task that Freud did not shrink from, and we can do no less.

I believe that nothing should be taken for granted in the training of the leader of a group. Psychoanalytic group therapists should be required to study, as part of the training, the philosophical issues inherent in science and social science: freedom and determinism, the role of value judgments, reductionism, and paradoxes in the concept of autonomy.

All of this will bring forth charges of "elitism." The careful delineation of human behavior and the problems of the culture are not fashionable in a climate of "anti-intellectualism." But it is no surprise (Lipset and Raab 1970) to note the narrow ideological commitments of the majority of Americans which lead them periodically to flirtations with extremist politics as well as extremist psychotherapies. Our training should equip us to be both elitist and democratic. The majority of "middle Americans" (55-63% of the 1969 population) described life in America as meaningless. It is part of our responsibility to develop and delineate a higher purpose of life (Lemon 1970). Rousseau stated that the highest good for man is the maximization of freedom in community, a concept that many scientists attack as too visionary and abstract. But is Pareto's dictum (1935) that it is not in the nature of science to provide the ends men ought to pursue, a dictum that any ethical practitioner would ally himself with? So we must define, work through, and move toward a higher level of living, and we must come to grips with those so-called "leaders" who would have us settle for dross.

Finally, the thoughtful and trained leader of the group will integrate some techniques of the encounter movement, but these techniques will be used against a background of experience and clinical maturity. As the culture changes, so will techniques.

Through the years Alexander Wolf, as one of the pioneers in the field of group psychotherapy, has consistently expressed his point of view cogently and has not permitted himself to be caught up in the latest fads. He has set an example of what honest leadership is all about. This writer, too, encourages the innovative use of new approaches in psychotherapy, but all of this must be against the background of a therapist's thought-through philosophy of psychotherapy practice.

REFERENCES

Back, K. W. *Beyond Words—The Story of Sensitivity Training and the Encounter Movement* (New York: Basic Books; Russell Sage Foundation, 1972).

Freud, S. *Group Psychology and the Analysis of the Ego*, Vol. 18. in *Complete
Psychological Works of Sigmund Freud* (London: Hogarth Press, 1955).

Lemon, R. *The Troubled American* (New York: Simon & Schuster, 1970).

Lipset, S. M., and Raab, E. *The Politics of Unreason: Right-Wing Extremism in
America, 1790-1970* (New York: Harper & Row, 1970).

Pareto, V. *A Treatise on General Sociology* (New York: Dover Publications,
1935).

Rogers, C. "The Process of the Basic Encounter Group." Bugental, J. F., ed.,
Challenges of Humanistic Psychology (New York: McGraw-Hill, 1967),
p. 261.

Rogers, C. *The Process of the Basic Encounter Group* (La Jolla, Calif.: Western
Behavioral Sciences Institute, 1968).

Rosenbaum, M. "The Responsibility of the Psychotherapy Practitioner for a
Therapeutic Rationale." *Journal of Group Psychoanalysis and Process* 3,
2 (Winter 1969-70):5-17.

Rosenbaum, M. "Responsibility of the Therapist for a Theoretic Rationale."
Group Process 3, 2 (Winter 1970-71):41-47.

Rosenbaum, M. "An Overview of Group Psychotherapy and the Present Trend."
Group Process 4, 2, (Spring 1972):19-32.

Schutz, W. *Joy* (New York: Grove Press, 1967).

Skinner, B. F. *Beyond Freedom and Dignity* (New York: Knopf, 1971).

37. The Psychoanalyst As Leader in a Community Service

SERGE LEBOVICI

The purpose of this article is to describe the functions and responsibilities of leadership as it has been assumed by psychiatrists and psychoanalysts within both a Parisian psychiatric service and the community of 165,000 people that it serves. The socio-economic and socio-cultural level of this community was rather poor until recent improvements forced the most deprived families into the outlying areas. A young population of a higher socio-economic stratum has moved into the large blocks of apartment dwellings which have replaced unsanitary dwellings and factories.

The psychiatric facility is composed of two departments: one is for children; the other is for adults and the aged. The theory guiding the service, and its practical implications, are best explicated in *The Psychoanalyst Without a Couch*, by P. C. Racamier (1970). At the heart of the different teams working full or part-time in the two departments (which have various institutions at their disposal) are psychoanalysts who assume the role of leaders—a development which has numerous consequences.

In the department of child and adolescent psychiatry (the project to which we will primarily refer) the presence of psychoanalysts has a particularly heavy impact due to the fact that there are so many employed there. Identification, however, is mainly with the director of the service—a well-established psychoanalyst who is surrounded by the aura of national and international recognition.

During the first fifteen years of its existence, the personnel of this service were divided into two classes, the psychoanalysts and their assistants (that is, all of those who assisted the psychoanalysts in any

283

way). The former were regarded as being imbued with special powers of omniscience—as though they were capable of examining everyone's unconscious. Identified with the leader (i.e., the director of the service), the psychoanalysts were regarded as the bearers of the ego-ideal, therefore receiving all the narcissistic projections and being the object of the prevalent belief that psychoanalysts are endowed with unequalled phallic powers.

The intensity of this projection deserves to be analyzed. The weight of psychoanalytic theory in clinical and therapeutic activity, in research and in teaching seems to justify this splitting, but there can also be more complex processes of identification in situations such as the community service. Freud (1948), for example, in *Group Psychology and the Analysis of the Ego,* described how the libidinal nature of ties in identification is well-founded and how the conflictualization of this identification is also valid.

This dichotomy came to light in May, 1968. The leader of the services was accused of accumulating "the knowledge and the power" in his hands. The young rivals of the psychoanalyst advocated the separation of the psychoanalyst's knowledge from the direction of the service. They claimed that in this type of service, the psychoanalyst should only embody the psychoanalytic attitude, listen with his "third ear," and in essence limit his activity to interpretations. According to his opponents, the director should be a screen for transferential projections which must remain pure of all contamination by external reality—in particular, the functioning of the service.

During a heated meeting at the center, one which focused on the above problem and triggered intense and long-winded dissertations, a guinea pig escaped from the cage in which it had been enclosed, whereupon the young revolutionaries betrayed phobic manifestations by leaving the meeting as quickly as possible. This illustrates that as in all phobias, the superego can be conceptualized as floating and ready to crystallize on a phobogenic object with symbolic value—in this case the psychoanalyst leaders. These leaders had not interpreted anything, but their presence in a situation which would clearly confirm Freud's death instinct precipitated the revolutionaries' reaction. Masochism, which had been expressed diffusely in verbal aggression, found a projection on which to focus.

This anecdote is comprised of facts which cannot be overlooked. It is difficult for a psychoanalyst who is used to being a screen for ambivalent projections to respond with reciprocally ambivalent counter-attitudes. However, his role as leader should not be confused with that of a psychoanalyst in a group united by professional functions. One can say that the countertransference to which he is constantly liable puts him in an inevitably painful situation. There is the basic assumption that he is the leader, father-mother, thanks to whom the ties of identification are built. At the same time, being concerned with efficiency and coherence, he must exercise a certain authority that, whether he likes it or not, places him in a hierarchically-defined position.

These facts lead to a consideration of the traditional definitions of interdisciplinary teamwork. The concordance which must define it is, in fact, only made possible by the presence of a leader whose role transcends the functional and organizational realities. It has often been said that the team leader must sufficiently master group dynamics since one finds in them the necessary foundations of identification. Nevertheless, libidinal ties must be tempered by the realities of the individual work of each team member and by the necessity of decision-making which is only possible within the framework of assumed responsibilities.

These remarks are necessary when one is aware of the impact of the projections directed onto the psychoanalyst being judged as omnipotent. We observed, for example, that the representatives from diverse disciplines working with the service gradually became contaminated with the ego-ideal projected onto psychoanalysis and psychoanalysts. Everyone wanted to be a psychoanalyst. A number of co-workers in the service, regardless of their professional orientation, were tempted by the idea of being psychoanalyzed. This was complicated by the fact that often enough the psychoanalysis was justified by the existence of neurotic troubles or by the particular nature of mental functioning. What was generally not understood was that being psychoanalyzed does not make one a psychoanalyst. Hence, dual phenomena exist which explain the distortion of identification. After being psychoanalyzed there are risks both of losing one's professional identity and of becoming an "underground analyst," without the benefit of regular and continuous training. In the service we have been describing, an attempt was made to minimize this difficulty by creating a training center for child psychotherapists.

We also observed, particularly in the institutions attached to this service, the difficulties often brought to light by the presence of psychoanalysts of whom everything is asked in order to facilitate their rejection, or even worse, to keep them ineffectual, separated from the daily functioning of the service and institutional life. (In this case, the situation was even more difficult because of the large number of psychoanalysts.) The problems of identification were compounded by an "as if" attitude. That is, the technicians pretended they were psychoanalysts and indulged in games of interpretation which soon resulted in an extreme diffusion of transference. The effect of this behavior on the patients was that there was no longer a distinction between the place where one lived and had to adapt to reality and the place where interpretation takes place and where reality must be allowed to elaborate itself in the framework of understanding of fantasy life and distribution of drives.

Such effects could only be corrected by considering the work of the team and the role the psychoanalyst-leader can play within that team—a role which stresses his active presence more than his interpretive statements. I believe the importance of a psychoanalyst lies more in what he is than in what he says. Indeed, what he is allows him to maintain an observer's attitude, not to behave as a disembodied person, and to facilitate concurrence in decisions. Everyday experience shows that decision-making necessitates calling upon patients, provided they have not been made insecure by an environment of continuous interpretation. Likewise, their families can participate in meetings in which the role of the leader, although not explicitly evident, can take on its total significance when it is assumed by a psychoanalyst used to group work.

The foregoing notes have attempted to portray the consequences introduced by the presence of a psychoanalyst in a psychiatric service when he assumes the role of leader. We will now turn our attention to his role in the work carried on in the community with examples referring to the same project.

In community work the image of the leader is quite different than it is in the service itself. The fact that he is a psychoanalyst does not pose the same problems as those which have been examined above. One can say that his ability, his knowledge of interpersonal as well as intrapsychic processes, and his comprehension of group dynamics naturally designate him representative of the psychiatric service in all cases where there are tasks concerning mental health problems, particularly in the field of preventive action.

Nevertheless, opposition to this point of view is frequently observed. It is certain that in a number of cases, there is no reason for the psychoanalyst to actually assume the role of leader, a situation which occurs in many institutional services concerned with infancy or adolescence. A distinction is easily made between the organic role of leader, which is not necessarily that of being responsible for the institution, and his actual role, which stems from his knowledge of the problem treated and his understanding of the group process. For example, in the case of institutions which attend to the health of young children, it is most desirable for the pediatricians to treat mental health problems themselves, the parents being somewhat reluctant to accept the idea that their young children need psychiatric help. Consequently, in many situations the psychoanalyst working in a community service must confine himself to the role of consultant.

We will now turn to two concrete examples of this type: services intended for infants in good health—The Maternal and Infant Protection Services, as they are called in France—and the School Services. The Maternal and Infant Protection Services function to assure the surveillance of the health of young children. They administer necessary vaccinations at parental request and perform compulsory medical check-ups during childhood, of which the parents must show proof in order to receive certain state allowances. Outpatient services are often annexed to the medical check-ups of preschool children.

In our project, the leader psychoanalyst contacted the district Maternal and Infant Protection Service and proposed to provide them with assistance in detecting the existence of mental health problems and in undertaking prophylactic activity affecting the parents. The leader was received very cordially, but it was not difficult for him to ascertain that they merely wanted to keep him amused.

Consequently, cases which in the opinion of the pediatricians indicated mental health problems were referred to him, although they could have been completely examined at the mental health center for children. Nevertheless, the director accepted this task and rapidly discovered that the time he was able to devote to the Maternal and Infant Protection Service was very quickly taken up by the assessment of cases referred to him. He therefore suggested another means of collaboration. This consisted in discussions about the cases in which the pediatricians would be able to play a more complete role, gain a better understanding of the psychological problems which they were faced with, and resolve them in the actual circumstances of their experience—in other words, brief and sporadic contacts with young mothers and their infants.

A work group was formed accordingly. It brought together pediatricians and their assistants, public health nurses, specialists in infant welfare, and psychologists. Once more, the group had to work against an artificial identification with the psychoanalyst. It was necessary to show members of the group that it was not a matter of copying what was visible in the psychoanalyst's attitude, but to accept their own roles. For example, we had to recognize the fact that young mothers sought the pediatricians' advice and expected a certain steadfast, concerned attitude when this advice was given.

Our purpose is not to enter into the details of the development of the work group whose existence was prolonged for so many years but to emphasize that in this case, we did not intend to copy the functioning of the training group that Balint (1965) described. The structure of our group was gradually determined by the study of actual case material. It seemed to us that the groups formed according to Balint's method were organized to study the responsibility of the technician presenting the case, with the purpose of more fully understanding his behavior and psychology in order to produce certain modifications of mental functioning that would permit him to better assume the responsibilities he holds. Here, the situation seemed to be different, inasmuch as the specialists from one discipline, the pediatricians and their collaborators, sought a better understanding of the mental hygiene problems with which they were faced. Accordingly, it has always been our opinion that the psychoanalysts must not refuse to furnish the keys to comprehension of each case. The organization of our group permitted it to identify with the psychoanalyst through the information he had provided them, which was received by the group as if it were a gift.

It soon became evident, in the course of discussion, that what was valued was not so much the content of what the psychoanalyst had provided, as the fact that he did not take refuge in silence and psychoanalytical pseudo-listening. This willingness to share information modified the ambivalence of the group toward the psychoanalyst-leader, so that it became less destructive. In addition, the fact that the leader exposed himself by revealing his ideas had a positive influence on the evolution of the group, based on the better insight afforded its various members.

Another example to which we would like to refer is the role of the leader in the public services of National Education. In France—and this exists in many other countries as well—the school services have their own mental health organizations. This duplication of services has deleterious effects, not only on the utilization of public funds, but on the families who are liable to be torn between two types of influences which are not coordinated.

It was therefore necessary for the representative of the community psychiatric service to persuade the school authorities not to organize two specialized services concerned with mental health in this district of Paris. As a result of the initial contacts established with the school authorities at the opening of the psychiatric service, it was impossible to avoid a situation which, from the beginning, was considered hazardous for the mental health of the population concerned.

It was understood that, in certain cases where the children could not be driven to the center, the psychiatric service would send a representative directly into the schools. In this manner, he could also help the teachers because of his knowledge of child development and mental health. It was under these circumstances that the work groups were created and the study of school-related problems made possible: those problems between the child and his family on the one hand, and those between the child and his teacher on the other.

After a few years it appeared that the teams formed by the National Educational Services to study adjustment problems were able to function at the core of the district schools and that the groups called psychopedagogical adjustment groups (d'adaptation psychopedagogiques) were able to be set up to study specific educational problems and to carry out remedial education, with particular emphasis on written language.

From that time on, it seemed fitting that the representatives of the psychiatric service stand aside and that a movement back toward the service take place in order to allow teams to take root and to give them a legitimate sense of security. It was imperative to establish a new collaboration at a sufficiently centralized level in order to compel recognition in all schools where the psychopedagogical action groups were set up. At the same time, it had to be arranged for the psychiatrist to play the role of consultant in these groups; not to examine the children directly but to discuss certain cases, using the information collected by the teachers and by members of the psychopedagogical action groups.

We had to convince the members of the psychiatric team to cease playing a direct role in the school, where they had gotten into the habit of working, and to assure the psychopedagogical teams that they were able to call upon the psychiatrist's services. This tactic, somewhat military in nature, of penetrating and subsequently decolonizing foreign territory, gives some idea of what appears to be indispensable in this type of action in community services.

Among the numerous difficulties implied by such a development, the following predominates: the leader inevitably had to collaborate with the school authorities and was then considered as a participant in the hierarchy established by the national educational services—a hierarchy which is quite pronounced in France. If, however, the leader had appeared to be representing only this hierarchy, he could not be accepted into the psychopedagogical groups which had been organized. Similarly, if he demonstrated more concern for his membership in these groups than in the National Education Services, he risked losing the confidence of the school authorities, who would be suspicious of the influence—probably too important from their point of view—that he could have exercised.

Once again, it was in having a specific role and assuming it as such that an ambiguous situation of this type did not have negative effects, but, to the contrary, seemed to permit a certain evolution. In the eyes of the school authorities as well as in the eyes of the members of the psychopedagogical team, the psychoanalyst had to appear to be playing a specific role.

The problems inherent in the situation were able to be alleviated by the presence of the psychoanalyst in "work days," the organization of which he had proposed. During the course of these work days, held periodically throughout the year, it had been agreed that the teachers would bring in specific cases relating to everyday life in the classrooms, for the purpose of group study.

The first day of study was devoted to the contacts between the families and the teachers with regard to the report card (carnet de notes). This is a booklet on which the marks received by the child during the month are written; the children must bring it to their parents who must give evidence of having looked at the marks by affixing their signature to the card. Because of this tradition, which has not changed very much in the past years, the signature on the carnet de notes is destined to become the object of numerous family crises. When the marks have not been good, the child is scolded or punished; if the mother wants to protect her child, she signs it herself in order to avoid any difficulties with the father. In other cases, which are frequent, the father's only educative function is his solemn signing of the carnet de notes, and in sanctioning the grades signed on it with either punishment or reward. The parents often write a few comments to the teachers with their signature, constituting one of the forms of communication the latter have with the families. Under the circumstances, it is understandable that returning the carnet de notes is an important—often a dreaded event in the scholastic life of children. It goes without saying that little schemes are often contrived for the occasion: amelioration of the grades by the child before having his report card signed, concealment of the card for several days when it is bad, etc.

During the course of this work day, the teachers studied these problems comprehensively, encountering a great deal of difficulty in transcending the assumptions by which they worked: namely, that the work of the child must be made known to the parents; that there are lazy children and hard workers; that the manner in which they work must be sanctioned; that there are good and bad students.

It was not a question of obtaining a radical change in the subject matter, because for many teachers in France the notion of effort in the field of education and the notion of boredom, of necessary sanctions, are too often profoundly united. Instead, it was necessary for the teachers to understand the concept of a child's educational contract with his parents and his school. This contract does not exclude the effort required to learn but must show the child, at an early stage in his schooling, that he has a certain autonomy in relation to the contract which he has accepted.

Thus, in the case of school services, the psychoanalyst-leader must impart the knowledge afforded by his experience and must furnish a model which allows those with whom he works to pass beyond the stage where they sit in judgment to the point where they offer new experiences to the children.

The psychoanalyst's background is probably most valuable in this situation, since it shows how neutrality, in the absence of internal reactions, of guilt feelings and aggression, can benefit the scholastic effort and the educational contract.

In the previous examples, it is clear that the psychoanalyst-leader, on the condition that he devote a sufficient amount of time to this type of work and has adequate knowledge of small group processes, can succeed, at least to some extent, in modifying the work of the institutions of the community to which he belongs, thus representing in an effective manner the psychiatric service. Within this range of experience, the psychoanalyst can find himself relatively comfortable, even if he must be capable of making an effort to identify with the representatives of the services with whom he comes into contact and with whom he works.

In some cases, though, training alone is not sufficient, especially in those cases which deal with what we refer to in France as atypical or multiple-problem families. These families are not necessarily miserable or poor: their standard of living is rather comparable to that of the working classes, but deprivation occurs primarily in the socio-cultural sphere. These families have often resided in a district for several generations and generally live in deteriorated dwellings, refusing relocation. They have a unique life style, in that their expenses generally exceed their income and they live in a state of constant debt. Nevertheless, they continue to buy powerful cars and useless household appliances on credit, without having the money to pay for them. Alcoholism is rampant and drug addiction is becoming a problem. This psychopathic style of behavior can be observed in all the generations and is characterized by a propensity to act out, which is the fundamental problem of the children. The school is not used as a channel of communication and information is not disseminated through discourse. The children get knocked around and fight back.

Under such conditions, one can say with regard to psychopathology that no solid psychological framework can be observed to develop. The psychoanalyst is evidently not well equipped to intervene in this case and act as an acceptable leader. Various services have been organized to respond to the psychiatric needs of this type of family.

In the department for adults, it appeared that treatment in the homes allowed the psychiatric teams to intervene under more positive conditions, and that psychotherapeutic action—non-codified psychotherapeutic action—with the family could be useful.

In the department for children, we felt that an action undertaken after school, in the evening, would establish a link between the child and his family, between the family and community institutions. In these cases, difficulties in learning how to read could not be considered as isolated from the child's personality organization but a reflection of the same. No systematic psychotherapy could have been undertaken, and we felt that the psychoanalyst had to intervene as a member of the team, representing verbal communication in the framework of daily action, which we hoped would be conducive to the circulation of language and to the development of an appreciation for written forms as well.

In this case, then, nonverbal communication had to be favored in the group and the psychoanalyst could not be an acceptable leader, either within the service or in relation to the families, without having prior prolonged and intensive experience in the ways of life particular to these groups. We can even go so far as to say that not all psychoanalysts can open up to this new way of thinking and acting, and under no conditions would we obligate them to do so merely out of concern for efficiency in carrying out an activity.

We hope to have shown that in a psychiatric service where psychoanalytic references prevail and the leader is usually a psychoanalyst, particular undertakings by the service do not lend themselves to the psychoanalyst's training. His personal manner may also be a constraining factor in considering him for the role of leader, in spite of the organization planned.

Finally, we would like to reiterate that in the service described here—both within the service and in the community—the psychoanalyst appeared as the natural leader and was generally accepted as such since he represented by an inner capacity, by his training, and through his practice the very image the service wished to communicate. We have shown how his knowledge is elevated into power, even within the service, and that the power bestowed on him can lead to difficulties in interpersonal relationships in the course of daily affairs. In any case, this power emanates neither from the power projected onto him because of psychoanalytic training nor from the realities of the power conferred on him by the administrative structure of the service where he has a directive role. It seemed essential for us to point out that the leader's authority, in such conditions, stems not only from the specific qualities of his experience but more importantly from what he is as a person and as a psychoanalyst—in other words, from his ability to not react to conflicts and rivalries in the usual manner.

In these circumstances, it is not evident that the principles of team work can be applied as easily as is generally assumed. The responsibility for decisions and action cannot be neglected for the benefit of a pseudo-democratic egalitarianism. Such a conception of the leader's role does not in any way preclude interdisciplinary discussion or the possibilities for interprofessional identification.

The psychoanalyst, who generally belongs to the upper middle class and who, more often than not, has completed graduate studies, cannot identify with every situation or every stratum of population. We have attempted to show that his knowledge and his power come up against barriers of identification, leaving him incapable of responding to all situations, as in the case of the problem families described above.

The knowledge and the power bestowed on the psychoanalyst-leader thus have limits. The recognition of these limits is imperative so that actions undertaken can be carried out successfully under certain specified conditions. This is especially necessary if the various members of the team are to accept the fact that the leader's authority does not rest on an illusion, but has very real foundations.

We have not been concerned with giving an idealized picture of the functions and role of this type of leader in the service chosen as an example. We have seen that the conflicts are numerous and that in certain circumstances they reveal themselves subtly.

The example was, nevertheless, chosen of a project probably original to France, where psychoanalysts did not hesitate on occasion to leave their offices and easy chairs and devote part of their time to psychiatric community work, embarking on activities in conditions relatively alien to their everyday experience, but where their particular training proved to be especially fruitful.

REFERENCES

Racamier, Paul Claude. *Le Psychoanalyste Sans Divan* (Paris: Payot, 1970).

Freud, Sigmund. *Group Psychology and the Analysis of the Ego* (London: Hogarth Press, 1948).

Balint, Michael. *Primary Love and Psychoanalytic Technique* (New York: Liveright, 1965).

A MEMORIAL TO THE LEADERSHIP
OF EMANUEL K. SCHWARTZ

Leadership and the Psychotherapist

EMANUEL K. SCHWARTZ

The nature of human relationships is only ideally equalitarian. But it is a human goal toward which all societies must strive and toward which each social unit, even the family, ultimately aspires. The wish for equalization of status or role function is a basic human experience and colors interpersonal transactions. The hierarchical relationship between authorities and subordinates, and even among authority figures and among peers—since functional co-equals exist only as ideals—is best illustrated in the family. The eldest child and the youngest child of a family with five siblings are hardly co-equal. Any attempt to deny the difference between parents and children or among the children returns us to the medieval concept of the child as a miniature adult or to the dehumanizing attitude which denies differences. Diversity is in the nature of nature and so long as this reality is recognized, there will be differences in role, status, power, position, and responsibility.

Psychotherapy is a bipersonal transaction between one individual seeking help, called the patient, and the helper, called the therapist, who represents the authority, expert, or leader in the social dynamics of the therapeutic system. Every relationship between one person and another involves a contractual arrangement which is either conscious or unconscious, expressed or implied. Too often the social contract remains tacit, different for the participating parties, and results in frustrated expectations, mistrust, and failure in the accomplishment of outcomes. An early first step in developing a therapeutic relationship is to explicate the terms of the interpersonal contract governing the transaction.

One more generalization needs to be made. Democracy and therapeutics should not be confused. It is probable that a democratic at-

297

mosphere is therapy-facilitating. But democratic politics are not curative of emotional disturbance in persons. The subject matter of this
presentation is an exploration of the relationship of the patient and the
therapist. Even in a treatment group of eight to ten persons, there
is multiplicity of relations among co-patients; but each has a special,
specific, and dynamic involvement with the psychotherapist who, by
virtue of the social reality, is the leader of the group (Wolf and
Schwartz, 1962). No attempt will be made to investigate social dynamics, the interrelated action systems operative in the group
(Kardiner 1945).

As has already been indicated, human interaction takes place on a
multiplicity of levels. When we talk about leadership in a group, or
in the dyad, we are talking about roles, and a sharp distinction must
be made between symbolic and real roles. This does not mean that
symbolic roles are not real and have no psychological reality, but
distinction must be made between the roles which are the result of the
realities of the social interaction and those which are projected onto
the person of the leader. Tarachow (1963) discusses simply and well
the real and the as if in the treatment situation.

To be sure, there is always an interpenetration of the symbolic and
objective roles of the leader. This is clearly seen in the charismatic
effect. Charisma inspires followership, the real terms of the contractual
arrangement are not explicated, are left implicit, and expectations are
projected but never bilaterally agreed upon. In psychotherapy, symbolic roles and expectations projected onto the therapist by the patient
are subsumed under the rubric of transference phenomena. The therapist, as well, is capable unconsciously of demanding the patient play
a symbolic role in the therapist's psychodynamics; this, too, is
transference. These two sets of projected anticipations may dovetail;
this is countertransference. The transference reactions of the patient
and the transference reactions of the therapist may, however, clash. If
either state persists, therapy is bound to fail (Schwartz and Wolf,
1964).

In a true therapeutic relationship, the conditions of the social contract must be explicit, bilaterally understood and agreed to, at least
consciously. It is important not only for the cure but also for the
theory and practice of therapy and the advance of the science of
psychology, that we attempt to make as explicit as possible what is
implicit in our activity as therapists in the individual setting or the
group setting.

At this time in this culture, most persons place great stress upon the expert, the leader. There is concomitantly a tendency for leadership to take on increasing significance in all social interactions, including psychotherapy. The social and psychological antecedents of this trend can be explicated (Freud 1921, 1939; Kardiner 1945), but I wish to restrict myself to the field of psychotherapy.

In the historical development of psychotherapy, we have seen a shift from the patient, his intrapsychic life, his dynamics, his pathology, his experience in the therapeutic situation, to an emphasis on the therapeutic situation in which the patient experiences the basis for change and presently to a deepening involvement with the person of the therapist. The therapeutic encounter is seen as an interpersonal transaction involving a helper and a helped seeking jointly a common experiential goal. The current literature in the field of psychotherapy is less concerned with patient's psychodynamics and the interactional dynamics and more with the therapist. What are the therapist's psychodynamics, his values, his prejudices, his origins, his identity (Schwartz and Abel, 1955; Strupp 1960; Wolf and Schwartz, 1964)? As this trend becomes stronger, we begin to see, as was the case with patients, a preoccupation with the psychopathological aspects of the leader and leadership, namely the transference and countertransference aspects of the therapist's activity (Schwartz and Wolf, 1963). In contemporary fiction, what is almost exclusively depicted is the acting out of the psychiatrist. "Many fictional psychiatrists appear to be using such (Svengalian) methods to achieve satisfaction for themselves rather than for the patients . . ." (Winick 1963).

Many parameters that enter into this complicated situation need to be specified: Who becomes a leader and why? What kind of leadership are we talking about? Individual therapists and group therapists, like leaders and fanatics, tend to define for themselves their roles. They enter into a bilateral relationship with patients and have certain preconceptions of themselves as therapists which are sometimes partially conscious and sometimes partially unconscious. Similarly, they have anticipations about patients. These self- and other-assigned expectations of the therapist are confronted by the self- and other-assigned expectations of the patients. Generally a compromise, again too often implicit, results. There are, then, self-assigned roles of the patient, self-assigned roles of the therapist, and the roles assigned by each to the other, with more or less awareness.

I am always fascinated by the first phase of psychotherapy, whether it is in the individual or the group setting. My clinical experience with patients, my supervisory experience with other therapists, and reading case reports of my colleagues impress me that regardless of the antici-pations a patient brings with him, the therapist tends to put the patient, in the beginning, through a training period. Persons, even peripatetic patients, do not come into a therapist's office as patients but as persons, and each learns to become a patient of the specific therapist. Being a patient of one therapist is different from being a patient of any other, and every person must experience what it means to be a patient of a particular therapist.

This is seen most dramatically in psychoanalytic groups, especially if they are continuous (Wolf and Schwartz, 1962). A person will react quite differently in one group from the way he behaved in another. This is due in part to a group climate, the dynamics of the particular group of patients, the role assignments, and role expecta-tions of the membership. Often the role assigned to a patient in a group is determined by the leader, especially in the early phase of the therapeutic participation of a particular patient. Foulkes states that the therapist is an orchestra leader, a conductor, in the group (Foulkes and Anthony, 1957). This, too, is a self-assigned role which the thera-pist may get the members of the group to accept as his role by convincing them that if he plays such a role it will be in their ultimate interest.

It has been my experience with therapists working with groups of patients that many have a need to view the group as a democratic microsociety and their self-assigned roles with regard to the patients is to be democratic. In this attitude, they feel obligated to provide something for every patient. This kind of therapist often gets quite anxious if a patient or a group of patients leave a session without re-ceiving something. I had a grandmother who was somewhat like this. After a family visit with her, you could not leave unless all of the grandchildren got something. On the other hand, she was not pseudo-democratic in that she did not feel that each one of the children had to take home the same thing. It was possible for her to differentiate between one and another. I am suggesting that this possibility is a necessity for the group therapist. Different patients may take different things from the experience with the leader and with the other patients, and each may take home with him after each session something different, something quite specific in terms of his own necessities.

In this connection, even the silent member of the group, who is not always a patient but is sometimes the therapist, will take home something from the experience in the group. And I am not sure that being silent is a nonactive or inactive role, for even in a state of silence on the part of patient or therapist, I think a level of interaction goes on. What do I mean by interaction? Is it the words we use? The tones? The feelings? Our personality? The way we sit? The way we talk? The kinds of things we approve or disapprove?

In preparation for this presentation, I listened more carefully (yes, even this is possible) and more pointedly to my patients. I listened to children and parents talking about themselves and about each other in family groups, and I listened to patients in nonfamily groups, and to patients in individual treatment. I noted in each instance that the patient was ascribing a role to me, that each one had a multiplicity of levels of expectation of me. Each wanted me to do something, wanted something of me, and I listed some of these wishes. I am certain each therapist can prepare such a list of his own many times the length of this one.

Patients wanted me, among other things, to comfort them, to help them, to gratify or support them, to advise or counsel, to inhibit or condemn, to arbitrate or mediate among various persons, to align myself with one against another, to feed one or another. In one of my groups the other day, I was to have been the scapegoat for what had been going on elsewhere. I happen to wear several hats in the training institution in which I work. In one setting I am an administrator, in another a therapist. Both are leadership roles. In the therapeutic group, the members decided this was the time to use me and to abuse me for some of the administrative situations that had been frustrating them. They denied and rejected their own problems, refused to talk about themselves. They wanted me to play the role of the scapegoat. They also wanted me to be a magician. They were convinced that I could do magic, that I had ways of dealing with the administrative reality, a power far beyond the realistic limitations they were refusing to face.

Like all of us, I am often put in the position where one or another patient wants me to be a mind reader, a punisher, an attacker, a sympathetic fellow mourner for lost object relations, or an inspirer. I have had patients who wanted me to be a co-patient, co-delinquent. I even had a pass made at me; a patient who wanted me to be her lover; another desired that I father her child.

As I have already indicated, this is only a partial listing. I tried, however, to integrate the varieties of role assignments and expectations in light of my own commitment to psychoanalytic therapy. I recognized that each patient wanted me to be some significant family member—father, mother, uncle, grandfather, old-maid aunt—in the reconstitution of the real, illusory and symbiotic relationships of his early life experiences.

In addition to the role assignments that patients make to us, we might ask what roles we as therapists think we ought to play or have to play. An equally long list of self-assigned roles of the therapist could be constructed. Some therapists feel that they have to listen, to reflect, to be a mirror, to be a passive target for the feelings, attitudes, and demands of the patients. An occasional therapist wants to be an active target, that is, he invites attack upon himself. Some therapists want to be the comforter, the frustrator, "the pointer outer," the questioner, the interpreter, the explainer, the teacher, the philosopher, the desensitizer, the supporter, or the social reformer of the patient. Sometimes a therapist feels he has to be the negotiator and help patients come to a compromise with reality or come to grips with a difficult life situation, because life is not easy. Some therapists play the role of the persuader, the director of the life of the patient, or the manager of the life of the group of patients. Or desire to be a group or family member. Occasionally, a therapist re-enacts the succoring mother, the punitive father, the competitive brother, or the seductive sister, and even insists that such roles are appropriate to his activity as a therapist.

One therapist thought his function was to entertain his group of patients. One of his partial objectives was to get the group to enjoy the therapy experience with him. Another wanted to be a relaxer; all the patients in the group had to leave the session much more relaxed than when they came. It was his primary responsibility to bring about this state of increased relaxation. A therapist said he was a "reconditioner," to which he added the words "of the ailing ego." Another wanted to be the "destroyer" of the superego. Still another wanted to be a "hypnotizer." The therapist did not use this word, but in some way he felt he could supply patients with an experience in ecstasy and so demonstrate his powers to relieve suffering. One often gets the feeling from patients who ask for hypnosis in treatment that they want to have something taken away—the illness, or evil, their pain or guilt, a recollection or confession.

The therapist may discriminatingly play a variety of conscious roles with different patients at different times under different conditions. Or he may rigidly adhere to one role for all under every circumstance. He may even consciously enter into collusion with his patients by being seduced by "the principal temptation [of both the analyst and psychotherapist, which is] to play the role of mother" (Tarachom 1963). It is obvious, in comparing the roles, functions, demands or expectations assigned to the therapist by the patients and those assigned to the therapist by himself, that there are many parallels, many areas of overlap. It would be noteworthy to discover which are the most frequent role assignments of the patient and the most frequent self-assigned roles of the therapist. A single list might be prepared to include most but no therapist could, would, or should play all the roles.

A large number of questions like the following arise: Are the conscious and unconscious demands of the patient and those of the therapist always, sometimes, or never congruent? Is the therapist never the lover of a patient or co-patient, or co-delinquent with a patient? Is the therapist sometimes counselor, advisor, and educator of the patient? Is the therapist always to be frustrator, or only sometimes, or never? Are we always helpful, as we conceive our functions and play our roles? When considering such questions, there is always the subsidiary one, namely, of which patients in what context are we talking? Obviously, we may always, sometimes, or never fulfill one or another set of expectations of one patient or one group of patients, depending on our awareness and our evaluation of what is appropriate. By appropriate, I mean therapy facilitating rather than therapy impeding for this particular group of patients in contrast to any other patient or group of patients (Schwartz and Wolf, 1964).

Serious study is needed of these many factors. I should like to suggest a research design in which the conscious and unconscious, self-assigned and other-assigned roles of patients and therapists are explored and compared. Not only conscious or aware roles interlock, but patient and therapist may act, react, and interact out of unconscious provocation and resonance. Through such explorations we may learn about the real and illusory needs of the patient and of the therapist and the extent of congruence between these two sets of expectations or roles, for what kinds of patients under what kinds of conditions.

Finally, it is important to resist referring to the therapist as leader. The word "leader" seems to imply a role which tends to prevent transactions among peers. A leader has the latent motivation to prevent peers, the patients, from communicating to one another, from relating to one another in meaningful ways. You may have heard of the group therapist who insisted at the end of each session that patients leave his office in Indian file, so that no two patients leave in the same elevator. This therapist leader had a need for constant surveillance and control over his patients so they not experience one another except under his supervision. An antipodal quality of leadership is reflected in the use of the alternate session, the meeting of the patients of a therapy group without the physical presence of the therapist (Schwartz and Wolf, 1963; Wolf and Schwartz, 1962). This therapeutic regimen has been largely rejected by those who are leaders in the sense that they tend to inhibit and proscribe the interaction among the peers. Within current clinical experience and knowledge, the most effective arrangement for therapist and patient can be conceptualized only in terms of a reasonable flexibility in a situation of antagonistic cooperation.

BIBLIOGRAPHY OF ALEXANDER WOLF

1931-1940

"The Effective Use of Small Non-Dehydrating Doses of Epsom Salt in Epilepsy: Study of 109 Cases." *Journal of Neurology and Psychopathology* 16 (1936):213-218.

"Quinine: An Effective Form of Treatment for Myotonia: Preliminary Report of Four Cases." *Archives of Neurology and Psychiatry* 36 (August 1936):382-383.

"The Relationship of Intellect to Speech Defect in Aphasic Patients, with Illustrative Cases." A. Wolf and Foster Kennedy. *Journal of Nervous and Mental Diseases* 84, 2 (August 1936):125-145; 84, 3 (September 1936):293-311.

"Experiments with Quinine and Prostigmin in the Treatment of Myotonia and Myasthenia." A. Wolf and Foster Kennedy. *Archives of Neurology and Psychiatry* 37 (January 1937):68-74.

"Quinine in Myotonia and Prostigmin in Myasthenia: A Clinical Evaluation." A. Wolf and Foster Kennedy. *Journal of the American Medical Association* 110 (January 1938):198-202.

"The Use of Quinine in Myotonia." *Transactions of the American Therapeutic Society* 37 (1938):90-91.

"The Respiratory 'Fingerprint' of Nervous States." A. Wolf, G. F. Sutherland and Foster Kennedy. *Medical Record* 148 (August 1938): 101-103

"A Method for Shortening the Duration of Lower Motor Neurone Paralysis by Cholinergic Facilitation: A Preliminary Report." *Transactions of the American Neurological Association* 64 (1938):205207.

"The Treatment of Encephalitis with Roentgen Ray: A Preliminary Report." A. Wolf and S. Rubenfeld. *American Journal of Roentgenology* 42, 4 (1939):561-564.

"A Method for Shortening the Duration of Lower Motor Neurone Paralysis by Cholinergic Facilitation." *Journal of Nervous and Mental Diseases* 92 (November 1940): 614-622.

1941-1950

"The Dynamics of the Selective Inhibition of Specific Functions in Neurosis: A Preliminary Report." *Psychosomatic Medicine* 5, 1 (January 1943). Reprinted in the Section on Experimental Psychopathology in *Contemporary Psychopathology: A Source Book* (Cambridge, Mass.: Harvard University Press, 1943), pp. 398-413.

"The Effective Use of Thyroid in Periodic Paralysis." *New York State Journal of Medicine* 43, 20 (October 15, 1943):1951-1963.

✳ "The Psychoanalysis of Groups." *American Journal of Psychotherapy* 3, 4 (October 1949):525-558; 4, 1 (January 1950): 16-50.

1951-1960

"On the Irrelevance of Group Psychotherapy in Mass Conflict." *Group Psychotherapy* 5, 1, 2 and 3 (April, July and November 1952): 78-79.

✳ "The Psychoanalysis of Groups: The Analyst's Objections." A. Wolf et al. *The International Journal of Group Psychotherapy* 2, 3 (July 1952):221-231.

"Sexual Acting Out in the Psychoanalysis of Groups." A. Wolf et al. *The International Journal of Group Psychotherapy* 4, 4 (October 1954):369-380.

"The Psychoanalysis of Groups: Implications for Education, Forthcoming Proc. of the Interamerican Soc. of Psych." A. Wolf and E. K. Schwartz. *The International Journal of Social Psychiatry* 1 (August 1955):9-17.

"Psychoanalysis in Groups: Three Primary Parameters." A. Wolf and E. K. Schwartz. *The American Imago* 14, 3 (August 1957):281-297.

"Code of Ethics of Group Psychotherapists, Comments." *Group Psychotherapy* 10, 3 (September 1957):221-223. Also in *Psychodrama and Group Psychotherapy Monographs*, No. 31, by J. L. Moreno et al. (Boston: Beacon House, 1962), pp. 6-8.

Discussion of "Psychic Structure and Therapy of Latent Schizophrenia," by Gustave Bychowski. *Psychoanalytic Office Practice*, edited by Alfred H. Rifkin (New York: Grune & Stratton, 1957), pp. 135-139.

"Acting Out in Group Psychotherapy: A Panel Discussion." H. Durkin, H. T. Glatzer, W. C. Hulse, A. L. Kadis and A. Wolf. *American Journal of Psychotherapy* 12, 1 (January 1958):87-105.

Book Review of *Psychotherapy of Chronic Schizophrenic Patients* edited by C. Whitaker (Boston: Little, Brown & Co., 1958), pp. ix and 219. A. Wolf and E. K. Schwartz. *AMA Archives of Neurology and Psychiatry* 80, 4 (October 1958):530-531.

"The Advanced and Terminal Phases in Group Psychotherapy" and "The Development of Group Psychotherapy Programs in Various Existing Settings." *Proc. of the Second Annual Institute of the American Group Psychoth. Assoc.*, edited by M. M. Berger and M. E. Linden (January 22-23, 1958):66-79.

"Potentialities of Group Therapy for Obesity." *International Record of Medicine* 171, 1 (January 1958):9-11.

"Irrational Trends in Contemporary Psychotherapy: Cultural Correlates." A. Wolf and E. K. Schwartz. *Psychoanalysis and the Psychoanalytic Review* 45, 1 and 2 (Spring-Summer 1958):65-74.

"Irrational Psychotherapy: An Appeal to Unreason (I)." A. Wolf and E. K. Schwartz. *American Journal of Psychotherapy* 12, 2 (April 1958):300-314.

"Irrational Psychotherapy: An Appeal to Unreason (II)." A. Wolf and E. K. Schwartz. *American Journal of Psychotherapy* 12, 3 (July 1958):508-521.

"Irrational Psychotherapy: An Appeal to Unreason (III)." A. Wolf and E. K. Schwartz. *American Journal of Psychotherapy* 12, 4 (October 1958):744-759.

"Irrational Psychotherapy: An Appeal to Unreason (IV)." A. Wolf and E. K. Schwartz. *American Journal of Psychotherapy* 13, 2 (April 1959):383-400.

"Psychoanalysis in Groups: The Role of Values." A. Wolf and E. K. Schwartz. *American Journal of Psychoanalysis* 19, 1 (1959):37-52.

Book Review of *Group Psychoanalysis*, by B. Bohdan Wassell (New York: Philosophical Library, 1959), p. 339. A. Wolf and E. K. Schwartz. *AMA Archives of General Psychiatry* 1, 3 (September 1959):130-131, 346-347.

"Psychoanalysis in Groups: Clinical and Theoretic Implications of the Alternate Meeting." Proc. of the Second International Congress of Group Psychotherapy (Zurich, Switzerland: May 29-31, 1957), in A.

Wolf and E. K. Schwartz. *Acta Psychotherapeutica* 7: *Supplement*, edited by B. Stokvis (Leyden, Basel and New York: S. Karger, 1959), pp. 404-437, 540-573.

"The Quest for Certainty." A. Wolf and E. K. Schwartz. *AMA Archives of Neurology and Psychiatry* 81, 1 (January 1959):69-84.

"Psychoanalysis in Groups: The Alternate Session." A. Wolf and E. K. Schwartz. *The American Imago* 17, 1 (Spring 1960): 101-108.

Book Review of *From Death Camp to Existentialism* by Viktor Frankl (Boston: Beacon Press, 1959). A. Wolf and E. K. Schwartz. *American Journal of Psychotherapy* 14, 2 (April 1960):418-419.

"Psychoanalysis in Groups: The Mystique of Group Dynamics," *Sources of Conflict in Contemporary Group Psychotherapy*, edited by W. C. Hulse (New York: S. Karger, 1960).

1961-1970

"Psychoanalysis in Groups: Some Comparisons with Individual Analysis." A. Wolf and E. K. Schwartz. *Journal of General Psychology* 64 (January 1961):153-191.

Book Review of *Psychoanalysis and the Family Neurosis* by Martin Grotjahn (New York: W. W. Norton & Co., 1960). A. Wolf and E. K. Schwartz. *Archives of General Psychiatry* 4, 2 (February 1961): 127-128, 213-214.

Psychoanalysis in Groups. A. Wolf and E. K. Schwartz (New York: Grune & Stratton, 1962).

Discussion of Anonymous (Richard Abell's) article "How Patients Reacted to Viewing a Television Series Based on Their Own Group Sessions" (pp. 92-93). *Journal of Psychoanalysis in Groups* 1, 1 (1962):86-91.

"The Psychoanalysis of Groups." *Group Psychotherapy and Group Function*, edited by Max Rosenbaum and Milton Berger (New York: Basic Books, 1963), pp. 273-327.

"Psychoanalysis in Groups: Resistance to Its Use." A. Wolf and E. K. Schwartz. *American Journal of Psychotherapy* 17, 3 (July 1963): 457-464.

"Psychoanalysis in Groups: As Creative Process." A. Wolf and E. K. Schwartz. *American Journal of Psychoanalysis* 24, 1 (1964):46-59.

"Psychoanalytic Group Therapy." *Current Psychiatric Therapies*, Vol.
IV (New York: Grune & Stratton, 1964), pp. 166-174.

"Short-Term Group Psychotherapy." *Newsletter of the Society of
Medical Psychoanalysts* 5, 2 (June 1964):1 and 12.

Discussion of Dr. Sidney Rose's paper "Values of the Analyst as a
Therapeutic Factor in Group Psychoanalysis." *Journal of Psychoanalysis in Groups* 1, 2 (1964):7-9.

"On Countertransference in Group Psychotherapy." A. Wolf and
E. K. Schwartz. *International Journal of Group Psychotherapy* 15, 4

Book Review of *Therapeutic Group Analysis* by S. H. Foulkes (New
York: International Universities Press, 1964), p. 320. A. Wolf and
E. K. Schwartz. *International Journal of Group Psychotherapy*, 15, 4
(October 1965):528-529.

"Short-Term Group Psychotherapy." *Short-Term Psychotherapy*,
edited by Lewis R. Wolberg (New York: Grune & Stratton, 1965),
pp. 219-255.

"The Absence of Face-to-Face Contact in Training in Psychoanalysis
in Groups." I. Goldberg, C. McCarty, E. K. Schwartz and A. Wolf.
The International Handbook of Group Psychotherapy, edited by J. L.
Moreno (New York: Philosophical Library, 1966), pp. 533-534.

Comments on J. L. Moreno's "Code of Ethics for Group Psychother-
apists: Moreno's Proposal." *The International Handbook of Group
Psychotherapy*, edited by J. L. Moreno (New York: Philosophical
Library, 1966), pp. 112-113.

"Psicoanalisis en Grupos." A. Wolf and E. K. Schwartz. *14th Colec-
cion Ciencias del Hombre*, editorial Pax-Mexico, Libreria Carlos
Cesarman, S. A. Rep. Argentina 9, Mexico 1, D.F., 1967, pp. 1-383.

"Group Psychotherapy." *Comprehensive Textbook of Psychiatry*,
edited by A. M. Freedman and H. I. Kaplan (Baltimore, Md.: Williams & Wilkins, 1967), pp. 1234-1241.

"Psychoanalysis in Groups: The Role of Values." A. Wolf and E. K.
Schwartz. *Morality and Mental Health*, edited by O. Hobart Mowrer
(Chicago: Rand McNally, 1967), pp. 104-117.

"The Interpreter in Group Therapy: Conflict Resolution Through
Negotiation." A. Wolf and E. K. Schwartz. *Archives of General
Psychiatry* 18, 2 (February 1968):186-193 (New York: American
Medical Association Publication).

"The Problem of Infidelity." *The Marriage Relationship: Psychoanalytic Perspectives*, edited by S. Rosenbaum and I. Alger (New York: Basic Books, 1968), pp. 175-195.

"Psychoanalysis in Groups." *Basic Approaches to Group Psychotherapy and Group Counseling*, edited by G. M. Gazda (Springfield, Ill.: Charles C Thomas, 1968), pp. 80-108.

"The Discriminating Use of Feeling in Group Psychotherapy." *New Directions in Mental Health*, Vol. I, edited by B. F. Riess (New York: Grune & Stratton, 1968), pp. 173-186.

"On Countertransference in Group Psychotherapy." A. Wolf and E. K. Schwartz. *New Directions in Mental Health*, edited by B. F. Riess (New York: Grune & Stratton, 1969), pp. 21-32.

"The Schizophrenic Wallet: Where is the Money?" A. Wolf and E. K. Schwartz. *Psychiatric Opinion* 6, 3 (June 1969):32-36.

"Training in Psychoanalysis in Groups Without Face-to-Face Contact." A. Wolf et al. *American Journal of Psychotherapy* 23, 3 (July 1969):488-494.

"Money Matters." A. Wolf and E. K. Schwartz. *International Mental Health Research Newsletter* 9, 2 (Summer 1969):1-7.

"Training in Psychoanalysis in Groups Without Face-to-Face Contact," A. Wolf et al. *Mental Health Digest* 1, 11 (November 1969): 33-35.

"The Psychoanalysis of Groups." *Group Therapy Today*, edited by H. M. Ruitenbeck (New York: Atherton Press, 1969), pp. 67-96.

"Acting Out in Group Psychotherapy." A. Wolf et al. *Group Therapy Today*, edited by H. M. Ruitenbeck (New York: Atherton Press, 1969), pp. 103-120.

"Sexual Acting Out in the Psychoanalysis of Groups." A. Wolf et al. *Group Therapy Today*, edited by H. M. Ruitenbeck (New York: Atherton Press, 1969), pp. 162-173.

Discussion of Dr. Lillian A. Tamarin's paper "Violence and Alcohol." *Journal of Psychoanalysis in Groups* 2, 3 (1969):11-13.

"The Interpreter in Group Therapy: Conflict Resolution Through Negotiation." A. Wolf and E. K. Schwartz. *New Directions in Mental Health*, edited by B. F. Riess (New York: Grune & Stratton, 1969), pp. 33-40.

"Psychoanalysis in Groups: As Creative Process." A. Wolf and E. K. Schwartz. *New Directions in Mental Health*, edited by B. F. Riess (New York: Grune & Stratton, 1969), pp. 57-68.

"Irrational Psychotherapy: An Appeal to Unreason." *New Directions in Mental Health*, edited by B. F. Riess (New York: Grune & Stratton, 1969), pp. 124-185.

"Irrational Trends in Contemporary Psychotherapy: Cultural Correlates." A. Wolf and E. K. Schwartz. *New Directions in Mental Health*, edited by B. F. Riess (New York: Grune & Stratton, 1969), pp. 186-195.

"The Quest for Certainty." A. Wolf and E. K. Schwartz. *New Directions in Mental Health*, edited by B. F. Riess (New York: Grune & Stratton, 1969), pp. 242-257.

"Training in Psychoanalysis in Groups Without Face-to-Face Contact." I. Goldberg, G. McCarty, E. K. Schwartz and A. Wolf (New York: Grune & Stratton, 1969), pp. 368-374.

"Psychoanalysis in Groups." A. Wolf and E. K. Schwartz. *Comprehensive Group Psychotherapy*, edited by H. I. Kaplan and B. J. Sadock (Baltimore, Md.: Williams & Wilkins, 1971), pp. 241-291.

Beyond the Couch: Dialogues on Teaching and Learning Psychoanalysis in Groups (New York: Jason Aronson, 1970), 364 pp.

1971-1974

"Psychoanalyse in Gruppen." *Psychoanalytische Therapie in Gruppen*, edited by S. de Schill (Stuttgart, Germany: Ernst Klett Verlag, 1971), pp. 145-199.

"The Dynamics of the Selective Inhibition of Specific Functions in Neurosis." *The Development of Behavior*, edited by Victor H. Denenberg (Stamford, Conn.: Sinauer Associates, 1972), pp. 256-268.

"Psychoanalysis in Groups: Contrasts with Other Group Therapies." I. Goldberg, G. McCarty, E. K. Schwartz and A. Wolf. *Progress in Group and Family Therapy*, edited by Clifford Sager and Helen Kaplan (New York: Brunner Mazel, 1972), pp. 47-53.

"Morality and the Population Explosion." *Moral Values and the Superego Concept in Psychoanalysis*, edited by Seymour C. Post (New York: International Universities Press, 1972).

"Psychoanalysis in Groups." *Major Contributors to Modern Psychotherapy* (Hoffman-LaRoche, 1972), pp. 5-26.

"The Arcadian Ingredient in Group Psychotherapy." *Group Therapy: 1973—An Overview*, edited by L. R. Wolberg and E. K. Schwartz (New York: International Medical Book Corp., 1973), pp. 1-11.

"Psychoanalysis in Groups." *The Challenge for Group Psychotherapy*, edited by S. deSchill (New York: International Universities Press, 1974), pp. 120-172.

"Psychoanalysis in Groups." *Current Psychiatric Theories, 1974*, edited by J. Masserman (New York: Grune & Stratton, 1974), Vol. 14, pp. 219-221.

ACKNOWLEDGMENTS

The editor would like to thank the publishers and copyright holders for permission to reprint the following material. Selections are numbered as they appear in the book.

1. A. WOLF, An Early View of the Role of the Group Leader, from "The Psychoanalysis of Groups," *American Journal of Psychotherapy* 3, 4 (October 1949):525-528; 4, 1 (January 1950):16-50.
2. A. WOLF, On the Irrelevance of Group Psychotherapeutic Leadership in Group Conflict, from "The Irrelevance of Group Psychotherapy in Mass Conflict," *Group Psychotherapy* 5, 1-3 (April, July, and November 1952):78-79.
3. A. WOLF, The Role of the Leader in the Advanced and Terminal Phases of Group Psychotherapy, from "The Advanced and Terminal Phases in Group Psychotherapy: The Development of Group Programs in Various Existing Settings," Proceedings of the Second Annual Institute of the American Group Psychotherapy Association, January 22-23, 1958, edited by M. M. Berger and M. E. Linden, pp. 66-79.
4. A. WOLF and E. K. SCHWARTZ, The Role of the Leader's Values, from "Psychoanalysis in Groups: The Role of Values," *American Journal of Psychoanalysis* 19, 1 (1959):38-51.
5. A. WOLF and E. K. SCHWARTZ, The Absent Leader, from "Psychoanalysis in Groups: Clinical and Theoretical Implications of the Alternate Meeting," Proceedings of the Second International Congress of Group Psychotherapy, Zurich, Switzerland, May 29-31, 1957, published in *Acta Psychotherapeutica* 7, supplement edited by B. Stovkis and S. Karger (Leyden, Basel, and New York, 1959), pp. 404-437, 540-573.
6. A. WOLF and E. K. SCHWARTZ, The Leader in Uncertainty, from "The Quest for Certainty," *AMA Archives of Neurology and Psychiatry* 81, 1 (January 1959):75-76, 81-82.
7. A. WOLF and E. K. SCHWARTZ, The Mystique of Group Dynamics in Psychoanalytic Leadership, from "Psychoanalysis in Groups:

313

The Mystique of Group Dynamics," *Sources of Conflict in Contemporary Group Psychotherapy*, edited by W. C. Hulse (New York: S. Karger, 1960), pp. 129, 139-141.

8. A. Wolf and E. K. Schwartz, "The Role of the Leader as Psychoanalyst," *Psychoanalysis in Groups* (New York: Grune & Stratton, 1962), pp. 38-44.

9. A. Wolf and E. K. Schwartz, "The Leader and the Homogeneous or Heterogeneous Group," *Psychoanalysis in Groups* (New York: Grune & Stratton, 1962), pp. 73-78.

10. A. Wolf and E. K. Schwartz, "The Leader and the Use of Dreams," *Psychoanalysis in Groups* (New York: Grune & Stratton, 1962), p. 151.

11. A. Wolf and E. K. Schwartz, "The Leader and the Process of Working Through," *Psychoanalysis in Groups* (New York: Grune & Stratton, 1962), pp. 163-165, 170-171.

12. A. Wolf and E. K. Schwartz, Resistances on the Part of Group Leaders, "Psychoanalysis in Groups: Resistance to Its Use," *American Journal of Psychotherapy* 17, 3 (1963):462-463.

13. A. Wolf and E. K. Schwartz, The Creative Leader, from "Psychoanalysis in Groups: As Creative Process," *American Journal of Psychoanalysis* 24, 1 (1964):46-59.

14. A. Wolf and E. K. Schwartz, The Leader and Countertransference, from "On Countertransference in Group Psychotherapy," *Journal of Psychology* 57 (1964):135-137, 139, 141.

15. A. Wolf, Short-Term Leadership, from "Short-Term Group Psychotherapy," *Short-Term Psychotherapy*, edited by Lewis R. Wolberg (New York: Grune & Stratton, 1965), pp. 244-246.

16. A. Wolf, The Discriminatingly Affective Leader, from "The Discriminating Use of Feeling in Group Psychotherapy," *New Directions in Mental Health, Vol. 1*, edited by B. F. Riess (New York: Grune & Stratton, 1968), pp. 174-177.

17. A. Wolf and E. K. Schwartz, The Responsible Leader, from "Irrational Psychotherapy: An Appeal to Unreason," *New Directions in Mental Health, Vol. 2*, edited by B. F. Riess (New York: Grune & Stratton, 1969), p. 164.

18. A. Wolf, E. K. Schwartz, G. McCarty, and I. Goldberg, "The Leader as Human Being," *Beyond the Couch: Dialogues on Teaching and Learning Psychoanalysis in Groups* (New York: Jason Aronson, 1970), pp. 22-26.

19. A. WOLF, The Loving Leader, from "The Arcadian Ingredient in Group Psychotherapy," *Group Therapy: 1973—An Overview,* edited by L. R. Wolberg and E. K. Schwartz (New York: Stratton Intercontinental Medical Book, 1973), pp. 1-11.

Memorial. E. K. SCHWARTZ, "Leadership and the Psychotherapist," ✳ *Topical Problems in Psychotherapy* 5 (1965):72-79.

Index

acting out, 124
activism, 116
activity, 92
  demanding of patients, 61
  group as initiating, 167
Adler, A., 274
affect
  expression, as more enlightening than logic or reason, 28
  fleeting, 74
  hiding, 42
affiliation, 105
aggression, as not integrated with libidinal goals, 221
aggressor, widespread identification with, 248
alcoholics, 98, 264
alienation, 72, 93
allegiances, family, changed by exposing complementarity of needs, 178
alliances, concealed group, 42
alternate sessions, 58, 192, 267, 304
  constructive use, 31-32
ambiguity, 290
Americans, 281
analysis
  educational aspects, 67
  group therapists unable to understand individual, 57
  movement from individual to group, 59
analysts, 283
  aging, 146-150
  artificial identification with, 288
  background as benefiting scholastic effort, 291
  balance of theory and practice, 43
  group, as leaders, 87
  group therapist must be, 38
  indicating trust of patients, 58
  judged as omnipotent, 284-285
  knowledge elevated into power, 293
  limits of knowledge and power, 294
  no reason to assume role of leader, 286-287

not taking refuge in silence and pseudo-listening, 288
as parameter of freedom, 68
particular undertakings by a service do not lend to training, 293
personal qualifications, 41
qualifications and functions of successful group, 38-44
see also therapists
analytic attitude, of leader, and new perspectives, 101
anonymity, classical, of therapist, 16
answers, by leader, 109
antagonistic cooperation, 304
anti-intellectualism, 273
anxiety, 158
apartness, physical, allowing speech without permission from others, 177
application, conscious, planned, and goal-directed, 54
approaches, more effective group therapeutic, 123
arrangement, traditional analytic, 14
art, taking social form in schools, 261
articulation, verbal, 190
"as if" attitude, 286
assistants, psychoanalytic, 283
attack and counterattack, 20
atypical media, 187-202
audiovisual methods, 187-202
authoritarianism, 46-47, 95
authority
  given by rank and position, 86
  group as whole as last, 110
  masochistic submission to, 248-249
  right to criticize, 16
awareness
  appeal to participants, of self-, 205
  fuller, 39
  of self and others, 26
  of what one really wants to say or do, 211

Balint, M., 217, 226, 227, 231, 288
Basel Psychiatric University Hospital

sides, taking, 11-12
silence, role of, 300-301
"single parent anxiety," 236
s (internal stimuli), 152
Skinner, B. F., 277-278
Slavson, S. R., 102
small-group dynamics, 104
social contract, conditions must be explicit, 298
social control, 277-278
socialization, 24, 25
society, functioning based on power structure whose goal is to broaden itself, 247
speaking, conversing about, 209
splitting, 219-222, 237-238
spontaneity, personal, 174
Stanford University, 120
statements, one at a time, 210
state yourself, 208
status, denial, 16
strangers, nation of, 115
Strong's Vocational Interest Inventory, 126
structure, 28
  homogeneous or heterogeneous, 45-51
"structured interactional psychotherapy," 174
study group, 255
styles, leadership, study, 270
subculture, group, as microcosm of total society, 25
submission, masochistic patterns, 250
suffering, 31
suggestion, 85
superego demands, expectation that patient will fulfill therapist's, 61
*super*transference, 119
supervisees, criticism, 139
supervisor, and analytic climate of empathic neutrality, 139
symbiotic tie
  patient seeking emancipation of with therapist, 233
  relinquishing, 76
syndromes, obsessional or hysterical, 192
systems, scrutiny, and focus on members' conflicting allegiances, 171

talk, defensive, to obscure and subvert communication, 73
Taylor, G., 167
teacher(s), 290-291

VTR serving as, 191
teaching-model role, of therapist, 127
team, 286, 289, 293
teamwork, interdisciplinary, traditional definition, 285
techniques, workable with one group and unsuccessful with another, 135
television, techniques in group therapy, 187
temptation, of therapist toward patients, 149
tension, group, intervention dissolving, 158
T-group theory, 255
Thanatos, 275
theme-centered interactional method, 203, 206
Therapeutic Group Analysis, 83
therapists
  acceptance of limitations as freeing patient from desire for certainty and perfection, 70
  active in introducing new techniques, 124
  affect-committed, 64
  affection for a patient, 147
  artists as best, 78
  as if he were his own favorite patient, 150
  auxiliary, 97
  believing in group therapy, 131
  charismatic qualities of group, 120
  communicating to patient what's right and wrong, 67-68
  couples group, 175-177
  deepening involvement with, 299
  desired as some significant family member, 302
  and dilemma of schizoid patient, 228-230
  direct relationship between viewpoint and outcomes, 124
  empathy, genuineness, and warmth to therapeutic outcome, 126
  family group, 177-179
  first important element is relationship with patients, 125
  fundamental importance as group architect, 135
  goals and personal qualifications, 184
  good qualities becoming ideals for patient, 66
  group, 173